THE FINAL ISLAND

Paris, January 1973. Photo: Anne De Brunhoff.

THE FINAL ISLAND

The Fiction of Julio Cortázar

Edited by Jaime Alazraki and Ivar Ivask

Norman
University of Oklahoma Press

By Jaime Alazraki
Poética y poesía de Pablo Neruda (New York, 1965)
Jorge Luis Borges (New York, 1971)
La prosa narrativa de Jorge Luis Borges (Madrid, 1974)
Jorge Luis Borges: el escritor y la crítica (Madrid, 1976)

By Ivar Ivask
Luminous Reality: The Poetry of Jorge Guillén (coed.) (Norman, 1969)
The Cardinal Points of Borges (coed.) (Norman, 1971)
The Perpetual Present: The Poetry and Prose of Octavio Paz (ed.) (Norman, 1973)
World Literature Since 1945 (coed.) (New York, 1973)

The Final Island.

   Bibliography: p.
   1. Cortázar, Julio—Criticism and interpretation—Addresses, essays, lectures. I. Alazraki, Jaime.   II. Ivask, Ivar, 1927–
PQ7797.C7145Z66   863   77–21912
ISBN 0–8061–1436–3

Preface

> . . . but openness continues there, pulsation of stars and eels, the Möbius strip of a form of the world where conciliation is possible, where the obverse and reverse will cease to part company, where man will have his place in this jubilant dance which we at times call reality.
>
> J. Cortázar, *Prosa del observatorio*

The leading contemporary writers of Latin America tend to be not only Argentine, Chilean or Mexican writers but continental authors, even intercontinental ones at home both in South and North America. Hardly any North American writer could hold forth on the Spanish American classics as Borges does on Hawthorne, Poe, Emerson, and Whitman; or as Octavio Paz writes on Pound, Eliot, Frost, e. e. cummings, W. C. Williams and Elizabeth Bishop. And how could one understand fully the achievement of Pablo Neruda's American poetry without the example of Whitman, or the achievement of the novels of Gabriel García Márquez without taking into account such a forerunner as William Faulkner? The best Latin-American writers are equally at home on the European literary scene: one has only to read Borges on Kafka, or analyze Neruda's, Paz's and Cortázar's relationships with French surrealism to comprehend how much they owe to Europe. In short, these—and other—Latin American authors aim at nothing less than universality in their poetry, fiction and criticism.

The Final Island fills the need for criticism in English of Julio Cortázar's work. It is a study in depth by twelve Cortázar specialists who either analyze individual outstanding works or interpret certain central motifs.

Roberto González Echevarría and Jaime Alazraki deal with two early works; Margery A. Safir and Saúl Yurkievich analyze from different perspectives the novels *Hopscotch* and *Libro de Manuel*; Ana María Hernández takes up the motif of vampires in the novel *62: A Model Kit*; Evelyn Picon Garfield examines the despair which underlies the short story collection *Octaedro*. The following critics look at Cortázar's work in a more synoptic way by tracing certain motifs or themes: Malva E. Filer stresses the significance of the hand in his fiction; the presentation of male and female protagonists has caught the attention of Martha Paley Francescato; Sara Castro-Klarén formulates Cortázar's theory of literature; and both Lida Aronne Amestoy and Saúl Sosnowski interpret the pursuer motif.

A general overview is offered in the introduction, "Toward the Last Square of the Hopscotch," by one of the editors, Jaime Alazraki. Gregory Rabassa, the principal translator of Cortázar (and of most other leading Latin American novelists), shares his observations about Cortázar's Art of Fiction. The opinions of the critics, however, are balanced by three texts contributed by Cortázar himself: a recent short story, "Second Time Around," translated by Gregory Rabassa; and two essays of fundamental importance for the understanding of this major Argentine author, "The Present State of Fiction in Latin America" and "Politics and the Intellectual in Latin America."

We would like to express our cordial gratitude to the following individuals for their help in the preparation of this book: Julio Cortázar, who placed at our disposal most of the rare photographs reproduced here; Gregory Rabassa, Margery A. Safir, Mary E. Davis, and Irene Salazar for their translations from the Spanish; William Riggan, Associate Editor of *World Literature Today*, who helped edit the manuscript for publication.

IVAR IVASK

Norman, Oklahoma

Contents

Illustrations

THE FINAL ISLAND

Presentation and Texts

Introduction: Toward the Last Square of the Hopscotch

By JAIME ALAZRAKI

Julio Cortázar, the most Argentine among Argentine writers, is also, together with Borges and Octavio Paz, the most universal in a generation of Spanish American writers which has so definitely changed the status of its literature and its place in the letters of our time. *Hopscotch* was the turning point. Published in Spanish in 1963, it was successively translated into French, English, Italian, Polish and Portuguese. The English translation by Gregory Rabassa received the first National Book Award given in this country for the work of a translator. It was greeted by *The New Republic*'s reviewer, C. D. B. Bryan, as "the most powerful encyclopedia of emotions and visions to emerge from the post-war generation of international writers," by the London *Times Literary Supplement* as the "first great novel of Spanish America" and by Carlos Fuentes, who reviewed the book for the prestigious magazine *Commentary*, as the novel which "in its depth of imagination and suggestion, in its maze of black mirrors, in its ironical potentiality-through-destruction of time and words, marks the true possibility of encounter between the Latin American imagination and the contemporary world."[1] Donald Keene reviewed *Rayuela*'s English version for *The New York Times Book Review* and concluded that if *The Winners*, published in English a year earlier, "earned respectful reviews, *Hopscotch*, a superb work, should establish Cortázar as an outstanding writer of our day."[2] A year later the American reader was to discover that the author of one of the most prominent novels of the century was also a master of the short story. A selection of his short fiction, translated by Paul Blackburn, was published under the title *End of the Game and Other Stories* (Pantheon, 1967).

*

Cortázar was born in Brussels in 1914 of Argentine parents whose descent included Basque, French and German forebears. This apparent non-Argentine background is, however, his most Argentine asset, if one remembers that 97% of the population in Argentina is of European extraction. About the circumstances of his birth, he has explained:

> My birth in Brussels was the result of tourism and diplomacy. My father was on the staff of a commercial mission stationed near the Argentine legation in Belgium, and since he had just gotten married he took my mother with him to Brussels. It was my lot to be born during the German occupation of Brussels, at the beginning of World War I. I was almost four when my family was able to return to Argentina. I spoke mainly French and from that language I retained my rolling *r* which I could never get rid of. I grew up in Banfield, a town on the outskirts of Buenos Aires, in a house with a large garden full of cats, dogs, turtles and parrakeets: paradise. But in that paradise I was already Adam, in the sense that I don't have happy memories from my childhood—too many chores, an excessive sensitivity, a frequent sadness, asthma, broken arms, first desperate loves (my story "The Poisons" is very autobiographical).[3]

As for his beginnings as a writer, he made the following comments:

Like all children who like to read, I soon tried to write. I finished my first novel when I was nine years old . . . And so on. And poetry inspired by Poe, of course. When I was twelve, fourteen, I wrote love poems to a girl in my class . . . But after that it wasn't until I was thirty or thirty-two—apart from a lot of poems that are lying about here and there, lost or burned—that I started to write stories. I knew instinctively that my first stories shouldn't be published. I'd set myself a high literary standard and was determined to reach it before publishing anything. The stories were the best I could do at the time, but I didn't think they were good enough, though there were some good ideas in them. I never took anything to a publisher.

I'm a schoolteacher. I graduated from Mariano Acosta School in Buenos Aires, completed the studies for a teacher's degree, and then entered the Buenos Aires University School of Liberal Arts. I passed the first-year exams, but then I was offered a teaching job in a town in the province of Buenos Aires, and since there was little money at home, and I wanted to help my mother, who educated me at great cost and sacrifice—my father had left home when I was a very small child and had never done anything for the family—, I gave up my university studies at the first chance I had to work, when I was twenty years old, and moved to the country. There I spent five years as a high school teacher. And that was where I started to write stories, though I never dreamed of publishing them. A bit later I moved West, to Mendoza, to the University of Cuyo, where I was offered to teach some courses, this time at the university level. In 1945–46, since I knew I was going to lose my job because I'd been in the fight against Perón, when Perón won the presidential election, I resigned before I was backed against the wall as so many colleagues who held onto their jobs were. I found work in Buenos Aires and there I went on writing stories. But I was very doubtful about having a book published. In that sense I think I was always clear-sighted. I watched myself develop, and didn't force things. I knew that at a certain moment what I was writing was worth quite a bit more than what was being written by others of my age in Argentina. But, because of the high idea I had of literature, I thought it was a stupid habit to publish just anything as people used to do in Argentina in those days when a twenty-year-old youngster who'd written a handful of sonnets used to run around trying to have them put into print. If he couldn't find a publisher, he'd pay for a personal edition himself . . . So I held my fire.[4]

Cortázar's reference to the anonymous twenty-year-old author of a book of sonnets describes his generation's hasty attitude toward publishing, but it also alludes to his own first collection of sonnets published in 1938 under the title *Presencia* and pseudonymously signed Julio Denís. This is, so far, the earliest evidence of his writings and the only book he never allowed to be reprinted. Copies of this limited first edition, not available today in most libraries or collections, circulate nonetheless among friends and devotees, sometimes in xeroxed copies of the original. Cortázar doesn't care to talk about this early volume and discards the collection altogether as a "very Mallarméan" type of poetry. The presence of Mallarmé is apparent, but in addition Baudelaire, Rosetti and Cocteau are quoted in three epigraphs, and two poems are devoted to Góngora and Neruda. His reading of Rimbaud is also evident, supported by one of his earliest prose pieces, "Rimbaud," published in 1941 in the literary magazine *Huella*. Cortázar acknowledges Rimbaud as one of the most influential poets on his generation and on surrealism because, he explains there, "Rimbaud is above all a man. His problem was not a poetic problem but one posed by an ambitious human realization, to which end the Poem should be the key. This brings him near to those of us who see poetry as the fulfillment of the self, as its absolute embodiment and its entelechy."[5] In later essays Cortázar further elaborates and refines this point concerning surrealism as a world view and poetry as "an extension of life." As a young poet he voiced some of the preoccupations of his generation: poetry as a journey to the self; life as an insoluble mystery; authenticity as the ultimate test; time, solitude and death. The tone is grave, elegiac and at times sibylline: "Because this that you call my life / Is my death feigning my life."[6] One thinks of Quevedo, but from the quotation heading the poem Cortázar makes clear that his context is not the Spanish conceptist, but a writer who is to leave a strong impression on him—Jean Cocteau. *Presencia* also reveals Cortázar's early enthusiasm for music in general and for jazz in particular, and more revealing still is one sonnet in which his fascination for the fantastic finds a first formulation in a closing triplet:

> And what once was true is no longer true,
> And night enters through the windows
> Open to the realm of the unknown.[7]

One can understand Cortázar's reluctance to permit the reedition of this early volume and his dismissal of its literary merits. As much as he displays profuse and at times cryptic language and handles the sonnet form with the skill of a virtuoso, this poetry is still the probing of a poet attitudinizing, echoing the prestige and elegance of a polished dictionary, conjuring the spell of the old masters. Cortázar has not yet found his own poetic voice, which when fully achieved in his more mature poetry of *Pameos y meopas*, published in 1971 but including poems written as early as 1951, will prove to be of such different tenor and timbre—straightforward, attuned to his circumstance, free of any affectation, masterfully plain and yet by far more complex and intense than his early attempts. His first volume of poems is reminiscent of the literary beginnings of another Argentine, Borges, who never allowed the reprinting of his first three volumes of essays because, he has explained,

> I began writing in a very factitious and baroque style. I believe that what happened to me was happening to many young writers. Out of timidity, I thought that if I used a plain language people would suspect that I didn't know how to write. I felt compelled to prove that I knew many rare words and that I knew how to combine them in a surprising way.[8]

Curiously, it was Borges who published Cortázar's first short story, "House Taken Over," in *Los anales de Buenos Aires*, a literary journal he edited and which, together with *Sur*, was among the most influential literary magazines published in Argentina at the time. The year, 1946. Talking about these early contacts with Cortázar, Borges observed:

> I don't know Cortázar's work at all well, but the little I do know, a few stories, seems to me admirable. I'm proud of the fact that I was the first to publish any work by him. When I was the editor of a magazine named *Los anales de Buenos Aires*, I remember a tall young man presenting himself in the office and handing me a manuscript. I said I would read it, and he came back after a week. The story was entitled "La casa tomada" (House Taken Over). I told him it was excellent; my sister Norah illustrated it.[9]

It couldn't have been a more auspicious beginning for Cortázar as a fiction writer. A year later the same journal published his second short story, "Bestiary," and a third, "Lejana" (The Distances), appeared the year after in *Cabalgata*, a Buenos Aires monthly magazine of arts and letters. It was not until 1951, the year he left for France not to return except for occasional visits, that he collected these three stories together with five others in a volume entitled *Bestiario*. The book was published at the insistence of a few close friends who read the stories in manuscript form. About his unhurriedness, Cortázar has explained: "I was completely sure that from about, say, 1947, all the things I'd been putting away were good, some of them even very good. I am referring, for example, to some of the stories of *Bestiario*. I knew nobody had written stories like those before in Spanish, at least in my country. There were others, the admirable tales by Borges, for instance, but what I was doing was different."[10]

And indeed it was. There are some stories whose subjects bring to mind those of Borges, sort of variations on a same theme; but even when that is the case, the common subject only underlines the differences. A good example is Borges's "Streetcorner Man" and Cortázar's "El móvil" (The Motive). Both stories deal with a similar character (the *compadre* as the city counterpart in courage and sense of honor to the gaucho in the countryside), both present a similar plot (an infamous act that must be avenged), and both surprise the reader with an unexpected turn in the sequence of events leading to their denouement. Yet Cortázar's treatment of this common theme differs considerably from the one adopted by Borges. While Borges follows a linear unfolding of the basic conflict, in Cortázar's story the plot ramifies into a double conflict, thus creating within a single narrative space two spaces that the reader must discover as a hidden double bottom. Stylistically, Borges has fused some living speech patterns of the *compadre* with a language in which the reader recognizes the traits of Borges's own playful style. This deliberate hybridization works, because in recreating the *compadre*'s speech as the narrator of the story, Borges proceeds with the knowledge that the problem confronting a writer is not that of reproducing with the fidelity of a tape recorder the voice of his protagonists but that of producing the illusion of his voice, and this illusion is based on a literary convention. Cortázar's stylistic solution, on the other hand, is different. Since his character-narrator lives in an Argentina contemporaneous with his own writing, he rejects the use of an exclusive vernacular to adopt instead a Spanish closer to that used by a *Porteño* type he is fully familiar with and not too different from his own—in summary, a Spanish which best captures the tone of the narrative, which best fits the theme and intention of the story and which becomes its most powerful vehicle of characterization.

This stylistic answer typifies Cortázar's overall approach to the use of language in his stories. He himself has pointed out that:

> . . . in a great style language ceases to be a vehicle for the expression of ideas and feelings and yields to a borderline state in which it is no longer a mere language to become actually the very presence of what has been expressed. . . . What is told in a story should indicate by itself who is speaking, at what distance, from what perspective and according to what type of discourse. The work is not defined so much by the elements of the *fabula* or their ordering as by the modes of the fiction, tangentially indicated by the enunciation proper of the *fabula*.[11]

In most of his stories the challenge lies precisely in the search for a voice without falsetto, a genuine voice through which his characters embody themselves. In a strange way, mimesis at its best, the author keeps quiet so that the narrative can speak for itself, from within, and find the language which suits in the most natural manner its inner needs and own intents, a paradoxical immanence by means of which the characters lend their voices to the author.

It has also been a facile operation to throw Borges and Cortázar into the same bag loosely labeled as the fantastic. The truth is that neither of them has much in common with the nineteenth-century European and American writers who, between 1820 and 1850, produced the masterpieces of the fantastic genre.[12] Sensing the imprecision of the designation, Cortázar himself has said about this, "Most of the stories I have written belong to the genre called fantastic for lack of a better name."[13] And on the same subject, he has explained to the interviewer of *La Quinzaine Littéraire*:

> Le grand fantastique, le fantastique qui fait les meilleurs contes, est rarement axé sur la joie, l'humour, les choses positives. Le fantastique est négatif, il approche toujours de l'horrible, de l'épouvante. Ça a donné le roman "gothique," avec ses chaînes et ses fantômes, etc. Puis ça a donné Edgar Allan Poe qui a vraiment inventé le conte fantastique moderne—toujours horrible aussi. Je ne suis pas arrivé à savoir pourquoi le fantastique est axé sur le côté nocturne de l'homme et non sur le côté diurne.[14]

Neither Borges nor Cortázar is interested in this nocturnal side of man, in assaulting the reader with the fears and horrors which have been defined as the attributes of the fantastic.[15] Yet it is clear that in their stories there is a fantastic dimension which runs against the grain of the realist or psychological forms of fiction, allowing for uncanny events intolerable within a realist code. Accepting this fact, and acknowledging at the same time that the definition of "fantastic" for this type of narrative is incongruous, I have suggested elsewhere to refer to them as "neofantastic" as a way of distinguishing them from their distant, nineteenth-century relatives.[16] This is not the place to expand on a proposal for a poetics of this new genre, but it seems reasonably acceptable to view certain works by Kafka, Blanchot, Borges, Cortázar and several others in Latin America as expressions of the neofantastic. Rather than "playing with the readers' fears," as the fantastic sought, the neofantastic, as Cortázar has put it in defining his own short fiction, "seeks an alternative to that false realism which assumed that everything can be neatly described as was upheld by the philosophic and scientific optimism of the eighteenth century, that is, within a world ruled more or less harmoniously by a system of laws, of principles, of causal relations, of well defined psychologies, of well mapped geographies." Cortázar concludes, "In my case, the suspicion of another order, more secret and less communicable, and the fertile discovery of Alfred Jarry, for whom the true study of reality did not rest on laws but on the exceptions to those laws, were some of the guiding principles of my personal search for a literature beyond overly naïve forms of realism."[17]

Much as Borges and Cortázar approach the fantastic in an effort not to terrify the reader but to shake his epistemological assumptions, to immerse him in a world where "the unreal" invades and contaminates the real, their stories can be described as the obverse and the reverse of that same effort. Borges has said that everything that has happened to him is illusory and that the only thing real in his life is a library. This would be a dubious statement were it not for the fact that the world, as we know it, is a creation of culture, an artificial world in which, according to Lévi-Strauss, man lives as a member of a social group.[18] Leaning on the nature of culture as a fabrication of the human mind, Borges has written, "We have dreamed the world. We have dreamed it strong, mysterious, visible, ubiquitous in space and secure in time; but we have allowed tenuous, eternal interstices of unreason in its structure so we may know that it is false."[19] Borges penetrates these illogical interstices in an attempt to unweave that tidy labyrinth of reason woven by culture to find finally that art and language (and science, for that matter) are, can only be, symbols—however, "not in the sense of mere figures which refer to some given reality by means of suggestion and allegorical renderings, but in the sense of forces each of which produces and posits a world of its own."[20]

Motivated by this inference, Borges finds the road that leads to the universe of his fiction: "Let us admit what all idealists admit: the hallucinatory nature of the world. Let us do what no idealist has done: let us seek unrealities that confirm that nature."[21] He has found those unrealities not in the realm of the supernatural or the marvelous but in those symbols and systems which define our own reality, in philosophies and theologies which in some way constitute the core of our culture. Hence the countless references in his stories to authors and books, to theories and doctrines; hence the aura of bookishness and intellection that pervades his work; and hence his constant insistence on his having said nothing new, because what he wrote was already written in other literatures. It was written in the same way that the *Quixote* had been written before Pierre Menard, but Menard's merit lies in his reading the *Quixote* as it couldn't have been read in Cervantes's time. Borges, for whom "one literature differs from another, either before or after it, not so much because of the text as for the manner in which it is read,"[22] reads that "respected system of perplexities we call philosophy" in a new context. The ingredients do not change, just as the number of colored glass bits contained in a kaleidoscope is always the same, but with each movement of the tube the symmetrical image does change. Borges deals with human culture as if he were holding a kaleidoscope, but after his master stroke the image is no longer the same. The alchemy consists in presenting our reality, what we have come to accept as our reality, transfigured in a dream, in one more phantasmagoria of the mind which has little or nothing to do with the real world it seeks to penetrate.

Cortázar's fictional world, on the other hand, rather than an acceptance, represents a challenge to culture, a challenge, as he puts it, to "thirty centuries of Judeo-Christian dialectics," to "the Greek criterion of truth and error," to the homo sapiens, to logic and the law of sufficient reason and, in general, to what he calls "the Great Habit." If Borges's fantasies are oblique allusions to the situation of man in a world he can never fully fathom, to an order he has created as a substitute labyrinth to the one created by a divine mind, Cortázar's stories strive to transcend the schemes and constructs of culture and seek precisely to touch that order Borges finds too abstruse and complex to be understood by man. The first stumbling block Cortázar encounters in this quest is language itself: "I've always found it absurd," he says, "to talk about transforming man if man doesn't simultaneously, or previously, transform his instrument of knowledge. How to transform oneself if one continues to use the same language Plato used?"[23] He found a first answer in surrealism. As early as 1949 he defined surrealism as "the greatest undertaking of contemporary man as an anticipation and attempt toward an integrated humanism."[24] Cortázar saw in surrealism not a mere literary technique or a simple esthetic stand, but a world view or, as he said in the same article, "not a school or an ism but a Weltanschauung." When surrealism settled for less than "an integrated humanism," Cortázar confronted some of its inconsistencies through the pages of *Hopscotch*. One of its characters, Étienne, says in chapter 99:

> The surrealists thought that true language and true reality were censored and relegated by the rationalist and bourgeois structure of the Western world. They were right, as any poet knows, but that was just a moment in the complicated peeling of the banana. Result, more than one of them ate it with the skin still on. The surrealists hung from words instead of brutally disengaging themselves from them, as Morelli would like to do from the word itself. Fanatics of the *verbum* in a pure state, frantic wizards, they accepted anything as long as it didn't seem excessively grammatical. They didn't suspect enough that the creation of a whole language, even though it might end up betraying its sense, irrefutably shows human structure, whether that of a Chinese or a redskin. Language means residence in reality, living in a reality. Even if it's true that the language we use betrays us . . . , wanting to free it from its taboos isn't enough. We have to relive it, not reanimate it.[25]

The second obstacle Cortázar stumbles upon in this search for authenticity is the use of our normative categories of thought and knowledge, our rational tools for apprehending reality. He believes in a kind of marvelous reality (here again the affinity with surrealism is obvious). "Marvelous," he explains, "in the sense that our daily reality masks *a second reality* which is neither mysterious nor theological, but profoundly human. Yet, due to a long series of mistakes, it has remained concealed under a reality prefabricated by many centuries of culture, a culture in which there are great achievements but also profound aberrations, profound distortions."[26]

Among those distorted notions which obstruct man's access to a more genuine world, Cortázar points a finger to our perception of death and to two of the most established concepts in the Western grasp of reality—time and space.

> The notions of time and space, as they were conceived by the Greeks and after them by the whole of the West, are flatly rejected by Vedanta. In a sense, man made a mistake when he invented time. That's why it would actually be enough for us to renounce mortality, to take a jump out of time, on a level other than that of daily life, of course. I'm thinking of the phenomenon of death, which for Western thought has been a great scandal, as Kierkegaard and Unamuno realized so well; a phenomenon that is not in the least scandalous in the East where it is regarded not as an end but as a metamorphosis.[27]

As much as Cortázar sees the East as an alternative to this preoccupation with time and space, he also realizes that it cannot be an answer for Western man, who is the product of a different tradition, a tradition one cannot simply undo or replace. If there is an answer to the questions of time and space, it lies in a relentless confrontation with them in a manner similar to the struggle Unamuno memorably represented in the fight between Jacob and the Angel. "*Rayuela*, like so much of my work," Cortázar says, "suffers from hyperintellectuality. But, I'm not willing or able to renounce that intellectuality, insofar as I can breathe life into it, make it pulse in every thought and word."[28]

It is this kind of coalescence between two diametrically opposed dimensions—one natural and one supernatural, one historical and one fantastic—that constitutes the backbone of Cortázar's neofantastic short fiction. The beggar whom the protagonist of "Lejana" meets in the center of a bridge in Budapest, the noises that expel the brother and sister from their "house taken over," the rabbits that the narrator of "A Letter to a Lady in Paris" helplessly vomits, the tiger that roams freely through the rooms of a middle-class family's house in "Bestiary," the dead character who is yet more alive than the living ones in "Cartas de mamá," the dream that becomes real and converts its dreamer into a dream in "The Night Face Up," the reader who enters the fiction and ends up fictionalizing reality in "Continuity of Parks"—these are but a few examples of how the realist code yields to a code which no longer responds to our causal categories of time and space. In these stories the reverse side of the phenomenal world is sought, an order scandalously in conflict with the order construed by logical thinking; hence the incongruities we call "fantastic."

But the fantastic event in these tales does not aim, as it did in the nineteenth century, at assailing and terrifying us with "a crack," as Roger Caillois says of the fantastic genre.[29] From the outset the realist scale is juxtaposed with the fantastic one. In "Axolotl" the opening paragraph reads, "There was a time when I thought a great deal about axolotls. I went to see them in the aquarium at the Jardin des Plantes and stayed for hours watching them, observing their immobility, their faint movements. Now I am an axolotl."[30] In this text there is not, as is the case in most neofantastic fiction, a gradual process of presentation of the real which finally yields to a fissure of unreality. In contrast to the nineteenth-century fantastic fiction in which the text moves from the familiar and natural to the unfamiliar and supernatural, like a journey through a known and recognizable territory which eventually leads to an unknown and dreadful destination, the writers of the neofantastic bestow equal validity and verisimilitude on both orders. They have no difficulty in moving with the same freedom and ease in both. This unbiased approach is in itself a profession of faith. The unstated assumption declares that the fantastic level is just as real (or unreal, from a realist standpoint) as the realist level. If one of them produces in us a surreal or fantastic feeling, it is because in our daily lives we follow logical notions similar to those that govern the realist mode.

The neofantastic writer, on the other hand, ignores these distinctions and approaches both levels with the same sense of reality. The reader senses, nevertheless, that Cortázar's axolotl is a metaphor (a metaphor and not a symbol) that conveys meanings unconveyable through logical conceptualizations, a metaphor that strives to express messages inexpressible through the realist code. The metaphor (rabbits, tiger, noises, axolotl, beggar) provides Cortázar with a structure capable of producing new referents, even if their references are yet to be established or, to use I. A. Richards's terminology, the *vehicles* with which these metaphors confront us point to unformulated *tenors*. We know we are dealing with vehicles of metaphors because they suggest meanings that exceed their literal value, but it is the reader's task to perceive and define those meanings, to determine the tenor to which the vehicle points.

When personally asked about the meanings implied in those metaphors, Cortázar has answered: "I know as much as you do." This is not a subterfuge. He once explained, "The great majority of my stories were written—how should I say—in spite of my own will, above or below my reasoning consciousness, as if I were but a medium through which a strange force passed and manifested itself."[31] Some even originated as dreams or nightmares:

> Il est vrai que certain de mes contes sont nés directement de cauchemars ou de rêves. Un des premiers contes que j'ai écrits, "La maison occupée", procède d'un cauchemar. C'en est la transcription très fidèle bien que travaillée littérairement, évidemment. . . . Si je faisais une statistique de ceux de mes contes que je dois aux rêves, ils se situeraient en nette minorité. Quelques-uns évidemment sont faits de lambeaux de rêves, mais c'est lorsque je suis éveillé que le fantastique tombe sur moi comme une pierre.[32]

All this may sound too close to the surrealist explorations of the unconscious, to the prescriptions included by Breton in the *Manifestos* regarding automatic writing and transcription of dreams. Any page written by Cortázar will suffice, however, to dispel that impression. If he, on one hand, acknowledges the strong influence surrealism had on him at the beginning of his work, it is equally true, on the other, that it was an influence on outlook and philosophy rather than on technique and style. Cortázar's stories are built with the rigorous precision and, at the same time, subtle naturalness of a cobweb. The text flows with the same perfection one finds in those fragile fabrics beautifully spun between two wires of a fence or in the branches of a tree. But there is nothing fragile in the texture of any of his stories. Quite the contrary. The text displays such an economy of means, it streams with such ease and determination, it arrives so convincingly at its destination, one is tempted to say the story has been told by itself, that what the reader has in front of him is a structure woven by the text itself and that, like those seashells which have engraved on themselves with silent perfection traces of undefiled beauty, on that limpid surface nothing is in excess and nothing is lacking.

*

Cortázar likes to think that with his novels, and more specifically with the long story "The Pursuer," he begins to unloose the stylistic perfection with which his stories are knitted. He also believes that with this change he moves to a new stage in his development as a writer.

> When I wrote "The Pursuer," I had reached a point where I felt I had to deal with something that was a lot closer to me. I wasn't sure of myself any more in that story. I took up an existential problem, a human problem which was later amplified in *The Winners*, and above all in *Hopscotch*. Fantasy for its own sake had stopped interesting me. By then I was fully aware of the dangerous perfection of the storyteller who reaches a certain level of achievement and stays on that same level forever, without moving on. I was a bit sick and tired of seeing how well my stories turned out. In "The Pursuer" I wanted to stop inventing and stand on my own ground, to look at myself a bit. And looking at myself meant looking at my neighbor, at man. I hadn't looked too closely at people until I wrote "The Pursuer."[33]

But, of course, the new linguistic mood he finds in this long story, and later in his subsequent novels, is not the deterioration of his previous style but a new form of expression which tackles more effectively the nature of his new concerns. Cortázar defines those new concerns as "existential and metaphysical" as opposed to his esthetic pursuits in the short story.

The truth is, though, as Cortázar well knows, that his short stories and his novels are motivated by a common search, by a quest for authenticity which is of one piece in both genres. Otherwise, how does one understand his own definition of *Hopscotch* as "the philosophy of my stories, as an examination of what determined, throughout many years, their substance or thrust"?[34] *Hopscotch* articulates the same questions around which the stories are built; but if the novel is a reflection, an effort to brood upon those questions, the stories are narrative translations of those same questions. *Hopscotch* traces the mandala through which the characters of the stories are constantly journeying. Those characters do not speculate or intellectualize; they simply deliver themselves to the passions and games sweeping their lives, moved and battered by forces they don't understand. *Hopscotch* seeks to understand those forces, and as such it represents the intellectual bow from which the stories were shot. The proof that this is indeed the case lies in the fact that some of the central inquiries found in *Hopscotch* were already outlined in the early essays and reviews Cortázar wrote before and during his writing of the short stories. His tales were fantastic responses to those problems and questions which occupied his mind at the time and which eventually found a masterful formulation in *Hopscotch*. It goes without saying that *Hopscotch*'s hyperintellectual ponderings alone do not explain the stories; Cortázar combined his intellectual spurs with his own passions and phobias, and the latter are as enigmatic to him as to the reader.

If Horacio Oliveira seeks through the pages of *Hopscotch* a second reality which has been covered by habit and culture in our present version of reality, and Johnny Carter in "The Pursuer" perceives through intuition and artistic imagination dimensions of reality which have been buried by conceptualization, the characters of the stories also find their ultimate realization on a fantastic plane that is the reverse of that stiff reality to which habit and culture have condemned them. In "Lejana," for instance, one of Cortázar's earliest short stories, the protagonist searches for a bridge at whose center she hopes to find that part of her self rejected and suffocated by family, friends and environment. She does find it, as a beggar waiting on a Budapest bridge, a beggar in whom she recognizes her true self, a sort of double whose reality bursts from her imagination, like a fantastic event, onto a historical plane. Similarly, the protagonist of "The Pursuer," a jazzman modeled after saxophonist Charlie Parker, searches for "a reality that escapes every day" and that sometimes presents itself as "holes": "In the door," he explains, "in the bed: holes. In the hand, in the newspaper, in time, in the air: everything full of holes, everything spongy, like a colander straining itself . . . ."[35] Those holes, invisible or covered for others, are for Johnny the residence of "something else," of a second reality whose door Johnny senses and seeks to open: "It's impossible there's nothing else, it can't be we're that close to it, that much on the other side of the door . . . Bruno, all my life in my music I looked for that door to open finally. Nothing, a crack. . . ." (215–16). What is behind that door is a world that Johnny sees only on one occasion, through his music, but whose substance one glimpses throughout the narrative. A good example is the biography of Johnny written by Bruno: very well informed, very complete, very successful, but with one omission—the biographee. Or as Johnny puts it, "It's very good your book. . . . You're much better informed than I am, but it seems to me like something's missing. . . . Don't get upset, Bruno, it's not important that you forgot to put all that in. But Bruno, . . . what you forgot to put in is me" (207, 212).

Cortázar has acknowledged that Johnny Carter is a first draft of Horacio Oliveira, a precursor in that search which takes the protagonist of *Hopscotch* into a revision of the very foundations of Western culture—its writers and artists, its music and language, its philosophy and ethics, its religion and science—a task Oliveira undertakes together with his friends of the Serpent Club with the casualness and poignancy that makes fiction more credible and convincing than pure intellection. Jung has said of Freud that "he has given expression to the fact that Western man is in danger of losing his shadow altogether, of identifying himself with his fictive personality and of identifying the world with the abstract picture painted by scientific rationalism."[36] This is also Oliveira's concern; but to show that man has become "the slave of his own fiction, and that a purely conceptual world progressively replaces reality," as Jung has said of the products of man's conscious activity, Cortázar proceeds to disassemble that fictitious apparatus manufactured by culture to show that it has become a substitute of reality, a mask that must be removed if man is to regain touch with the real world and with himself. In this sense, *Hopscotch* is a devastating criticism of rationalism:

> . . . this technological reality that men of science and the readers of *France-Soir* accept today, this world of cortisone, gamma rays, and the elution of plutonium, has as little to do with reality as the world of the *Roman de la Rose*. . . . Man, after having expected everything from intelligence and the spirit, feels that he's been betrayed, is vaguely aware that his weapons have been turned against him, that culture, *civiltà*, have misled him into this blind alley where scientific barbarism is nothing but a very understandable reaction. (444–45)

As in "The Pursuer," in *Hopscotch* reality lies also somewhere behind: "Behind all that (it's always behind, convince yourself that this is the key idea of modern thought) Paradise, the other world, trampled innocence which weeping darkly seeks the land of Hurqalyā" (377). How does one get there? How does one reach that center, the "kibbutz of desire" which Oliveira seeks? In his short stories the road is a fantastic event; the conflict between a hollow reality and one which, like an epiphany, reveals to the characters a time outside time and a space that transcends geometric space, resolves itself in metaphors that by defying physical laws appear as fantastic occurrences. In "The Pursuer" Johnny Carter peeps through those "holes" of a second reality via his jazz music; the artistic phenomenon becomes what it has always been—"a bridge toward true reality," in Nietzsche's dictum—but now Johnny transports his visions to the trivial act of riding a subway and indicts the fallacy inherent in our concepts of time and space. In *Hopscotch* our logical order of reason and science is described as totally absurd: "Reason is only good to mummify reality in moments of calm or analyze its future storms, never to resolve a crisis of the moment. . . . And these crises that most people think of as terrible, as absurd, I personally think they serve to show us the real absurdity, the absurdity of an ordered and calm world" (163–64). Oliveira muses on this absurd world when he concludes that "only by living absurdly is it possible to break out of this infinite absurdity" (101). *Hopscotch* offers an answer different from the one found in the short stories and even in "The Pursuer," where Johnny, as much as he lives a life which in Bruno's eyes can only be described as "absurd," engages in a life style of a musical genius who indulges in his allotted share of "absurdity"; it is music which in the end provides for Johnny a bridge to those "holes." The characters of *Hopscotch*, on the other hand, are unprofessional, simple, though extremely well-read and informed people who, as much as they live a bohemian life, share the pettiness and trivia of plain people.

Thus the solution *Hopscotch* presents to Cortázar's basic quest for authenticity is a kind of existential absurdity, a solution that also had a very strong appeal to surrealists since Mallarmé's *Igitur*: "Igitur is a person 'who feels in himself, thanks to the absurd, the existence of the Absolute.' After him the Surrealists will enlarge and maintain the domain of the absolute through this very same type of cult of the absurd which will tend to become the basis of artistic creation and a means of liberating art from the finite or natural aspects of things and beings."[37] It is in this context that some of the most momentous chapters of *Hopscotch* should be read: the concert by Berthe Trépat, the death of Rocamadour, the encounter with the *clocharde*, the episodes of the board, the circus and the mental clinic. These seemingly preposterous situations impress us as absurd because they run against the grain of our accepted order, which for Oliveira has become absurdity at its best. For him, reason contains a sophism as huge as the world it has created, and logic leads to a gargantuan and catastrophic nowhere. To pull out from this dead end, Oliveira embarks on feats and situations which, though they offer him on one hand a route to further exploration of that dead end, act on the other hand as a modified virus of the same disease which hopefully will immunize him. And although *Hopscotch* presents no answers, no prescriptions for guaranteed salvation, it offers a possibility of reconciliation. Toward the end of his absurd odyssey Horacio meditates on the significance of his friend Traveler's last efforts to lend him a helping hand. Horacio seems to have reached the last square of his hopscotch:

> After what Traveler had just done, everything had something like a marvelous feeling of conciliation and that senseless but vivid and present harmony could not be violated, could no longer be falsified, basically Traveler was what he might well have been with a little less cursed imagination, he was the man of the territory, the incurable mistake of the species gone astray, but how much beauty in the mistake and in the five thousand years of false and precarious territory, how much beauty in those eyes that had filled with tears and in that voice that had advised him: "Throw the bolt, I don't trust them," how much love in that arm that held the waist of a woman. "Probably," Oliveira thought while he answered the friendly gestures of Dr. Ovejero and Ferraguto, . . . "the only possible way to escape from that territory is to plunge into it over one's head." (347)

Cortázar's next novel, *62: A Model Kit*, derives from chapter 62 of *Hopscotch* and represents his novelistic answer to Oliveira's search for alternatives to that fabricated reality criticized in the earlier novel. In chapter 62 Morelli sketches the outline of "a book he had been planning but that never got beyond a few scattered notes." "If I were to write this book," he continues, "standard behavior . . . would be inexplicable by means of current instrumental psychology. . . . Everything would be a kind of disquiet, a continuous uprooting, a territory where psychological causality would yield disconcertedly, and those puppets would destroy each other or love each other or recognize each other without suspecting too much that life is trying to change its key in and through and by them, that a barely conceivable attempt is born in man as one other day there were being born the reason-key, the feeling-key, the pragmatism-key" (363). *62: A Model Kit* is the implementation of this attempt.

The novel is, as Cortázar advances in the foreword, a transgression, not only at the most manifest level of language but also as an effort to understand life by cognitive means other than the ones rationally codified by science. Hence psychology is no longer the yardstick. What replaces psychology as the criterion to measure human behavior? A mixture of game, vampirism[38] and an intangible magnetic force that groups people into what Cortázar calls *figuras* or human constellations. The notions of time and space as traditionally accepted are no longer the ordinate and the abscissa which frame and regulate life. In *62* the action takes place in Paris, London and Vienna, but the characters move and act in these different cities as if they were one single space referred to as *la ciudad* (the city). This new space is no longer a confining area which imposes on the characters the limitations of its own perimeter; it is a new medium that the characters stretch, shape and dispose of like a chessboard to play their own games. It matters not if Marrast and Nicole are in London, Hélène and Celia in Paris, Juan and Tell in Vienna; they move and interact from one city to the other horizontally, vertically and diagonally, using the cities as square spaces for their traps, gambits and inevitable checks. But they ignore the rules of the game they play. Their movements are controlled by forces they dimly grasp and which ultimately escape their consciousness, like chess pieces unaware of the player's designs and strategies. Physical or conventional time also recedes to a sort of mythical time in which "the before and the after touch and are one and the same."[39] The characters' nights and days are pivoted around the ominous and invisible rule of the Countess (Erszebet Báthory), whose legendary past marks the birth of vampirism. That past becomes present, and the present in which the characters reside sends them back to that legendary past, in which context one begins to understand in part the patterns that shape their destiny.

The model kit in the title alludes, as Cortázar points out in the foreword, not so much to the structure of the novel as to the task of assembling an intimated meaning by putting together the various elements of a possible *combinatoria*. In form, the novel is built with the precision and cleverness of a clockwork. The first thirty pages that introduce the rest of the narrative contain, like the slide in Nicolas Roeg's memorable film *Don't Look Now*, the basic ingredients of which the novel is made: the name of the restaurant, the mistranslation of a customer's order, Juan's own order of a bottle of Sylvaner, the book Juan carries and opens by chance to a certain page, the date (Christmas Eve) and fragments of the story the novel is about to unfold. In this long soliloquy that streams through Juan's consciousness as he sits facing a mirror in the restaurant, Cortázar has disclosed the leading strands that tie together the meandering ramifications of the entire novel. In this sense, the overture is like a cocoon which already holds the full length of the thread the text patiently and skillfully unwinds. The mirror Juan faces in the restaurant anticipates the reflective quality of the introductory passage and also defines the mirrorlike symmetries with which the novel is constructed. Each character seems to be a reflection or double of another: Frau Marta echoes Erszebet Báthory, and the English girl she violates has a counterpart in Celia, who is violated by Hélène, who in turn seems to be under the spell of Countess

Báthory; Marrast loves Nicole, who loves Juan, who loves Hélène; the seduction of an adolescent girl (Celia) is matched by the seduction of an adolescent boy (Austin); Polanco and Calac are each like the inverted image of the other; the long section about Frau Marta and the possession of the English girl parallels and crisscrosses, at the same time, the equally long section about the possession of Celia by Hélène, and the doll made by monsieur Ochs that Juan gives to Tell and Tell sends to Hélène bridges the two sections as the clue to both stories. Finally, Hélène is guilt-ridden by the death of one of her patients, who hauntingly reminds her of Juan, and toward the end of the novel she is killed by Austin, who loves Celia; Hélène is thus the vertex of two triangles, in each of which there is a deceased and in each of which a member of one sex is linked to two of the other: Hélène-Patient-Juan and Austin-Hélène-Celia.

The text itself, as discourse, shares these equidistances: first, in the relation between the introduction and the body of the novel in a proportion similar to the one between a code and its decoder; second, in the way the myth of the Countess Báthory and the "blood castle" at the very beginning of the novel exchanges signals toward the end with a second myth, the story of Diana and Acteon from Greek mythology, mentioned by Juan on page 235 and subsequently discussed by him and Hélène in the following pages; and third, the black pontoon that mysteriously appears at the end of the introduction carrying Frau Marta and reappears towards the end of the novel with Frau Marta on it, but this time bewitching Nicole, who also travels through the canal on "the same" black pontoon. In addition, the scene in the restaurant is described as the point where the various pieces of a puzzle finally fall into place, bringing the bizarre and liquid ingredients of Juan's blood story to "coagulation," to a curdling point and a frozen time where for Juan "the before and the after had fallen apart in his hands, leaving him a light, useless rain of dead moths" (24).

But if for a moment this curdled *figura*, which creates its own space and generates its own time, which seeks to perceive and define reality in terms that defy causality, makes us think of or suspect a flight from history, it is only so because we have tended for too long to associate the concern for man and his social plight with facile pamphlets mistakenly taken as "literature" of protest. Cortázar knows too well that there are no easy answers, that the fires and horrors of history cannot be put out or even placated by making literature impersonate roles and gestures which create false illusions and hollow expectations and end up adulterating and finally canceling its true capabilities. His next and latest novel so far, *Libro de Manuel*, is an effort to show that a writer can undertake to deal with the social problems of his time without turning into a puppeteer whose script has been set beforehand as an adaptation of political slogans and ideological platitudes. Cortázar is torn in this novel between his responsibilities as a writer who respects and values his craft and his responsibilities as a man who lives immersed in his time and feels part of the Latin American destiny. And again the answer is neither simple nor clear-cut. In *Hopscotch* Horacio ponders the dilemma and its double-edged nature:

> Besides, what was the true morality of action? A social action like that of the syndicalists was more than justified in the field of history. Happy were those who lived and slept in history. . . . There was no objection to that action as such,

but he pushed it aside with doubts about his personal conduct. He would suspect a betrayal the moment he gave in to posters on the street or activities of a social nature; a betrayal disguised as satisfactory work, daily happiness, satisfied conscience, fulfilled duty. He was too well acquainted with certain communists in Buenos Aires and Paris, capable of the worst villainy but redeemable in their own minds by "the struggle," by having to leave in the middle of dinner to run to a meeting or finish a job. Social action in those people seemed too much like an alibi, the way children are usually the alibi for mothers' not having to do anything worth while in this life, the way learning with its blinders is useful in not learning that in the jail down the street they are still guillotining guys who should not be guillotined. False action is almost always the most spectacular, the kind that tears down respect, prestige, and whequestrian wheffigies. (417-18)

Andrés, the protagonist of *Libro de Manuel* and a sort of outgrowth of Horacio Oliveira, seeks a political answer without suppressing his human condition and without impinging on his individual rights and endeavors. Thus his political search becomes an act of assertion of his freedom and of his personal realization. The road leading to this ultimate goal is a tortuous and agonizing one, since in the long run any genuine social struggle implies the suppression or assimilation of personal struggles, or at least their postponement, to the cause one is engaged in. In his last conversation with Lonstein, Andrés defends his rights up to the last, sensing that the slightest form of mutilation conceals a betrayal:

> —You, *sir*, want a lot of things, but you don't give up any.
> —No, I don't give up anything, pal.
> —Not even a tiny bit? Say, an exquisite author? A Japanese poet known only to you?
> —No, not even that.
> —What about your Xenakis, your aleatory music, your free jazz, your Joni Mitchell, your abstract lithographs?
> —No, brother. Nothing. I take everything with me wherever I go.
> —You really have it your way. don't you?—said Lonstein—. You want to have the pie and eat it too, right?
> —Yes sir—said Andrés.[40]

But as much as this novel takes Cortázar into exploring his own social and political concerns, *Libro de Manuel* is also, like his previous works, part of his relentless effort to liberate man. This new man should be the product of a new kind of humanism Cortázar has striven to outline throughout his poetry, essays and fiction. Each of them is a stretch of a route seeking to arrive at a center, at a final island, at a world that "exists in this one" but that "one has to create like the phoenix." As there are no easy answers for Cortázar, there are no final answers either. He is a nonconformist, a rebel or, what amounts to the same thing, a poet who searches through literature "to earn the right to enter the house of man."

[1] Carlos Fuentes, "A Demanding Novel," *Commentary* (New York), October 1966, pp. 142-43.

[2] Donald Keene, "Moving Snapshots," *The New York Times Book Review*, 10 April 1966, p. 1.

[3] Graciela de Sola, *Julio Cortázar y el hombre nuevo*, Buenos Aires, Sudamericana, 1968, p. 9 (my translation).

[4] Luis Harss, Barbara Dohmann, *Into the Mainstream*, New York, Harper & Row, 1967, pp. 214-15.

[5] Julio Denís (Julio Cortázar), "Rimbaud," *Huella* (Buenos Aires), no. 2 (July 1941). Quoted by G. De Sola, p. 14.

[6] Julio Denís (Julio Cortázar), "Quitadme," from his *Presencia*, Buenos Aires, El Bibliófilo, 1938, p. 40 (my translation).

[7] Ibid., p. 94 (my translation). The Spanish pun *cierto/incierto* is lost in translation.

[8] James E. Irby, "Encuentro con Borges," *Vida universitaria* (Monterrey, Mex.), 12 April 1964, p. 14.

9 Rita Guibert, *Seven Voices*, New York, Vintage, 1973, p. 108.

10 Harss, p. 61.

11 Julio Cortázar, *La vuelta al día en ochenta mundos*, Mexico City, Siglo XXI, 1967, p. 94. In the second part of the quotation Cortázar cites a passage by Michel Foucault, as he clearly indicates in his book.

12 See Roger Caillois, *Imágenes, imágenes . . .* , Buenos Aires, Sudamericana, 1970, pp. 23–24.

13 Julio Cortázar, "Algunos aspectos del cuento," *Casa de las Américas* (Havana), 1962, nos. 15–16, p. 3 (my translation).

14 C. G. Bjurström, "Julio Cortázar, Entretien," *La Quinzaine Littéraire* (Paris), 1 August 1970, p. 17.

15 See Caillois, op. cit.; Louis Vax, *L'art et la littérature fantastique*, Paris, 1960; and Peter Penzoldt, *The Supernatural in Literature*, New York, 1965.

16 See my article "The Fantastic as Surrealist Metaphors in Cortázar's Short Fiction," *Dada/Surrealism* (New York), 1975, no. 5, pp. 28–33.

17 "Algunos aspectos del cuento," pp. 3–4.

18 See Claude Lévi-Strauss, *Arte, lenguaje, etnología (Entrevistas con Georges Charbonier)*, Mexico City, Siglo XXI, 1968, p. 132.

19 Jorge Luis Borges, *Other Inquisitions*, R. L. Simms, tr., New York, Washington Square, 1966, p. 120.

20 See Ernest Cassirer, *Language and Myth*, New York, Dover, 1953, p. 8.

21 Borges, p. 120.

22 Ibid., p. 173.

23 Harss, p. 235.

24 Julio Cortázar, "Irracionalismo y eficacia," *Realidad: revista de ideas* (Buenos Aires), nos. 17–18 (September–December 1949), p. 253.

25 Julio Cortázar, *Hopscotch*, Gregory Rabassa, tr., New York, Pantheon, 1966, p. 441. Subsequent quotations are taken from this edition.

26 Margarita García Flores, "Siete respuestas de Julio Cortázar," *Revista de la Universidad de México* (Mexico City), vol. 21, no. 7 (March 1967), p. 11 (my translation).

27 Harss, p. 219.

28 Ibid., pp. 244–45.

29 Caillois, p. 14.

30 Julio Cortázar, *Blow-Up and Other Stories*, Paul Blackburn, tr., New York, Collier, 1968, p. 3.

31 "Algunos aspectos del cuento," p. 7.

32 Bjurström, p. 17. In this regard Cortázar also noted in one of his lectures at the University of Oklahoma in November 1975: "And since I have mentioned dreams, it seems appropriate to say that many of my fantastic stories were born in an oneiric territory and that I had the good fortune that in some cases the censorship was not merciless and permitted me to carry the content of the dreams into words. . . . One could say that the fantastic which they contain comes from archetypal regions which in one way or another we all share, and that in the act of reading these stories the reader witnesses or discovers something of himself. I have seen this phenomenon put to the test many times with an old story of mine entitled "The House Taken Over," which I dreamed with all the details which figure in the text and which I wrote upon jumping out of bed, still enveloped in the horrible nausea of its ending." From "The Present State of Fiction in Latin America," Margery A. Safir, tr., *Books Abroad* 50:3 (Summer 1976), p. 522–32, and included in this volume.

33 Harss, p. 224.

34 *La vuelta al día*, p. 25.

35 *Blow-Up and Other Stories*, pp. 190–91. Subsequent quotations are from this edition.

36 C. G. Jung, *The Undiscovered Self*, Boston, Little, Brown, 1957, p. 82.

37 Anna Balakian, *Surrealism: The Road to the Absolute*, New York, Noonday, 1959, p. 12.

38 On game, see Linda Cummings Baxt, "Game in Cortázar," unpublished Ph.D. dissertation (Yale University), 1974; and also my article "*Homo sapiens* vs. *homo ludens* en tres cuentos de Cortázar," *Revista Iberoamericana* (Pittsburgh University), nos. 84–85 (July–December 1973), pp. 611–24. On vampirism in *62: A Model Kit*, see chapter 8 of Baxt's dissertation; and also Ana María Hernández, "Vampires and Vampiresses: A Reading of *62*," *Books Abroad* 50:3 (Summer 1976), pp. 570–76, included in this volume.

39 Julio Cortázar, *62: A Model Kit*, Gregory Rabassa, tr., New York, Pantheon, 1972, p. 148. Subsequent quotations are from this edition.

40 Julio Cortázar, *Libro de Manuel*, Buenos Aires, Sudamericana, 1973, p. 343 (my translation).

Chronology

By EVELYN PICON GARFIELD

1914	26 August: Julio Cortázar is born in Brussels, Belgium of Argentine parents.
1918	Returns to Argentina to live in Banfield, a suburb of Buenos Aires.
1932	Earns a degree as an elementary school teacher.
1935	Earns a degree as a secondary and preparatory school teacher.
1936	Passes first-year examinations at the university.
1937–44	Leaves studies to work as a high school teacher in Bolívar and Chivilcoy. Starts to write short stories.
1938	Publishes *Presencia* (Presence), a collection of poems, and signs it with the pseudonym Julio Denís.
1944–45	Teaches courses in French literature at the University of Cuyo. Participates in the occupation of the university in protest against Peronism. Is arrested but freed shortly afterward. Renounces his post.
1946–48	Moves to Buenos Aires where he works as the manager of the Argentine Publishing Association (Cámara Argentina del Libro). Earns a degree as a public translator after passing examinations in languages and law.
1948–51	Leaves the managerial position to begin work as a public translator.
1949	Publishes a dramatic poem, *Los reyes* (The Kings), using his own name for the first time.
1951	Is awarded a scholarship by the French government to study in Paris. Leaves Argentina the same month in which his first collection of short stories, *Bestiario* (Bestiary), is published.
1952	Remains in Paris and begins work as a free-lance translator for UNESCO.
1953	Marries Aurora Bernárdez, an Argentine and a translator. Visits Italy where he translates the prose works of Edgar Allan Poe for the University of Puerto Rico. Writes much of *Historias de cronopios y de famas* (*Cronopios and Famas*).
1956	Publishes the short story collection *Final del juego* (*End of the Game and Other Stories*) and *Obras en prosa* (Prose Works of Edgar Allan Poe).
1958	Publishes the short story collection *Las armas secretas* (Secret Weapons).
1960	Publishes his first novel, *Los premios* (*The Winners*). Visits the United States, in particular Washington, D.C. and Greenwich Village in New York.
1962	Publishes the anecdotes of *Historias de cronopios y de famas* (*Cronopios and Famas*).
1963	Publishes the novel *Rayuela* (*Hopscotch*). Makes first visit to post-revolutionary Cuba.
1965	*The Winners* is published in English translation by Pantheon in the United States.
1966	Publishes the short story collection *Todos los fuegos el fuego* (*All Fires the Fire*). *Hopscotch* is published in English translation by Pantheon in the United States.

1967   Publishes his first collage-book, *La vuelta al día en ochenta mundos* (Around
         the Day in Eighty Worlds). *Blow-Up and Other Stories* is published in
         English translation by Pantheon in the United States. Previously in hard-
         cover edition under the title *End of the Game and Other Stories*.

1968   Publishes the novel *62: Modelo para armar* (*62: A Model Kit*).

1969   Publishes his second collage-book, *Ultimo round* (Last Round). *Cronopios
         and Famas* is published in English translation by Pantheon in the United
         States.

1970   Publishes *Viaje alrededor de una mesa* (A Trip Around the Table).

1971   Publishes *Pameos y Meopas* (Pameos and Meopas), a collection of poems.

1972   Publishes *Prosa del observatorio* (Prose from the Observatory). *62: A Model
         Kit* is published in English translation by Pantheon in the United States.

1973   Travels to Argentina to commemorate the publication of his novel, *Libro de
         Manuel* (Book of Manuel). Also visits Peru, Ecuador and Chile. *All Fires
         the Fire* is published in English translation by Pantheon in the United States.

1974   Publishes the short story collection *Octaedro*. Participates in the P.E.N.
         Translation Conference in New York.

1975   Lectures at University of Oklahoma. Fifth Oklahoma Conference on Writers
         of the Hispanic World dedicated to Cortázar (21–22 November).

The above Chronology is reproduced from E. Picon Garfield's book, *Julio Cortázar*
(New York, Ungar, 1975), with permission of the publisher.

Second Time Around

By JULIO CORTÁZAR

We just waited for them, each one had his date and his time, but there was no rush about it, smoking slowly, every so often Nigger López would come by with coffee and then we'd stop working and talk about what was new, almost always the same things, the boss's visit, the changes higher up, the races at San Isidro. They, of course, had no way of knowing that we were waiting for them, what's called waiting, things like that had to happen without making waves, you people go ahead without worrying, the boss's word, he would repeat it every so often just in case, you people just go ahead nice and easy, when you come down to it, it was easy, if there was a slip they wouldn't take it out on us, the ones responsible were higher up and the boss was O.K., just rest easy, boys, if there's any trouble here I'll take the responsibility, the only thing I ask is that you don't get your subjects mixed up on me, an investigation first so you don't get involved where you shouldn't, and then you can go right ahead.

Frankly, they weren't any trouble, the boss had picked out functional offices so that there wouldn't be any crowding, and we received them one at a time, as it should be, with all the time necessary. Nobody with better manners than us, eh, the boss would say from time to time, and it was true, everything was synchronized in a way that would put IBM to shame, things worked vaseline-smooth here, no getting your piss hot or getting ahead of yourself. We had time for coffee and picking Sunday's races, and the boss was the first to come by to get the sure things because in that business Slats Bianchetti was a regular oracle. So the same thing every day, we'd arrive with the newspapers, Nigger López would bring the first round of coffee, and in a little while they would begin to come by for the procedure. The summons said that, a procedure which concerns you, and us, just there waiting. Now this is important, even if it is written on yellow paper, a summons always has a serious look about it; that's why María Elena had looked at it several times at home, the green stamp around the illegible signature and the date and the place. She took it out of her purse again on the bus and wound her watch just to be safe. They were summoning her to an office on the Calle Maza, it was strange that there should be a ministry there but her sister had told her that they were setting up offices all over because the ministries didn't have enough room any more, and as soon as she got off the bus she saw that it must have been true, the neighborhood was like any other, with three- or four-story houses and most of all a lot of retail stores, even some trees of the few left in the district.

"At least it most likely will have a flag," María Elena thought as she approached the seven-hundred block, it was probably like the embassies, which were in residential districts but could be spotted from a distance by the colored piece of cloth over one of the balconies. Although the number stood out quite clearly on the summons, she was surprised not to see the national flag and for a moment she stood on the corner (she was early, there was plenty of time) and for no particular reason she asked the man in the newsstand if the government office was on that block.

"Yes, indeed," the man said, "down there in the middle of the block, but first why don't you keep me company for a little while, see how all alone I am."

"On the way back," María Elena smiled at him, going away in no hurry and consulting the yellow paper once more. There was almost no traffic or people, a cat in front of a grocery store and a fat lady with a little girl coming out of a doorway. The few cars were parked by the government office, almost all of them with someone behind the wheel reading the newspaper or smoking. The entrance was narrow, like all those on the block, with a majolica-tile passageway and a stairway in the rear; the plaque on the door looked like one for a doctor or a dentist, that was all, dirty, and with a piece of paper pasted over the bottom part to cover that line of the inscription. It was strange that there was no elevator, a third-floor walkup after that paper which was so serious with its green stamp and signature and everything.

The door on the third floor was closed and she didn't see any bell or plaque. María Elena tried the knob and the door opened noiselessly; the tobacco smoke reached her before the greenish tiles of the hallway and the benches on both sides with people sitting on them. There weren't many, but with that smoke and such a narrow hallway their knees seemed to be touching, the two old ladies, the bald man, and the boy with the green necktie. They obviously had been chatting in order to kill time, for just as she opened the door María Elena caught the tail end of a phrase from one of the ladies, but, as always, they fell silent almost immediately as they looked at the latest arrival, and also as always and feeling so foolish, María Elena blushed and was barely able to raise enough voice for a good morning as she stood there by the door until the boy signaled to her, pointing to the empty space on the bench next to him. Precisely as she sat down, thanking him, the door at the other end of the corridor opened to let out a redheaded man who made his way between the knees of the others without taking the trouble to excuse himself. The clerk held the door open with his foot, waiting until one of the two ladies got up with difficulty and, begging their pardon, passed between María Elena and the bald man; the exit door and the office door closed at almost the same time, and those left began to chat again, stretching a little and making the benches creak.

Each one had his or her theme as always, the bald man about the slowness of the procedures, since this is my first time, what can I expect, tell me, over half an hour wasted for what in the end will probably be four or five questions and so long, at least that's what I imagine.

"Don't you believe it," said the boy with the green tie, "it's my second time and I can assure you that it's not so short, with everything that has to be typed up and some guy who can't remember a date, things like that, it ends up lasting quite a while."

The bald man and the old lady listened with interest because it was obviously the first time for them, the same as for María Elena, although she didn't feel she had the right to join in the conversation. The bald man wanted to know how much time there was between the first and the second summons, and the boy explained that in his case it had been three days. But why two summonses? María Elena wanted to ask, and once more she felt the color rising to her cheeks and she waited for someone to talk to her and give her confidence, let her form part of the group, not be the last one any more. The old lady had taken out a small vial with salts or something in it and took a whiff, breathing in deeply. It might have been all the smoke that was upsetting her, and the boy offered to put his cigarette out and the bald man said of course, this hallway was a disgrace, they'd better put out their cigarettes if she wasn't feeling well, but the woman said no, just a touch of fatigue which will go away immediately, her husband and sons smoked all the time at home, I practically don't notice it any more. María Elena, who had also had the urge to take out a cigarette, saw that the men were putting theirs out, that the boy was crushing his against the sole of his shoe, people always smoke too much when they have to wait, the last time it had been worse because there were seven or eight people then and in the end you couldn't see a thing in the hallway with so much smoke.

"Life is a waiting-room," said the bald man, carefully stepping on his cigarette and looking at his hands as if he didn't know what to do with them, and the old lady sighed an agreement of many years standing and put away the vial precisely as the door opened and the other lady came out with that air that they all envied, the almost compassionate good-by as she reached the exit door. It doesn't take so long after all, María Elena thought, three people ahead of her, let's say three-quarters of an hour, of course, in any one of the cases the procedure might take longer than in the others, the boy had already been there a first time and had said so. But when the bald man went into the office, María Elena got up the courage to ask in order to feel more secure, and the boy thought for a while and then said that the first time some had taken a long time and others less, you never could tell. The old lady called attention to the fact that the other lady had come out almost at once, but that the redheaded gentleman had been in there for an eternity.

"It's good there are only a few of us left," María Elena said, "these places are depressing."

"You have to be philosophical about it," the boy said, "don't forget that you're going to have to come back, so you might as well relax. When I came the first time there was no one to talk to, there was a whole bunch of us but, I don't know, no one hit it off, and today, on the other hand, the time has passed nicely from the moment I got here because ideas have been exchanged."

María Elena enjoyed chatting with the boy and the lady, she almost didn't feel the time passing until the bald man came out and the lady got up with a rapidity that one wouldn't have suspected at her age, the poor thing probably wanted to get the procedure over with quickly.

"Well, just us now," the boy said. "Would it bother you if I smoked a cigarette? I can't take it any more, but the lady there seemed so upset . . ."

"I feel like a smoke too."

She accepted the cigarette he offered her and they exchanged names, where they worked, it did them good to swap impressions and forget about the hallway, the silence which seemed too heavy at times, as if the streets and people had been left far behind. María Elena had also lived in Floresta, but when she was a child, now she lived in Constitución. Carlos didn't like that section, he preferred the west side, the air is cleaner, there are trees. His ideal would be to live in Villa del Parque, when he got married he'd probably rent an apartment over there, his future father-in-law had promised to help him, he was a man with a lot of connections and he could get something through one of them.

"I don't know why, but something tells me I'm going to spend the rest of my life in Constitución," María Elena said. "It's not so bad, after all. And if sometime . . ."

She saw the door in the rear open and she was almost surprised as she looked at the boy, who smiled at her as he got up, see how time flies when you talk, the lady gave them a friendly nod, she seemed so happy to be leaving, everyone had a younger, more agile look when they left, as if a weight had been lifted from them, the procedure over, one thing less to do and outside the street, the cafés where they would probably go to have a drink or a cup of tea in order to feel that they were really on the other side of the waiting-room and the forms. Now time would drag for María Elena, all alone, although if it kept on like that Carlos would come out fairly soon, but some took longer than others because it was the second time around and who could say what complications there might be.

She almost didn't understand at first when she saw the door open and the clerk looked at her and nodded for her to come in. She thought that's how it is, then, that Carlos would have to stay a while longer filling out forms and in the meantime they would take care of her. She nodded to the clerk and went into the office; scarcely had she gone through the door when another clerk pointed to a chair in front of a black desk. There were several people in the office, only men, but she didn't see Carlos. From the other side of the desk a clerk with a sickly face was looking at a form; without raising his eyes he held out his hand and it took María Elena an instant to realize he was asking for the summons, she suddenly understood and looked for it, a little flustered, murmuring excuses, she took two or three things out of her purse until she found the piece of yellow paper.

"Start filling this out," the clerk said, handing her a form. "Print it in capital letters, nice and clear."

It was the usual nonsense, first and last name, sex, address. In between two words María Elena got the feeling that something was bothering her, something that wasn't completely clear. Not on the form, where it was easy to go along filling in the blanks; something outside it, something that was missing or wasn't in its place. She stopped writing and took a look around, the other desks with the clerks working or talking among themselves, the dirty walls with posters and photographs, the two windows, the door she had come through, the only door in the office. *Profession*, and next to it the dotted line; she automatically filled in the blank. The only door in the office, but Carlos wasn't there. *Length of time in job*. Capital letters, nice and clear.

When she signed at the bottom, the clerk was looking at her as if she had taken too long in filling out the form. He studied the paper for a moment, found no errors, and put it into a folder. The rest consisted of questions, some of them unnecessary because she had answered them on the form, but about her family too, moves over the past years, insurance, whether she took many trips and where to, whether she had taken out a passport or was planning to. No one seemed very interested in the answers; in any case, the clerk didn't write them down. Suddenly he told María Elena that she could leave but to come back in three days at eleven o'clock; there was no need for a written summons, but she wasn't to forget.

"Yes, sir," María Elena said getting up. "Thursday at eleven, then."

"Have a good day," the clerk said without looking up at her.

There was no one in the hallway, and going along it was just as it had been for all the others, a haste, a lightness in her breathing, the urge to get out onto the street and leave the other thing behind. María Elena opened the exit door and as she started down the stairs she thought of Carlos again, it was strange that Carlos hadn't come out like the others. It was strange because the office had only one door, of course at some moment she may not have taken a good look because it couldn't be, the clerk had opened the door for her to come in and Carlos hadn't passed her, he hadn't come out first like all the others, the redheaded man, the ladies, everybody except Carlos.

The sun broke against the sidewalk, it was the noise and the smell of the street; María Elena walked a few steps and stopped, standing by a tree at a spot where no cars were parked. She looked back at the door of the building, told herself that she was going to wait for a moment to see Carlos come out. It was impossible for Carlos not to come out, they'd all left after the procedure was over. She thought that he was probably taking longer because he was the only one who had come for a second time; who knows, that must have been it. It seemed so strange not seeing him in the office, although there probably was a door hidden behind the posters, something she'd missed, but just the same it was strange because everybody had gone out through the hallway like her, all those who had come for the first time had left through the hallway.

Before leaving (she had waited a while, but she couldn't stay there any longer), she thought about the fact that she had to come back on Thursday. Maybe things would be different then and they would have her go out through the other side although she didn't know where or why. Not her, no, of course, but us, yes, we knew, and we'd be waiting for her and the others, smoking slowly and chatting while Nigger López brewed another of the many rounds of morning coffee.

The Present State of Fiction in Latin America

By JULIO CORTÁZAR

In light of the limited time we have tonight, I assume as a given that none of you has taken seriously the title of this lecture—"The Present State of Fiction in Latin America" —unless, of course, you suspect that the word "fiction" may refer more to the lecture itself than to its subject matter. I do not know exactly who is to blame for this title, although I confess—with obvious discomfort—that the list of suspects must be reduced to only two: Ivar Ivask and myself. Since it has been almost a year that Ivar and I have been exchanging letters about this conference, it is difficult to know in what precise moment the idea of this theme came up—whether it was proposed by me in a moment of delirium, or whether it resulted from a refined perversity on Ivar's part, a perversity directed somewhat against me but principally against you. The only thing which is certain is that the title of this talk does not correspond to anything realizable within the time alloted; and even if I were the Editor-in-Chief of *Reader's Digest*, my techniques of synthesis would not suffice to summarize here the present situation of fiction in all of Latin America.

Now then, it happens that in the stories and novels that I have written, the presence of what is called the "supernatural" or the "fantastic" is very strong and constitutes perhaps the dominant feature of my work. If the totality of any narrative work can be classified as "fiction," it is clear that fantastic literature is the most fictional of all literatures, given that by its own definition it consists of turning one's back on a reality universally accepted as normal, that is, as not fantastic, in order to explore other corridors of that immense house in which man lives. For reasons of this kind, which are not based too firmly on logic, as many of you will already have perceived, it occurs to me that this talk can have some meaning if we concentrate its scope in two ways: first, on the exclusive dimension of fantastic literature, and secondly, on that region of Latin America which, to date, has provided the greatest number of authors of this type of fiction. I refer to the area of the River Plate—not to its liquid part, of course, but to the two shores which delimit it: Uruguay and my own country, Argentina.

In proposing this partitioning of our theme, concentrating it on fantastic literature, which in turn is concentrated in a specific region of Latin America, I feel that I can count on the full understanding of those of you listening to me. I say this because, unlike other national literatures in which the fantastic appears only as a marginal manifestation, English literature in its entirety, with American literature as its most important projection outside of its original center, is in reality the chosen land of fantastic literature. It should be clear that in mentioning a given literature, one implicitly includes its readers as well, and in this case I know that I am addressing people who have been given the dimension of the fantastic since childhood through a literature which is exceptionally rich in it. This fact will allow us to reduce to a minimum the type of theoretical considerations of the genre of the fantastic which would be indispensable for a French audience, for example, since French literature, and thus readers in France, only accept the fantastic begrudgingly and with difficulty.

I will therefore limit myself to merely adjusting summarily the focus of our common point of view before going on to speak of fantastic literature in the River Plate area. For any sensitive reader the fantastic in literature is transparently clear; but it is also clear that when it comes to defining this perception in logical terms, doubts and difficulties arise which the critics of this type of literature have not yet been able to resolve. A definition of the fantastic in literature has been sought for a long time; personally, I have not seen any which satisfies me—and here I include everything from the merely psychological or psychoanalytical definitions to the most recent structuralist attempts. There is, to begin with, a problem of vocabulary: terms such as "marvelous," "fantastic," "strange," "startling," et cetera, change meanings according to their users. This first uncertainty is followed by another—I refer to the sensation of the fantastic itself when it is given to us through a literary text, a sensation which varies considerably throughout the course of history and from one culture to the next. Given this state of affairs, what can I do tonight to explain precisely that notion of the fantastic which I would like to show you in the literature of the River Plate? Not being a critic, my only possibility is to transmit as best I can my own experiences exactly as they have appeared to me since the time I was a child and just as they have been manifested in a series of stories and novels written over the course of thirty years. I will begin, then, by speaking about myself within this perspective, in order then to go on to other writers from the River Plate area. I realize that the Emily Posts of good social behavior would consider that in choosing this personal approach I am displaying a shocking lack of the most elemental modesty, but I see no other way to illuminate a field which is not distinguished by its clarity. To be honest, I prefer to pass for vain rather than for incomprehensible.

Chance (which for me is already a reference to the fantastic) comes to aid me today, because a short time ago I had to write an article on the influence of so-called gothic literature in Uruguay and Argentina, and that caused me to reflect on the relationship between my own childhood and my future as a writer. I think that it can be stated without fear of error, that except in cases where an implacable education cuts him off along the road, every child is, essentially, gothic; that is to say, that due not only to ignorance but above all to innocence, a child is open like a sponge to many aspects of reality that later will be criticized or rejected by reason and its logical apparatus. In the Argentina of my childhood, education was a long way from being implacable, and Julio Cortázar the child did not ever find his imagination shackled. On the contrary, it was encouraged by a mother who was very gothic in her literary tastes and by teachers who, pathetically, confused imagination with knowledge.

Naturally, the sense of the fantastic in a child's mind is always thick and truculent; and it is only much later, as adults, that some people will come to extrapolate from that first capability of being permeated when confronted with the startling or the inexplicable, in order to feel it and to verify it on much more subtle planes. The passage from the simply "marvelous," such as that which appears in the fairy tales that a child accepts in his earliest infancy, to what is called the "uncanny" only comes at the end of a long process of maturation. For me, in the beginning, the fantastic was an incessant producer of fear more than of marvel. My house, to begin with, was a gothic stage set, not because of its architecture, but because of the accumulation of terrors which were born from things and from beliefs, from the badly-lit hallways and from the after-dinner conversations of the grown-ups. They were simple people; their readings and their superstitions permeated an ill-defined reality, and from the time I was very little I learned that werewolves came out when there was a full moon, that the mandrake was a deadly plant, that in cemeteries terrible and horrifying things took place, that dead people's hair and fingernails kept growing interminably, and that in our house there was a basement to which nobody had the nerve to descend—ever. But curiously, that family given over to propagating the worst tales of terror and dread also maintained the cult of virile courage; from the time I was a child it was demanded that I go on nocturnal expeditions intended to temper me, and my bedroom became an attic illuminated by a stub of candle at the end of a staircase, where fear, dressed as a vampire or as a ghost, always awaited me. No one ever knew of this fear, or maybe they only pretended not to know.

Perhaps because of this, as pure exorcism and without clear consciousness of the compensatory reasons which moved me, I began to write poems and stories of which I prefer not to remind myself, pieces where the lugubrious and the necrophilic seemed very much at home. Since nobody watched over my reading, it did not take me long to devour all the fantastic literature within my reach. In general, it was very poor, and there is a certain irony in the fact that only ten or fifteen years later did I come to know the great authors of the gothic genre in their original languages—authors such as Horace Walpole, Sheridan Le Fanu, Mary Shelley and Maturin, not to mention modern masters such as Ambrose Bierce or Gustav Meyrink. As an admirable exception, however, Edgar Allan Poe did enter through the fearful door of my childhood, as did the Victor Hugo of *Hans of Iceland* and *The Laughing Man*, mixed ingenuously with Fu Manchu and other subproducts of the terrorific genre. Thus, with the way prepared by my childhood and by a natural acceptance of the fantastic in all its many forms, that literature, whether bad or good, found in me a reader like those of another time, a reader soon to play the game, to accept the unacceptable, to live in a permanent state of what Coleridge called "the suspension of disbelief."

Here we arrive at something which goes beyond my personal biography and which encompasses the attitude of almost all the writers of fantastic literature in the River Plate area. When I began to write stories that seemed publishable to me, I had already lived thirty-five years and read thousands of books. Because of this, despite my interest in fantastic literature, my critical sense made me find the mysterious and the startling in terrains very different from the traditional ones, although I am sure that without that tradition I would never have found them. The traces of writers such as Poe are undeniable on the deepest levels of many of my stories, and I think that without "Ligeia," without "The Fall of the House of Usher," I would not have found myself with this disposition toward the fantastic which assaults me in the most unexpected moments and which propels me to write as the only way to cross over certain limits, to install myself in the territory of *lo otro*—the Other. But—and in this there is clear unanimity among the River Plate writers of the genre—something indicated to me from the start that the formal road of this otherness was not to be found in the literary tricks on which traditional fantastic literature depends for its celebrated "pathos," that it was not to be found in that verbal scenography consisting of "disorienting" the reader from the start, conditioning him within a morbid climate in order to oblige him to accede docilely to the mystery and the dread. Of course, this critical attitude is not the sole possession of the novelists or short story writers of the River Plate, and in fact it even precedes our generation. It is enough to remember that during the height of English romanticism Thomas Love Peacock already mocked the gothic genre in his delightful *Nightmare Abbey*, a mockery which reached its peak at the end of the last century in the pages of Oscar Wilde's *The Canterville Ghost*.

When writing fantastic stories, then, my feeling in the face of what the Germans call *das Unheimliche*—the unsettling or the startling—came forth and continues to come forth on a plane which I would classify as ordinary. The fantastic had never seemed exceptional to me, even as a child, and now I had come to feel it as a calling, perhaps a warning originating from areas of reality which homo sapiens prefers to ignore or to relegate to the garret of primitive or animist beliefs, of superstitions and nightmares. I have said a calling, and in my case it always has been one; there are moments in my life (and they are not exceptional moments; they can occur during a subway ride, in a café, in the middle of reading a newspaper) in which for an instant I cease to be he who I habitually am in order to convert myself into a type of passageway. Something opens up in me or outside of me, an inconceivable system of communicating receptacles makes reality as porous as a sponge; for one moment, unfortunately short and precarious, what surrounds me ceases to be what it was, or I cease to be who I am or think I am, and in that terrain where words can only arrive late and imperfectly to try to say what cannot be said, everything is possible and everything can surrender itself. The variety of eruptions of the fantastic is inexhaustible; in one of my novels, *62: A Model Kit*, the first chapters try to reconstruct one of these multiple terrains of passage. A man hears an insignificant sentence in a restaurant, and suddenly the external reality ceases to surround him and to define him in order to give way to a kind of coagulation of elements which reason would reject as heterogeneous or illogical. Within the character what we could call an instantaneous constellation is constructed, a constellation whose isolated elements do not have, in appearance, anything to do with one another. The force of that constellation is so great that the character surrenders himself to it without consciously knowing it, carried along by forces that manifest themselves in that instant without apparent reason or logical explanation. The reader of the book, who indirectly receives the influx of these forces, will see them act in the course of the novel and influence the destiny of the characters, who, for their part, believe that they act freely and do not suspect that that first constellation already contained the integrally constructed model of which they are mere pieces and means.

All this, which is only one example within the infinite manifestations of that which I understand as the fantastic, is not presented in a traditional manner, that is, with premonitory warnings, ad hoc scenarios and appropriate atmospheres as in gothic literature or modern fantastic stories of poor quality. I repeat that the eruption of the Other happens in my case in a markedly trivial and prosaic fashion. It consists above all in the experience that things or facts or beings change for one instant their sign, their label, their situation in the realm of rational reality. Receiving a letter with a red stamp at the same moment that the telephone rings and that one's sense of smell perceives the odor of burnt coffee can convert itself into a triangle which has nothing to do with the letter, the call or the coffee. Rather, it is because of that absurd and apparently casual triangle that something else slips in—the revelation of a deception or of happiness, the real meaning of an act committed ten years earlier or the certainty that in the immediate future a given something is going to take place. I do not want in any way to say that in all cases that coagulation of heterogeneous elements translates itself into precise knowledge, because then we would be leaving the terrain of the fantastic and it would only be a question of scientifically verifying a system of laws or of rigorous principles of which we were simply not aware. In most cases that eruption of the unknown does not go beyond a terribly brief and fleeting sensation that there is a meaning, an open door toward a reality which offers itself to us but which, sadly, we are not capable of apprehending. In my case I am almost always not up to the message, to the sign that those constellations intend to transmit to me; but their force is such that I will never put in doubt the reality of the messages, and the only thing that I can deplore is my own poverty of psychic means, of capacity for entering into the Other. In the presence of the fantastic the same thing happens to me as happens with certain dreams whose intensity is dazzling. We will remember those dreams in the instant of awakening, but a well-known censorship implacably erases them, leaving us scarcely some raveled threads in our hands and the anguish of having touched closely something essential which, simultaneously, our own psyche shuts off to us. And since I have mentioned dreams, it seems appropriate to say that many of my fantastic stories were born in an oneiric territory and that I had the good fortune that in some cases the censorship was not merciless and permitted me to carry the content of the dreams into words. Curiously, those stories have had more effect on my readers than others, although the readers have no way of knowing their oneiric origin. One could say that the fantastic which they contain comes from archetypal regions which in one way or another we all share, and that in the act of reading these stories the reader witnesses or discovers something of himself. I have seen this phenomenon put to the test many times with an old story of mine entitled "The House Taken Over," which I dreamed with all the details which figure in the text and which I wrote upon jumping out of bed, still enveloped in the horrible nausea of its ending. That story, which I can say without false modesty does not seem very extraordinary to me, has nonetheless been reproduced in numerous languages and continues to fascinate its readers. This leads me to suggest that if the fantastic sometimes invades us in full light of day, it is also waiting for us in that oneiric territory in which, perhaps, we have more things in common than when we are awake.

As you can see, for me the idea of the fantastic does not mean only a rupture with the reasonable and the logical or, in literary and above all science fiction terms, the representation of unthinkable events within an everyday context. I have always felt that the fantastic does not appear in a harsh or direct way, that it is not cutting, but rather that it presents itself in a way which we could call interstitial, slipping in between two moments or two acts in order to allow us to catch a glimpse, in the binary mechanism which is typical of human reason, of the latent possibility of a third frontier, of a third eye, as so significantly appears in some Oriental texts. There are those who live satisfactorily in a binary dimension and who prefer to think that the fantastic is nothing more than a literary fabrication; there are even writers who only invent fantastic themes, without in any way believing in them. As far as I am concerned, what has been given to me to invent in this terrain has always been carried out with a sense of nostalgia—the nostalgia of not being capable of fully opening the doors which on so many occasions I have seen set themselves ajar during a few fleeting seconds. In that sense, literature has fulfilled and fulfills a function for which we should thank it: the function of taking us for a moment out of our habitual little boxes and showing us, although it might only be vicariously, that perhaps things do not end at the point where our mental habits fix them.

We thus arrive at a stage where, even without a precise definition of the fantastic, it is possible to recognize its presence, at least in its literary manifestations, within a much broader and more open range than in the era of gothic novels and of stories whose trademarks were ghosts, werewolves and vampires. Throughout the course of this century many writers in the River Plate area have contributed considerably to the type of fiction in which the fantastic has those subtle and often ambiguous characteristics that I have tried to sketch in their more general lines tonight. But before referring specifically to these writers, it is necessary to pose an enigma which in itself already seems fantastic and which is contained within this question: Why has the River Plate region been and why does it continue to be a chosen land of Latin American fantastic literature? Of course, writers from Mexico, from Colombia, from many other Latin American countries have written notable novels or stories where the fantastic is present; but it is enough to take a look at the general panorama of our continent to see that it is on the two sides of the River Plate where one finds the maximum concentration of this genre.

Many times critics have looked for the answer to this question; they have spoken of the cultural polymorphism of Argentina and Uruguay resulting from the multiple waves of immigrants; they have alluded to our immense geography as a factor of isolation, monotony and tedium, with the consequent refuge in the startling, the exceptional, in the search for an anywhere, out-of-the-world type of literature. As a participant in that literary current, I feel these explanations to be only partial; and in the end, instead of a rational explanation, the only thing that I can see is once more a mechanism of chance, that same chance which once, and in infinitely greater proportions, concentrated a creative explosion in Renaissance Italy and in Elizabethan England, which made possible the Pléiade in seventeenth-century France, and in Spain the generation of the Golden Age or the poets of the Spanish Republic in the 1930s. Suddenly, and without logical and convincing reasons, a culture produces in a few years a series of creators who spiritually fertilize each other, who emulate and challenge and surpass each other until, also suddenly, there enters a period of drying up or of mere prolongation through imitators and inferior successors.

That chance seems to have manifested itself in modest but clearly perceptible proportions in the cultural zone of the River Plate in a period that runs approximately from 1920 to the present. There, without too many premonitory signs, the dimension of the fantastic bursts forth in the principal works of Jorge Luis Borges. It erupts in Borges with a force so compelling that, seen from outside of the River Plate, it appears to concentrate itself almost exclusively in his works. We in Argentina, however, situate

Borges's narrative within a context which contains important precursorial and contemporary figures, and although we are not dealing here with a chronology or detailed criticism, I will give some summary indications to show that even before Borges the fantastic was already a familiar and important genre in our midst. Leaving aside the antecedents, above all the historical ones such as the stories of Juana Manuela Gorriti or Eduardo Ladislao Holmberg, faithful inheritors of the Anglo-Saxon gothic tradition with all its good and bad points, I will stop for a moment to take a look at a great Argentine poet, Leopoldo Lugones. A man of unbridled cultural voracity, Lugones found time, in the course of producing numerous books of poetry, to write a series of short stories which he collected under the title "The Strange Forces." Among the stories found in this collection, there is one entitled "The Horses of Abdera" which can be counted among the great readings of my adolescence. In this story a herd of horses that today we would call mutants rises up against the men and ends up by taking possession of the city of Abdera, which will only be liberated at the last moment by the arrival of Heracles, the slayer of monsters. The fantastic appears in Lugones with violent profiles and dramatic atmospheres. Nonetheless, it already contains that trait which I have suggested is peculiar to our literature in this area: a force which does not reside only in the narrative quality, but also in a drive which seems to come forth from dark regions of the psyche, from those zones where reality and unreality cease to confront and to deny each other.

In Jorge Luis Borges in our literature, a Uruguayan with a shadowy biography and a tragic destiny writes in Argentina a series of hallucinatory stories, many of which are truly fantastic. I am speaking of Horacio Quiroga, author of a book which would profoundly influence the men of my generation and whose title reflects both the merits and the weaknesses of its content: "Stories of Love, of Madness, and of Blood." For Quiroga the fantastic appears in a climate of which Edgar Allan Poe would have approved; to demonstrate this, one has only to summarize the plot of one of his best stories, "The Feather Pillow." In this story a girl dies from what appears to be some sort of anemia that no doctor is able to explain or contain. After the burial her husband and servant return to the death room to put the furniture and the bed back in order. The servant is amazed by the extraordinary and abnormal weight of the feather pillow where the head of the sick girl had rested. The girl's husband cuts the pillow open with a knife and then . . . I will leave it to you to deduce the monstrous and entomological ending of the story. But I would like to add something which is as obvious as it is sad for those who give lectures: any synthesis of a literary text automatically destroys it to the extent that, if such a synthesis were possible, literature would cease to be necessary and it would suffice to have lectures.

In Jorge Luis Borges, the leading figure of our fantastic literature, misunderstandings accumulate, usually to his great delight. I will limit myself here to pointing out that what some literary critics admire above all in Borges is a genius of geometrical invention, a maker of literary crystals whose condensation responds to exact mathematical laws of logic. Borges has been the first to insist on that rigorous construction of things which tend to appear, on the surface, as absurd and aleatory. The fantastic, as it appears in Borges's stories, makes one think of a relentless geometrical theorem—a theorem perfectly capable of demonstrating that the sum of the square of the angles of a triangle equals the execution of Madame DuBarry. Stories such as "The Circular Ruins," "The Garden of Forking Paths" and "The Library of Babel" reflect this type of theorem construction, which would seem to hide a secret dread not only of what Lugones called strange forces, but also of the imagination's own powers, powers which in Borges are subjected immediately to a rigorous intellectual conditioning.

Nonetheless, others of us feel that despite this rational rejection of the fantastic in its most irreducible and incoherent manifestations, Borges's intuition and sensitivity attest to its presence in a good portion of his stories, where the intellectual superstructure does not manage to, nor does it probably want to, deny that presence. When Borges entitles a collection of stories *Ficciones* or *Artifices*, he is misleading us at the same time that he winks a conspiratorial eye at us; he is playing with that old ideal of every writer, the ideal of having at least some readers capable of suspecting a second version of each text. I will limit myself, of necessity, to one example which hits close to home. In his story "The Secret Miracle" Borges plays with the idea that in certain circumstances a man can enter into another dimension of time and live a year or a century during what other men live as a second or an hour. There is already a story based on this idea in a medieval Spanish text, *El Conde Lucanor*, and Borges himself uses as an epigraph to his story a fragment from the Koran which reflects the same concept. The theme is also dealt with in the psychology of oneiric life, which shows that certain dreams encompass multiple episodes that would demand considerable time to be carried out consecutively, and that, nonetheless, the complex plot of such dreams can end, for example, with a shot from a gun which abruptly awakens us and makes us realize that someone just knocked at the door. It is clear that the dream has been integrally constructed in order to lead to that supposed shot from a revolver, a fact which obliges one to admit that the dream's fulfillment has been almost instantaneous while the fact of dreaming it seemed to transpire over a long period of time. In other words, one could say that on certain occasions we slip into a different time, and those occasions can be, as is always the case with the fantastic, trivial and even absurd.

But Borges does not want things to be trivial and absurd, at least not in his stories, and "The Secret Miracle" is based once again on the rational and erudite crystallization of something which others grasp only in its unrefined state. The story relates that Jaromir Hladik, a Jewish writer condemned to death by the Nazis, awaits with anguish the day of his execution by firing squad. This man has written philosophical texts in which the notion of time is examined and discussed, and he has begun a play whose ending suggests that the work is circular, that it repeats itself interminably. On the eve of his execution Hladik asks God to grant him one more year of life in order to finish this play, which will justify his existence and assure his immortality. During the night he dreams that the time has been given to him, but the next morning he realizes that it was only a dream, since the soldiers come and take him to the firing squad. In the moment that the rifles take aim at his chest Hladik continues to think about one of the characters in his play; and in that same moment the physical universe becomes immobile, the soldiers do not shoot, and the smoke of Hladik's last cigarette forms a small petrified cloud in the air. Only Hladik can know that the miracle has been fulfilled and that, without moving from his place, thinking it instead of writing it, he has been granted the year he had asked for to complete his play. During the course of this year Hladik creates and re-creates scenes, he changes the characters, he eliminates and adds on. Finally, he needs to find only one word, an epithet. He finds it, and the soldiers shoot. For them only an instant has passed.

This theme, which we also find in Ambrose Bierce's admirable story "An Occurrence at Owl Creek," is not, as Borges's story might pretend, simply a literary artifice. I have already noted the frequent presence of this theme in literature and in dreams, and I have even included it in a passage of my own story, "The Pursuer"; in my case, however, I have no reason to obscure the authenticity of my personal experience and to create of it an ingenious superstructure of fiction. In my story what happens is exactly the same as what has happened to me various times in analogous circumstances. During a subway ride the main character of "The Pursuer" enters into that state which we call distraction and into which the fantastic tends to slide very easily. In a vague semi-dream state the character reflects extensively on the past, he remembers infinite scenes, he mentally hums a song, the memories start to link themselves together endlessly. When the train stops in a station, the jolt abruptly brings the character back to his normal state; he then realizes that if he wanted to enumerate everything he had thought during those minutes, he would need at least a quarter of an hour—and yet everything took place between two stations situated only about two minutes apart. The subway has served as an exterior clock to show him that during those two minutes he was given fifteen minutes to think, just as during a few instants Jaromir Hladik was given a year to finish his play.

I think that at this point you have an idea of our way of living and writing the fantastic in the River Plate area; and so I can now refer to other Uruguayan and Argentine writers without being obliged to present them in too much detail, since within their differences—which fortunately are very great—all of them partake of that same capability of being permeated by the uncanny which I have tried to sketch. In the case of Adolfo Bioy Casares, for example, irony and a sense of humor replace the geometric constructions that we perceived in Jorge Luis Borges. *The Invention of Morel*, Bioy Casares's most famous novel, is closely related to a long-forgotten book by Jules Verne, *The Carpathian Castle*. In both cases a man in whom scientific genius appears mixed with a lover's great passion fights against that unacceptable scandal which is the death of a loved one. Instead of resigning himself, instead of giving in to the slow curtains of time, Morel creates a prodigious mechanical model, moved by the ocean tides, which allows him to repeat the past, to find himself once again with the image of his beloved and everything which had surrounded her in life. Those who are satisfied with the novel's final explanation, once the mechanism is discovered, will fail to have understood the permanent ambiguity which is established between the living and the dead, between the bodies and the images. Bioy Casares and Borges are not fans of the chiaroscuro, for while they present their fictions in violent contrasts of light and shadow, they do so in order to provide between the black and white a mysterious range of grays which is left for the reader to tune his eyes to and discover.

I am moved to mention here, already nearing the conclusion of this talk, the name of Silvina Ocampo. Discreet, distant Silvina has written memorable stories which have not always found the following accorded to some lesser works in our part of the world. Of her numerous fantastic stories I will cite one, "The Sugar House," in which a woman sees herself slowly taken over by the personality of another woman who long ago occupied the same house. The progression is presented with an admirable economy of means; through scant details and sometimes imperceptible changes Cristina sees herself becoming transformed into Violeta; she finally assumes the personality of Violeta. Rarely has this theme, which I think I know quite well, of the phantasmal possession of a living being by a dead one been presented with such narrative effectiveness; the admirable thing in Silvina Ocampo is the incessant and extraordinarily varied invention of fantastic climates and her simultaneous lack of interest in exploiting them in the most spectacular way. Her stories always seem timidly to offer an apology, when in reality it is the literary critics who should apologize to her for not having been capable of placing her on the level which she deserves. I think, moreover, that this same apology should be extended to other writers of fantastic themes from the River Plate area, principally to Enrique Anderson Imbert, who has lived among you as a professor at Harvard for so many years and whose works have not attained the recognition they deserve.

But what can be said about the last author I would like to mention on this brief voyage? I am speaking of a great Uruguayan writer named Felisberto Hernández, who lived a life as marginal and phantasmagoric as his stories, almost all of which are autobiographical, although in Felisberto, biography and imagination were always inseparably mixed. Poor, modest, earning a living as a piano player in cafés, giving concerts in pathetic provincial casinos, living in lugubrious hotels which would then be the setting or the point of departure for his stories—written always in the first person—Felisberto limits himself to demonstrating that that miserable existence co-existed with the marvelous and that this quality did not need special ornamentation or equipment in order to manifest itself at any moment. When he wishes, nonetheless, the fantastic bursts forth like an enormous harmony of sounds or colors, and then we have stories like "The Flooded House": a matron takes Felisberto into her lodging, and upon arriving, he discovers that all the furniture and objects float and move about in the salons and bedrooms, beginning with the landlady, sprawled out on her bed as if in a Wagnerian gondola—the entire scene illuminated by light bulbs placed in baking pans, which the gentle currents of water carry from one side of the house to the other without one's ever being able to know where the piano is or where the dining-room table lies.

I am obliged to stop myself in this chronicle, which I would have liked to continue indefinitely; but since we are not on a subway or in front of a firing squad, it is impossible to put into a few minutes everything that we could say about these subjects. At any rate, you have been able to catch a glimpse of how we sense the fantastic in the River Plate, and perhaps this is the moment to point out that that feeling of the fantastic also seems to have projected itself, until very recently, in our national history. In some way (and here I speak especially of Argentina, which I know better than Uruguay) one could say that my country only attained its independence at the beginning of the last century in order to enter, little by little, into a perspective which separated it more and more from universal reality. At the end of our endless civil wars, which coincided with the beginning of the industrial era and the growing consciousness that not only is no man an island, but that countries are not islands either,

Argentina often gives the impression of turning her back on herself, surrendering herself to a narcissistic game of mirrors and delusions. Mutatis mutandis, the entire country cultivates a fantastic history, perhaps thus preparing the soil for what I have tried to show tonight and which mere literary criticism does not suffice to explain.

But in contrast to a literature of the startling, which enriches us in the measure in which it accepts and cultivates a rupture with the excessive pragmatism of reality and reason, history does not seem ever to have received a dose of the fantastic without precipitating the worst catastrophes, because nothing fantastic is usable on a practical plane, and what one allows oneself to glimpse as an incitement to go beyond our hermetically sealed compartments becomes pure deception when one pretends to make it serve everyday reality. I think, somewhat metaphorically, of the attempts made by Heliogabalus or Nero to change the reality which surrounded them, of the fatal caprices of so many Oriental sultans and, almost in our own time, of the unrealizable dream of Ludwig II of Bavaria. In some much less typified and spectacular way Argentine history would seem to have consisted for many decades of orienting its mirrors toward impracticable European models, of allowing itself to be invaded by foreign interests which would suck its blood like Dracula preying on his victims, of ignoring the vigorous and still untamed body of the country in order to cultivate only the hyper-trophied head of its capital, Buenos Aires, blind with pride, with opera and with money. In this way many Argentines accepted an existence in which what was truly ours, from the color of our skin to our authentic language, was denied by a European-izing education which made us uncertain and vulnerable. At present, at the same moment that I am reading these final lines to you, the house of cards has collapsed, just as all the fantastic dreams in the world's history collapsed, and we are witnessing, in conditions which are almost always horrible, the anguished search for our identity, for our necessary and irreplaceable reality. I know that we will obtain it, because the sole fact of having destroyed the false façade of mirrors is already an irreversible triumph; I also know the price we have to pay for that still uncertain ultimate triumph.

In another talk we will speak of these things, which are very far removed from the fantastic. But the fantastic is something that one must never say good-bye to lightly. The man of the future, such as many of us in Latin America dream him, will have to find the bases of a reality which is truly his and, at the same time, maintain the capacity of dreaming and of playing which I have tried to show you tonight, since it is through those doors that the Other, the fantastic dimension, and the unexpected will always slip, as will all that will save us from that obedient robot into which so many techno-crats would like to convert us and which we will not accept—ever.

Politics and the Intellectual in Latin America

By JULIO CORTÁZAR

In Latin America (and in the rest of the world) politically committed intellectuals can be divided into two categories: those who understand political theory and know or think they know why they are engaged, and those who do not understand political theory but nevertheless are equally committed. Anyone who has read my books realizes that I belong to the second of these categories, and this should, in principle, disqualify me from speaking about this subject. I assume this challenge with perhaps irresponsible responsibility, because these two categories are in no way incompatible and since the relationship of the Latin American intellectual to politics can be discussed in a more flexible manner than that which would suit those devoted to logic.

I begin with a very clear affirmation: I detest false modesty; I detest those lecturers who, after saying that they know nothing of dinosaurs, speak for an hour and a half, explaining even the tiniest bones of the skeleton. Therefore, when I say that I don't know much about political theory, please understand that I am telling you the absolute truth. In its own way, politics is a science, and its practice develops from theory. My ideas in this field are vague, and each time that it has seemed necessary to fill in the enormous gaps that I have in this area, something within me has rebelled, because in that same moment an impulse of another kind has forced me to forge ahead in my natural direction. That direction is the one of a writer who was born to write fiction and who therefore moves around in a world of pure intuition, of vital but not always definable energy, having my imagination as a pilot and as my sail, passions, desires, love —all that vibrates around me—the street, houses, women and children, cats, crabs and poplars: elements which create in each place in the world a perfect moment of life, fleetingly beautiful and endlessly dramatic.

Using a scandalous comparison, if I had to choose between Machiavelli and Cesare Borgia, it would fall to me to be Borgia. In order to write *The Prince*, Machiavelli starts with the personal life of Borgia and extracts from it the principles of an efficient political theory. Meanwhile, Borgia lives these principles spontaneously; his technique is based on direct, vital motivation (greed, hatred, vengeance, lust, cruelty and the triumph of might over reason). With a much more subtle purpose, Machiavelli makes abstract and general that which Borgia lived amid curses, sweat, blows and betrayal. Mutatis mutandis, the reasons which provoke many Latin American intellectuals to commit themselves to the political struggle of their people are more vital than theoretical, more Borgia than Machiavelli. The scandalous aspect of this comparison is that in the case of Cesare Borgia his vital motivations are infamous but nonetheless vital, and in this sense my comparison is valid, with two primary differences. While a Borgia only fights for himself, we fight only for our countrymen. In the second place, our battle becomes a moral struggle. It is not a matter of greed or of personal ambition, of dividends or monopolies that brings the modern Borgias to battle. Rather, we fight for the freedom of our brothers and for social justice that would return them to the proper condition of men—men who could control their destiny as part of a community and as individuals.

I think that it is now clear that for many Latin American intellectuals political compromise is a question that forms a part of their living mental and moral personality and that for them writing books does not signify a task totally divorced from the multiple forms of the political struggle. If we understand politics as passion, as life, as destiny, what difference can there be between that and what we try to create or reproduce in our novels and short stories, although many times their subjects have nothing to do with what is happening in the street? When someone like Gabriel García Márquez writes *One Hundred Years of Solitude*, it is apparent that the marvelous habits and adventures of the citizens of Macondo are not the same as those of the citizens of Bogotá. Nevertheless, I am certain that when García Márquez leaves his typewriter, for example, to serve on the Bertrand Russell Tribunal, he does not change one tiny hair in his moustache. For him, as for me, the same thing is happening in the court and in our books. In both one deals with life and death, love and hate, justice and injustice, liberty and oppression. There are differences of an esthetic order, but the substance is the same, and we call it Latin America.

What has happened to many Latin American intellectuals is that meditation on the geopolitical reality of their countries is no longer left to specialists and thereby reduced to those writers who openly participate in political battles and many times write only as one of the forms of that participation. What is the reason for this change? Why do an increasing number of poets, novelists, artists and dramatists, who, without necessarily belonging to a political party or knowing in detail socialist ideology, participate through their work as well as through personal conduct in the struggle for the definitive independence of Latin Americans? The specialists could no doubt enumerate various reasons for this change. I, through the course of my life, have clearly observed only one, but that reason includes the others. The reason for committing oneself as an intellectual and as a person is the dropping of masks. On the one hand, imperialism has stopped pretending to what it maintained during many decades in Latin America— the part of protector, the function of big brother, the collaborator for the achievement of technological, intellectual and economic progress. The most isolated inhabitant of the remotest village in Latin America would not believe any of that. The mask of the enemy now does not hide his true face, the face that wishes to dominate and exploit. But at the same time our own masks have fallen or are falling, and with them our illusion of believing that dependence on foreign culture and patronage would encourage our development, the illusion of being the youngest and therefore the liveliest branch of that old tree, the West, and the dream of inheriting the maturity and knowledge of older nations, thereby becoming the captains of our fate.

All those masks have fallen with a crash during the twentieth century, and the real faces remain, naked, staring at each other. Today we are beginning to find out what our weaknesses are and thereby to know our real strength. This process, this crisis of conscience is not reserved only for specialists and the elite. If our crisis of conscience is still far from including all our people, if there are still innumerable Latin Americans with faces covered by the masks of illusion and deceit, of treason and venality, half a century has sufficiently awakened to reality enormous masses who until now lived in subjugation without realizing it, accepting domination because it was imposed upon them in the guise of culture and progress, beneath the technicolor deceit of infinite gadgets which made them forget that beyond the television and Coca Cola they were naked, alone and abandoned, victims of exploiters from without and opportunists from within. This amorphous but discernible awakening was summed up in a simple sentence by Ernesto Che Guevara: "These people have said 'That's enough,' and have begun to walk."

Within the general perspective of unmasking, intellectuals inescapably had to play a part or at least had to have a clear understanding of the process and to decide the course of their conduct. I do not refer to many who have preferred to leave their face masked, without realizing that the mask has become as rigid as the death mask of mummies. Instead, I would like to illustrate as carefully as possible the process by which an increasing number of Latin American intellectuals have been internalizing a new vision of their specific work, a new concept of literature and art. To some extent I have the impression that this new concept comes as a response to a profound change which worked itself out during the course of the century in regard to the specific nature of human activities.

Everyone knows that the notion of genre, as it was understood in the past, has crumbled. It becomes more difficult every day to know what a novel really is (or a musical or a poem) or, on a more global level, what is meant by anthropology or sociology. When I was a child, my aunt explained to me that in the movies a drama is a film that ends poorly, while a comedy contains parts that make one cry but always ends well. These ingenuous labels were not only the property of my aunt but also belonged to my university professors of that period. But little by little, that which physics calls the principle of indetermination became apparent in the rest of these formerly perfect pigeonholes. And at a given point the intellectuals felt that not only had genres ceased to make sense in themselves, since some of the most important works of our time made a clean slate of conventions (it suffices to mention James Joyce or Marcel Duchamp), but that their own notions as intellectuals broke into a thousand pieces when faced with the assault of an ordinary reality that no longer permitted a detached attitude but rather situated itself in the heart of the central laboratory of the artist, demanding from him participation and direct contact. Years ago, in a manifesto concerning the situation of the intellectual in Latin America, I wrote something that seems even more valid now:

> If at one time one could be a great writer without participating in the immediate historical destiny of man, now one cannot write without that participation which is his responsibility and duty; and only those works which unite them, although they be purely imaginative, although they invent the infinite, playful gamut of which the poet and novelist are capable, only they will contain in some inexplicable way that trembling, that presence, that atmosphere which makes them recognizable and necessary, which awakens in the reader a feeling of contact and closeness.

Therefore, as I see it, political participation in no way imposes a limitation of the artist's creative value and function; rather, his literary or artistic creation develops within a context that includes the historical situation and its political options, which, in a subtle or direct manner, will be reflected in the most vital aspect of his work. Latin American poetry, for example, has to a great extent stopped being primarily lyrical

poetry of the individual. Fortunately, poets will always sing of their loves and mis-
fortunes and of their most intimate feelings, but nowadays it is easy to see that they
do so more and more as the mouthpiece of many voices, of many loves, of much
sadness or hope. The *I* of our authentic poets means more as it changes to *we*.

Personally, since I years ago clarified my own commitment as a writer with respect
to Latin American politics in general, I will merely summarize my point of view, for
it is comparable to that of a majority of Latin American intellectuals who struggle for
the identity and sovereignty of their people. Many Marxist critics, who begin with the
notion of the class struggle, tend to consider as revolutionary only those writers who
belong to the dominated classes or who have broken off with the bourgeoisie in order
to join the ranks of the oppressed. They would consider that a writer like me, who in
birth and cultural formation belongs to the bourgeoisie, can only be a fellow traveler.
And it is necessary to add at this point that the most widely-read writers in Latin
America are from the bourgeoisie.

Faced with this fact, from the beginning I chose to accept a situation which seems
inevitable at this stage of our geopolitical evolution and to commit myself to the
struggle for a socialist future for Latin America, without thereby giving up all that
which is natural and familiar to me—a system of cultural values that has made me
what I am as a writer, and above all an individualism perhaps suspect on the level of
militancy but which on the level of literary creativity has not yet been replaced by any
collective identification, by teamwork or submission to any line of orientation based
on political criteria. In other words, I believe that whatever will be eliminated in the
socialist future of Latin America, when a plenitude is reached in all areas of life which
will permit the creation of new esthetic and intellectual products, continues today to
be one of the positive and fertile forces in the struggle to achieve this future change.
Paradoxically, I affirm that an intellectual like me has the right and duty to keep on
taking advantage of these forms of creation destined to disappear or to be radically
modified in the future and that one should do so precisely in order to bring about that
modification.

When I write a novel, many times I have the impression that I am creating a kind
of anachronistic monster, a dinosaur in a world which is moving toward other species,
and that the novel, like so many other esthetic forms today, will be replaced by new
vehicles for the transmission of ideas and emotions. None of this keeps me from
writing novels, because I am well aware that fiction is the type of literature that interests
me and the majority of readers (and writers) in Latin America. In writing our novels
in the manner that we do, completely rupturing internal and external tradition, we
facilitate future access to new esthetic vehicles which today we can hardly imagine.

This attitude has been severely attacked by many critics, but from what I know of
the artistic products of those who submit to this type of criticism and create "proletarian
literature" and other varieties of dead socialist realism, they have not achieved anything
that seems valuable for the present or for the transformation of the future. Some years
ago I participated in a polemic whose focal point was the concept of reality and which
revolved around how a revolutionary writer should confront and treat reality in his
work. On that occasion I did everything possible to show that any impoverishment of
the idea of reality in the name of a thematics limited to the immediate and concrete on

a supposedly revolutionary plane, on behalf of the capacity of less sophisticated readers, is no less than a counterrevolutionary act, since any impoverishment of the present weighs on the future and makes it seem farther away. On the contrary, nothing seems more revolutionary to me than enriching the notion of reality by all means possible for the reader of novels and short stories.

It is at this point that the relationship between the intellectual and politics becomes critical in Latin America, because precisely this continent provides irrefutable proof that the enrichment of reality through culture itself has had and now has a clearly demonstrable effect on the revolutionary capability of the people. I do not delude myself concerning the influence of literature and art on the geopolitical process; the petroleum industry, the multinational corporations and the many other forms of capitalist power are infinitely more powerful. But one can discover upon observing Latin America to what extent there is a growing popular consciousness of the devastation caused by imperialism and fascism in our countries. This new consciousness has been reached to a large extent by direct or indirect intellectual means.

In the course of the last two decades there has developed in Latin America an enormous mass of readers who are particularly interested in national authors. What has been termed the "boom" in Latin American fiction is not a commercial trick fabricated by publishers, as some would believe. It is, rather, the logical, capitalist reaction to the sudden demand by buyers for books written by national authors. This new interest resulted from a series of books capable of demonstrating the quality of our intellectuals and of creating confidence in them. And so it happened that this handful of books which exploded into the boom of editions and a concomitant boom of readers were written by bourgeois intellectuals who had awakened to the reality of the drama of Latin America in a more revolutionary manner than had the writers of an earlier generation, particularly more so than those writers who continued to create parochial realism. To mention only a few of the first stage of the new era, books like Carlos Fuentes's *Where the Air Is Clear*, Mario Vargas Llosa's "The Time of the Hero" and Gabriel García Márquez's *No One Writes to the Colonel and Other Short Stories* represent tentative efforts to present cross-sections of reality within the respective national context of each writer, to show with consummate literary beauty something that was more than a literary theme and, finally, to come to terms with our peculiar manner of being and suffering. The public felt and appreciated this, so that when the second wave of books arrived, it found millions of readers, young and old, educated and unsophisticated, bourgeois or not, all prepared by those first books, ready for the depth and meaning which these writers presented them in successive novels, short stories and poems.

Let me give a personal example. When my novel "The Book of Manuel" was published in Buenos Aires in 1973, after a week of sales in typical bourgeois bookstores, the book appeared in newsstands. Salesmen had realized that the ordinary population, who hesitated to enter a large bookstore, would buy, in the middle of the street, a book that intrigued them because of commentaries which they had heard or read. That is indeed what took place, in a manner quite moving to me, since I felt that barriers were now broken, that contact had been established on levels other than those supported by the bourgeois tradition in culture.

This panorama is of course partial and full of gaps, but it proves at any rate that the majority of committed writers can participate legitimately in the struggle for Latin American independence and that they carry out a task as revolutionary as that of writers whose work is the pure expression of party militancy. Nevertheless, it is necessary to emphasize an important aspect before continuing, an aspect which my own life has revealed to me. Nowadays readers do not content themselves with demanding from a writer a literary work which satisfies and moves them. In the days of Flaubert or Henry James the only thing that counted was the work itself; the moral relationship between the work and its author only interested a tiny nucleus, for reasons that had little to do with politics.

The situation is completely different today. When a Peruvian reads Mario Vargas Llosa, the character of Vargas Llosa is as vital for him as are the novels. Of course I do not refer to those readers who, like some intellectuals, have remained in their ivory tower and only utilize literature as an escapist or hedonistic resort. I speak of the majority of Latin American readers for whom literature, at the same time that it continues to be the satisfaction of esthetic and emotional needs, represents a testimony to our reality, an explication, a search, a road to follow, a reason to accept, reject or combat. Therefore, although a writer like me writes with complete freedom and independence with respect to any party line, with respect to any ideological choice that anyone would wish to impose on me for theoretical or pragmatic reasons, I am well aware that my readers are not content merely to read me as an author, but, rather, they look beyond the page for my face and my actions. They seek to find me physically and spiritually with them. They want to know that my participation in the struggle of Latin America does not end with the last page of my texts.

This new situation of the writer confronting his readers, that is, his countrymen, demands from him arduous (at times, even terrible) daily work. The intellectual who is born to write and is generally inefficient in other fields provides the moral guarantee of his work, and he should present proof that his guarantee is redeemable whenever necessary. Not all intellectuals are capable of this, but my lecture is not an accusation, since intellectuals ultimately must settle accounts with their own people and not with other isolated intellectuals. In my case I believe that the responsibility for our commitment reveals itself on two levels: that of our creation, which is based on the expansion rather than on the limitation of reality, and that of personal conduct regarding oppression, exploitation, dictatorship and fascism, which continue their terrifying work in so many Latin American countries. I would like now to add elements which illustrate this double aspect of the only legitimate relationship between politics and the intellectual.

I will begin with the part that concerns personal responsibility, the ethical conduct of the intellectual. In the history of Latin America I do not believe there is a more perfect example than that of the nineteenth-century Cuban, José Martí. Mentioning his name sufficiently illustrates what I am trying to say. Martí provides the pattern for the life of the intellectual at its highest level, a life given over completely to the struggle for the liberation of his country, a life terminated by the actual sacrifice of itself. No one, of course, would demand that intellectuals repeat this matchless example, but the highest model of conduct is there, forever, and within the limits of personal possibility the Latin American intellectual has the responsibility of following it. Now, the participation in the struggle for revolution admits multiple possibilities, since our battle is waged on multiple fronts, against multiple antagonists. The personal integrity of a writer or artist has to reveal itself, besides in his work itself, in his presence at these fronts. He must show his people that he does not live in hiding (behind his desk, within his professorial image or in a foreign country). He must, metaphorically or actually, enter the street, and in Latin America this street becomes more cluttered with barricades, snipers and painful confrontations every day.

Perhaps I can illustrate what I mean by personal conduct with a personal anecdote. When the people of Chile elected Salvador Allende as President in 1971, I understood that the most elemental obligation of a writer concerned about the future of socialism was to show his solidarity with this difficult, grand experience just beginning. Arriving in Santiago on the day of the inauguration of Allende, I felt a profound bitterness when I discovered how few intellectuals from my continent shared the attitude which seemed so natural to me. At the time when it became necessary to commit oneself to the present and future of Chile and to collaborate to the fullest with the efforts of that country, many writers and artists who could easily have traveled to Santiago stayed at home and limited themselves to showing their solidarity in writing. While groups of young people without a cent crossed the mountains to be present, while writers for whom traveling was at times a dangerous problem were there because it was their duty to be there, many others expected by the Chileans did not come.

You may ask: What good did it serve for me to have been there on that occasion? I would answer that it did not serve for much, but it did serve that thousands of Chileans who had appreciated me as a novelist or writer of short stories now understood my political support and my search for a direct dialogue with them. University students could exchange ideas with me for days on end. I could come to know the intellectual caliber of Chile, and on my return I could become a propagandist for Chile's new values. After the sinister coup of 1973 I was in a moral position to fight for Chile, to defend her people's cause before the Russell Tribunal and at the Helsinki Commission, and I could collaborate on a book denouncing the genocide committed by the fascist military junta. In other words, my presence effectively demonstrated that the intellectual's commitment to politics is more than the subject for lectures in universities. If the intellectuals of other countries had mutiplied this participation, the struggle of the people of Chile could have counted on more support than it ultimately had outside Chile.

My presence here with you is another proof of the personal responsibility of a committed writer. For ten years I declined to accept many generous, well-intentioned invitations from intellectual centers in the United States. In each case my refusal was clearly explained; in fact, the Dean of Columbia University, Frank McShane, published the text of my letter for this reason. The reasons for my former refusals have to do with my responsibility as a Latin American confronting the attitude of the government of the United States regarding Cuba and other countries of my continent and of other continents. That attitude, which unfortunately has not been substantially changed, has nevertheless undergone modifications imposed by a decade of unusually difficult history for this country. I could be mistaken, but I feel that a new point of view is beginning to appear among North Americans as a whole after experiences which have proven the will and capability of tiny nations to defend their liberty and sovereignty. Therefore the moment has arrived for that which is happening here tonight, a moment perfect for authentic dialogue, for a direct confrontation, for open contact in which everything can and should be said for the mutual good of our countries. It is for this reason that I came to New York a year ago to attend a seminar concerning the translation of Latin American works into English, and thus it is that I am here to contribute as much as possible to a better understanding of our literature.

At the same time—this must be clearly understood—I continue to struggle before the Russell Tribunal, denouncing actions such as the ominous intervention of North American multinational corporations in the local politics of our countries. If I did not make this clear, I would not be justified as a visitor to this university, in spite of the generosity of your invitation. I hope that these personal references illustrate better what I wished to say when I referred to the responsibility and moral integrity of the Latin American intellectual.

Now, in closing, let us return to the other aspect of that responsibility—the professional aspect. I would define it in a single sentence: Never to recede, for whatever reasons, along the path of creativity. It is hardly discouraging that the literature which we could term "avant-garde" still cannot count on the understanding of all the readers we might desire. It is precisely to reach that totality someday that one must fiercely search for new vehicles of creativity and language. One must hurl oneself toward the new, toward the unexplored, toward mankind's most unsettling reality. Any simplification in the name of the vast public is a treason to our people. Creation can be simple and clear at its highest level, as the poems of Pablo Neruda prove. But the poems of César Vallejo verify that it can be difficult and hardly accessible at the same high level. These two poets were faithful to themselves, and their political commitment was exercised totally without ever restraining their personal way of feeling reality and enriching it with their own voices. I understand the reproach of hermeticism which I have received through the years; it always comes from those who demand a step backward in creativity in the name of a supposed step forward in the political struggle. It is not in this way that we will contribute to the final liberation of our countries; rather, it will be by fighting with words and deeds, both along with and on the behalf of our people.

At the beginning of this lecture I said that I hoped to show how intellectuals who do not necessarily understand politics could efficiently commit themselves to the long struggle for our full identity as Latin Americans. I don't know if I have succeeded in showing this, but as for me, within my ignorance of so many things that I will never have time to learn, I follow a road in which my books and my character struggle to become a single will, feeling its way toward a more just future for my brothers in Latin America and all over the world.

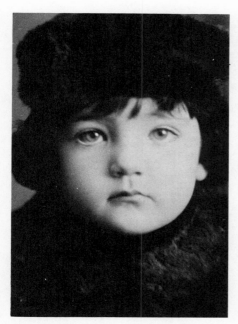

Julio Cortázar, age 2, in Switzerland, 1916.
Photo: collection of Julio Cortázar.

Klosters, Switzerland, 1916.
Photo: collection of Julio Cortázar.

Buenos Aires, 1939. Photo: collection of Julio Cortázar.

Paris, 1960. Photo: collection of Julio Cortázar.

Paris, 1966. Photo: Sara Facio-Alicia D'Amico.

An Argentine barbecue in Saignon, France, 1974. Photo: collection of Julio Cortázar.

An encounter and debate with students, Warsaw, 1974. Photo: Henryk Kimak.

With students, Warsaw, 1974. Photo: Henryk Kimak.

In Mexico for the seventieth birthday of Luis Buñuel, 1974. *Left to right*, Cortázar, Carlos Fuentes, Buñuel. Photo: Hector García.

At the grave of Raymond Roussel, Père Lachaise Cemetery, Paris, 1975. Photo: Anne De Brunhoff.

In Norman, Oklahoma, November 1975.

Blow-Up meets *Zabriskie Point*. Death Valley, 1975. Photo: collection of Julio Cortázar.

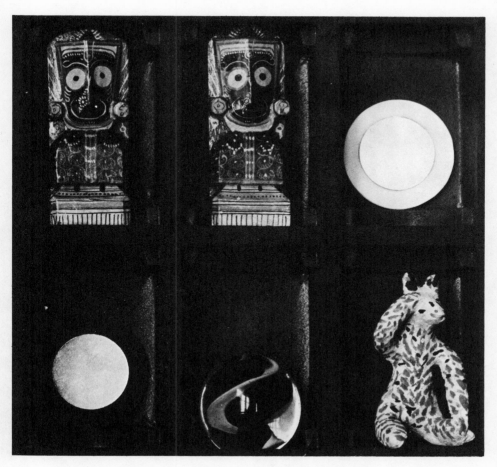

Object Destined to Irritate Art Critics, by Julio Cortázar. 1976, 25 x 25 cm.
Photo: Alfredo J. Zamora.

Visiting Cuban author José Lezama Lima in Havana, 1976. *Left to right*: Claude Gallimard, Cortázar, Ugnė Karvelis, Lezama Lima, Colette Duhamel, José Triana and Mrs. Lezama Lima. Photo: collection of Julio Cortázar.

Paris, 1976. Photo: Alberto Jonquières.

Essays

Lying to Athena: Cortázar and the Art of Fiction

By GREGORY RABASSA

In Book 13 of the *Odyssey*, when Odysseus has been put ashore on Ithaca at last, he encounters his patroness Athena, who is disguised as a shepherd. Almost at once he goes into the well-honed tale of his Cretan origins and all the great deeds to his credit. This stock-in-trade of his was useful for concealment, but the verve with which he tells the story and embellishes upon it betrays the joy of the bard, the creator. Finally the goddess is so pleased with him that she smiles and gives him a caress, shedding her mask and assuming female shape, as she reveals herself to him and says:

> "Whoever gets around you must be sharp
> and guileful as a snake; even a god
> might bow to you in ways of dissimulation.
> You! You chameleon!
> Bottomless bag of tricks! Here in your own country
> would you not give your stratagems a rest
> or stop spellbinding for an instant?
>
> You play a part as if it were your own tough skin.
>
> No more of this, though. Two of a kind, we are,
> contrivers, both. Of all men now alive
> you are the best in plots and story telling.
> My own fame is for wisdom among the gods—
> deceptions, too. . . ."[1]

Thus it is that fiction is a tool of wisdom and, indeed, one which is used with great joy, even by Athena herself. So that if our philosophic search for truth is to go on, we must cease to gather the shreds we take to be particles of the ultimate truth and, instead, fashion our own bits and pieces in the shape of that vague reality which Plato has described to us. This is precisely what the philosopher does at the end of the *Republic* with his myth of Er.

The Brazilian novelist Érico Veríssimo once said that his old *gaúcho* grandfather in Rio Grande do Sul was quite proud of the fame his grandson had acquired but that he had some serious reservations nonetheless because Érico was telling lies after all. This attitude is the heritage of the joyless nineteenth century, which tried to seek the truth directly, ignoring Plato's strictures concerning our incomplete grasp of reality. As thousands wheeze themselves to death, tobacconists say, "It hasn't been proven"; when someone says, "We must be realistic," another set of morals has gone down the drain. Myth may indeed be the closest we have come to truth, and if we put it to the mean and niggling test of realism, we retreat even deeper into Plato's cave, where so many of our critics deserve to be with their chopping blocks and single-edged cleavers. We think that the invention of devices improves upon our surroundings, and of late we even go on endlessly about life-style instead of life. Yet, if we turn our invention to words and concepts, we are given the lie. In his *Naufragios* the intrepid proto-anthropologist Alvar Núñez Cabeza de Vaca tells of how he had great difficulties in extracting facts from one certain tribe of Indians because they loved to novelize so much ("porque son grandes amigos de novelar"). This is certainly in the Odyssean spirit and that of tale-telling (even this last wonderful word has the connotation of something dirty), but it can also be the basis of Disneyland and other enforced hallucinations.

Julio Cortázar is a writer who has thrown off the restrictions of mental Calvinism imposed by the past century and still so much with us. Going along with Jarry, he finds that life imitates art and that homo ludens must precede homo faber ("homo faber & faber," as he calls him in *Libro de Manuel*). This is most evident in his conception of structure. A form is of its own making, an object is defined by its use, as Ortega y Gasset has said, and the reader really creates his own novel as he goes forward. This is the starting point of *Hopscotch*, where Cortázar gives us a carefully ordered alternate version and also invites us to go to work and bring forth further variations. We have before us a rich lode of chiastic possibilities. When the novel was first published in the United States, a great many critics did not know that along with the interesting possibilities put forth to them they were also being had. Cortázar shook his head in dismay at this straitlaced interpretation and agreed that it would be awful to have to read any novel through twice, this one above all. What he did do, however, was to point out the possibilities of reality, and this can best be done and perhaps only be done by recourse to fiction, to the lie. Our wisdom is still so limited that it most often needs to be primed with a cupful of untruth in order to start pumping up new ideas and concepts. Before we can begin to write, we must unwrite, as the mononymous Morelli says in *Hopscotch* (a fine and complex pun can be essayed in Spanish with the words *escribir* and *describir*).

As we put the pieces of *Hopscotch* together we find that the puzzle is the novel itself, that we are in a sense writing it as we read it, much in the way that Aureliano Babilonia in *One Hundred Years of Solitude* lives his life to the end and can only do so as he reads the manuscript of Melquíades, which is the book we are reading too. This is also the structure of *Don Quixote*, accepted as the first novel, although Homer and, indeed, Odysseus himself have some claim through the narrative techniques of the *Odyssey*. The Duchess recognizes Don Quixote because she has read the first part, just as we have, putting character and reader on the same level, giving the characters of the novel a real existence and making the reader a member of the cast.

Cortázar's art as seen in *Hopscotch* and its sequel *62: A Model Kit* is essentially indehiscent. The conclusion is vague, real rather than factual. Life cannot end so neatly and so precisely. When Allen R. Foley's Vermonter is asked, "Have you lived here all your life?" he answers, "Not yet."[2] Oliveira seeks truth and meaning in the accepted sense and finally comes to realize that they are elusive, that his illusions are closer to his goal. The very name of his friend Traveler is evidence that our words and labels in their assigned usage are apt ultimately to be a mockery of the very thing they are meant to represent. Oliveira's *nostos* is tragic, more like Agamemnon's than that of Odysseus, perhaps because, like the former, he is prone to accept standard definitions in spite of himself and only becomes a contriver when his mind begins to slip. Although he has traces of the grace entailed, Oliveira is not the thoroughgoing cronopio that Odysseus was.

Toward the end of the novel, in the madhouse already even though because of devious circumstances which ultimately prove meet, Oliveira finally has his katabasis as he descends into the refrigerated morgue, an image quite in keeping with the utter depths of Dante's Inferno rather than with the subsequent impression the world has come to give it. This would imply that Oliveira has plumbed the very bottom, where those punished as betrayers of benefactors are lodged. Here his revelation is negative. He loses his Eurydice as he kisses Talita, in whom he sees the lost Maga. He has looked back, but this time there is a reversal and it is the future which has disappeared; it is not the past reborn. Juno, counter-fate, has won out over Jupiter, fate, *furor* over *ratio*, and Oliveira goes mad in his labyrinth of string, basins and ball-bearings, or is it Agamemnon's net self-assumed?

The tragedy is that Oliveira had been following a process of rigidity until he became as cold and stiff and lifeless as the idems in the mortuary drawers, each of whom once had a life, a life befitting a nineteenth-century novel of the kind we call realistic. Oliveira had been lying to himself by following what he thought was true and reasonable instead of lying to Athena so that she would reveal herself and impart her wisdom. Suicide is rarely tragic, however, and if this is what Oliveira has done at the end of part two, the result is more pathetic. Cortázar in his scheme of things, however, in his reliance on the concept of quantum, has offered an alternative version in the dispensable chapters of part three. Oliveira is broken but saved. His body rather than his mind has cracked. This salvatory recourse brings to mind the treatment accorded the Hungarian suicide song of the late thirties, "Gloomy Sunday," which had ever so many people leaping into the Danube off the bridges between Buda and Pest. I recall that when Billie Holiday recorded the song here, lines were added to mitigate the urge and show that it was all a dream, that we could rest assured.

In Cortázar's perception of the truth the use of dreams and dreamlike states leads us in important directions. Much of this in *Hopscotch* is hallucinatory or a ribald caricature of surface reality, like the Berthe Trépat episode. (This section has the stuff of a happening about it and must be staged someday, replete with original music.) In *62* we meet the City, a vision shared by the characters and not really a dream. It is, rather, an epiphany which has a collective mise-en-scène. The City is, of course, a labyrinth and the hotel a labyrinth within a labyrinth. Here the direction of the elevator leads to anabasis before it turns horizontal. The coming up is frustrated, then, and the revelation incomplete, leading into difficulties on a higher level. This would bear out what has subsequently been discovered in mathematics regarding the so-called "Traveling Salesman Problem," a sort of maze puzzle which can be solved when it is in limited form but becomes insoluble when enlarged, showing that microcosmic solutions do not always obtain in the macrocosm. Returning to the Dis imagery of *Hopscotch*, we must wonder if the last scene in the City in *62* might not be Stygian in import, with the canal at the north end serving as the underground river.

It is also in *62* that the other self acquires more cohesion. In *Hopscotch* Traveler is seen as a kind of doppelgänger for Oliveira (the irony of names again: Traveler who has never left Buenos Aires, and Oliveira with the connotations of roots and staff of life, the trunk upon which the bed of Odysseus and Penelope was anchored). The idea of the double is broadened in *62*, and we have the notion of the *paredros*, the Egyptian concept of a guiding spirit, a fellow traveler, but one which here is shared and which possesses different people at different times, when that character, without being identified, is referred to simply as "my paredros." Able as she is to appear to or to influence the minds of whomsoever she chooses according to her will, Athena might well be called Odysseus's paredros. In his last novel, *Libro de Manuel*, Cortázar has a figure called "the one I told you," quite similar in concept to the paredros, but given an added dimension by the satanic suggestion of his title, so close to many Latin American euphemisms for the Prince of Darkness; and, of course, the name of God is never spoken in Hell except by the foul-mouthed Vanni Fucci. In classical mythology Hermes/Mercury, the messenger (*angelos*) of the gods, was given many of the mischief-making attributes later assigned to the Christian devil—Candanga, as he is known in some Asturian parts. Indeed, in Brazilian *candomblé* Exu, the messenger in the Yoruban pantheon, has often and mistakenly been coordinated with the devil.

Of all the Spanish American writers who have been said to practice a style called "magic realism," Cortázar is the one who might be closest to the mark. Straight fantasy is found more often in the short stories and is never explained. In the novels the case is more often one of creating fantasy out of the raw material of the reality at hand, as in the case of the Berthe Trépat episode in *Hopscotch* and Frau Marta in *62*. The most striking example of the creation of fantasy out of the stuff of reality is also in *62*, and it is most apt that the one who fashions this fantasy and turns it into reality (so that the real situation then ceases to exist and becomes fantasy) is the sculptor Marrast. His intervention perverts the aims of incongruent groups to such a degree that reality becomes what otherwise would be an absurd fantasy at the Courtauld Institute in London. Marrast here is being a cronopio, the figure Cortázar has invented and explained in *Cronopios and Famas* but who appears almost unobtrusively at times in the novels, where the cronopio is more often a spirit, like the paredros, who will overwhelm a character to make him reverse reality and fantasy. The only overt appearance of the battle between cronopio and fama is in *62* with Polanco and Calac. The two types are really well established in the brothers Shem (the Penman) and Shaun in Joyce's *Finnegans Wake*:

> Shem (Jerry), the introvert, rejected of man, is the explorer and discoverer of the forbidden. He is an embodiment of dangerously brooding, inturned energy. He is the uncoverer of secret springs, and, as such, the possessor of terrific, lightning powers. The books he writes are so mortifying that they are spontaneously rejected by the decent; they threaten, they dissolve the protecting boundary lines of good and evil. Provoked to action (and he must be provoked before he will act), he is not restrained by normal human laws, for they have been dissolved within him by the two powerful elixirs of the elemental depths; he may let loose a hot spray of acid; but, on the other hand, he can release such a magical balm of forgiveness that the battle lines themselves become melted in a bacchanal of general love. Such absolute love is as dangerous to the efficient working of society as absolute hate. The possessor of the secrets, therefore, is constrained to hold his fire. . . .
>
> Shem's business is not to create a higher life, but merely to find and utter the Word. Shaun, on the other hand, whose function is to make the Word become flesh, misreads it, fundamentally rejects it, limits himself to a kind of stupid concretism, and, while winning all the skirmishes, loses the eternal city.[3]

As is the case with Joyce, Cortázar and many of his Latin American contemporaries delve deeply into the real and the unreal and try to separate or conjoin them according to less traditional standards. Those who have been most successful in this penman's quest have been the ones who have undertaken cronopian means.

Another holdover from realism that Cortázar has been forced to grapple with is the element of time. His approach has not been as patently self-conscious as that of another neoteric Spanish American novelist, Mario Vargas Llosa, and it is therefore much more effective and "real." Although temporal changes are more clearly discerned in some of his stories, the stuff of time has also been manipulated in the novels. The pathetic and bitter death scene of Rocamadour shows how the time of going hence differs from the banal time roundabout, which seems static in comparison with the *hora de la verdad,* all too well reflected in Tirso de Molina's magnificently mediocre figure of Don Juan Tenorio and his shallow "tan largo me lo fiáis."

The time of the City becomes the time of Rocamadour's agony, brief and intense and existing amidst the superficiality of the other world or dimension, the one we see or see the shadows of. The infant Manuel, in some ways a Rocamadour redivivus, still exists in cradle time, still wet from the Lethe as well as other waters, as his parents devise a sort of scrapbook for him so that he will be aware of that other time in which he lives but which he has not fully entered as he pushes the memory of Limbo deeper into his unconscious. In *62* it is the residue of time past in the Blutgasse of Vienna which brings Tell and Juan to relive a vampiric episode in Mozart's room. This is another version of reality which Cortázar brings out and follows much in the spirit of a recent breakthrough in mathematics which has revealed that any infinite series of numbers contains within itself an infinite quantity of other series of infinite numbers. This was the basis of Borges's story "El libro de arena" in his latest collection of the same name. The paradoxical problem is that the universe (macrocosm) is finite and speckled with quanta, adding to the difficulties of finding reality or truth, if such there is. Pontius Pilate, a noble Roman who tarried too long in the Hellenistic world, has yet to receive a proper answer to his question.

Julio Cortázar is wise enough to know that there is no answer; for it is a question that can only be put to the gods, and ever since Eden and after Babel we are hard put enough to communicate with our fellows. While life as we see it in our daily rapidity has the feel of the flow of a *carmen perpetuum* about it, it is really made up of individual frames. As in the story "Blow-Up" and the subsequent film, when we examine these frames at our leisure, we see another reality, one which has come out of our own purview, however. Both aspects, then, are true, both are real; but as they are so different, can they both be such? Is Athena lying to us instead? Is our very wisdom, what we have of it, the culprit which leads us into conceptual error? The seemingly absurd becomes possible through words, but always with a mystery remaining as regards the fruition of our verbal notion. Cortázar has given us the wherewithal at least to move closer to the mouth of the cave and shake off the effects of the lottery of Babylonia.

The Cortazarian hero is, like all of us, schizophrenic in that he too is the heir to two distinct though superficially similar heroisms. Like Aeneas he is seeking his dutiful dose of *pietas* so that Rome can be built, the promised land, the *civis,* civilization; but the Odyssean element is too strong, the best he can do is preserve Ithaca and then go forth again in search of people who do not know what oars are for, much in the manner of the seeking narrator in Alejo Carpentier's *The Lost Steps,* trying to begin over again, to be Jung and unaFreud.[4] The origins of music as depicted in Carpentier's novel correspond to the Babelic universal sounds of Gliglish in *Hopscotch*, as basic elements are given a new structure but with the same implied meanings, just as concrete poetry attempts to become the mortar used to build another tower. In *One Hundred Years of Solitude*, again, José Arcadio Buendía, during the insomnia plague, wisely or unwisely, perhaps, labels things so that we will remember, thus cheating us out of the grace of an Adamic lexical renovation. From Gliglish and from the speech of Polanco and Calac in *62* or Lonstein in *Libro de Manuel* we can see that words are the real liars, that the truth is found in what is left unsaid, even though in English we cover those gaps with grunts while Spanish Americans use *éste* and Spaniards a rather more scabrous bit of putty. Borges has also shown us that the unsaid, the unwritten has as much significance as what has been articulated, perhaps even more, and the page of *blens* in Cabrera Infante's *Three Trapped Tigers* has more extensive meaning than can be found in the whole of *Fortunata y Jacinta*. (When will we purveyors of Spanish literature join Buñuel and celebrate *Nazarín*?) It is due time that our critical Perseuses turned and looked at the heads they have severed and shared with us the petrification we have suffered at their instance. If they are lucky, they might even turn to oilcloth stone.[5]

The approach to Cortázar's works, then, must be carried on in the same spirit as that with which they are written. We must prevaricate, we must lie to our wisdom, just as our wisdom itself lies to her peers on the Olympian level, elevated and beyond our ken. Then we will be proper readers, the kind that Cortázar pleads for and the kind that he does not always receive. I have found that my work with Julio has made me a better reader, and I have enough hubris to believe that I may have fooled Athena once or twice; in any case, I have felt her caress on occasion, and this is because, like Dante, I have been well guided by Julio and his paredroi.

[1] Homer, *Odyssey*, Robert Fitzgerald, tr., Garden City, N.J., Doubleday, 1963, p. 239.

[2] Allen R. Foley, *What the Old-Timer Said*, Brattleboro, Vt., Greene, 1971.

[3] Joseph Campbell, Henry Morton Robinson, *A Skeleton Key to Finnegans Wake*, New York, Viking, 1961, pp. 12, 13.

[4] William York Tindall has used this play on words in his classroom lectures at Columbia University.

[5] This is the stone that Marrast has come to England to buy. No definition or further description is given.

Los reyes: Cortázar's Mythology of Writing

By ROBERTO GONZÁLEZ ECHEVARRÍA

Although I refer to *Los reyes* in my title, I do not intend to carry out an independent literary analysis of what no doubt is a callow work of Cortázar's. My design, at once broad and reductive, is to deal with the somewhat dated and embarrassing problem of how to read an author, not a book.[1] Is "holistic" criticism viable? Is it possible, in other words, to read Cortázar instead of engaging in a series of isolated exegeses of his works? And if it is worth attempting such a reading, how does one avoid turning it into a thematic gloss, a formalistic reduction or a biographical narrative? How, other than as a rhetorical license, can we continue to use Cortázar's name in reference to what is already a vast and diverse body of writing, encompassing texts belonging not only to various genres but also to criticism and theory? And what can one make of a text as bizarre as *Los reyes*? In what way is it also Cortázar's?

These questions do not arise from an abstract, speculative whim, but from Cortázar's work itself. They are, as I hope to be able to argue here, the fundamental questions posed by Cortázar's texts, and not only by such obviously autobiographical books as *La vuelta al día en ochenta mundos*, *Ultimo round* and *Fantomas contra los vampiros multinacionales*. I intend to use *Los reyes* to sketch a primal scene, to delineate what might very broadly be called Cortázar's conception of writing—conception, that is, both in its etymological sense of insemination or generation, and in its more common meaning of notion or idea. By determining Cortázar's conception of writing in both these senses, I hope to legitimize a critical discourse that will atone for its reductiveness by providing a critical insight into the totality of a literary enterprise.

While discussing a problem similar to the one just sketched, Roland Barthes remarks in *Critique et vérité*:

> There is no doubt that the "civilized" work cannot be dealt with as myth, in the ethnological sense of the term. But the difference [between the "civilized" work and that of the "primitive"] has less to do with the signature of the message than with its substance. Our works are written; that imposes upon them certain constraints of meaning that the oral myth could not know. It is a mythology of writing that awaits us, which shall have as its object not certain *determined* works, that is to say, which are inscribed in a process of determination where a person (the author) would be the origin, but works *traversed* by the great mythic writing in which humanity tries out its significations, i.e., its desires.[2]

As often happens in discussions of myth, whether they be "civilized" or not, Barthes's own formulation has become part of the myth that it attempts to uncover. For if there is a modern mythology of writing, it centers on the question of authorship versus general determination—a question, in other words, of the origin or generation of writing. That "great mythic writing" of which Barthes speaks has as its object the disappearance of the author, or in more current critical idiom, the abolition of the subject; it is a search for meaning in a universe abandoned both by man and the gods.

While current and certainly modern, the abolition of the author is not new. In *The Dehumanization of Art*, synthesizing a whole current of modern thinking, Ortega

said that "the poet begins where man ends," and added, referring to Mallarmé, that
the fate of the "poor face of the man who officiates as poet" is to "disappear, to vanish
and become a pure nameless voice breathing into the air the words—those true protagonists of the lyrical pursuit. This pure and nameless voice, the mere acoustic carrier
of the verse, is the voice of the poet who has learned to extricate himself from the
surrounding man."[3] The work of philologists and mythographers during the nineteenth century (the Grimm brothers, later Bédier and Menéndez Pidal) brought to
the fore the question of authorship. As Foucault has shown, once representation as a
synchronic, complete system mediating between the subject and the world is shattered,
the various languages of literary expression, as well as the question of being, become
historical—language and being become a matter of depth.[4] Philology seeks the origin
of language, just as ontology seeks the origin of being in man's passions (Rousseau).
The urgency of this question of origins—in its double thrust: language, being—
determines that most salient characteristic of modern writing, self-referentiality. By
alluding to itself and by probing into its own mode of being, modern writing is always
in the process of offering an implicit statement about its own generation, a conception
of its conception, as it were.

   It would be a naïve and predictable undertaking to show that self-referentiality
occurs in Cortázar, since *Hopscotch* has already become a classic of self-referential
writing. But it is precisely in self-referentiality that the mythology which I intend to
isolate manifests itself. As Hyppolite has shown in his study of Hegel, self-reflexiveness
is a regressive movement, a circular journey back to the source.[5] In literature self-
referentiality is a return to origins in order to take away from conception its claim of
originality, of constituting a single, fresh moment of beginning, an ordering principle
and principium. Rather than the joyful game that it is often taken to be, self-referentiality is a deadly game in Cortázar, a violent ritual where Cortázar is at stake.
Los reyes, the first book that he signed with his own name (as is known, an earlier
work had appeared under a pseudonym), presents, under the guise of the Theseus
myth, this ritual. By the reenactment of this ritual, Cortázar's writing labors to define
itself, to cope with the opposition of the individual/original versus the general/collec-
tive, in short, the issue of generation. Who writes?

   The most superficial consideration of *Los reyes* immediately leads to the issue of
individuality and origin. The very appeal to classical mythology, to the dawn of
Western literary tradition, is suggestive of a concern about the beginning of writing.
The recourse to classical mythology is in itself hardly original, but rather a characteristic of the modern tradition: Nietzsche, Freud, Joyce, Pound, Unamuno; all take
recourse to classical figures. In Latin America there is a strain of classicism of this sort
that runs from Lugones and Borges through Reyes, Carpentier and Paz. It is not a
neoclassical spirit that leads these modern writers to the classical tradition, since they
do not imitate classical models, but instead (particularly in Nietzsche and Freud) a
philological quest for a mythology of origins: a perfect example of this would be
Carpentier's story "Like the Night," which begins and ends with an episode drawn
from the *Iliad*, a double thrust away from and back to the origin of Western literary
tradition. There is throughout Cortázar's work a recurrence of classical motifs and
figures that answers to this general philological trend.

All myths, as we know, appear in many versions; but if one reads the most complete account of the Theseus myth, that of Plutarch, one is struck by the confusing number of contradictory accounts extant of this particular story. The charm, in fact, of Plutarch's rendition is his juggling of so many different versions in one and the same text, versions that cancel each other and blur or abolish altogether the possibility of a master version. To read Plutarch is to realize that the myth, while organized around a certain implied narrative core, is not a fixed text but a set of superimposed narratives. Thus we already have in the myth chosen by Cortázar the outlines of the question of conception: while being set at the dawn of Western tradition that classical mythology represents, the myth cannot claim originality in the sense of constituting a single source.

If the versions of the myth of Theseus offer, simultaneously, the promise of uniqueness and multiplicity, of singularity and plurality, so do the many readings of which the particular incident of the Minotaur has been the object. Theseus's slaying of the Minotaur and his escape from the labyrinth have often been interpreted as the victory of reason over ignorance, so much so that to some the myth is a parable of the Greeks' founding of Western thought after conquering superstition. According to this reading the Theseus myth would mark the birth of reason. Moralistic interpretations also abound in the form of allegories, particularly in the Middle Ages. A creature half bull and half man is the image of man driven by his lower instincts, imprisoned in the materiality of his senses, unable to exercise his spiritual and intellectual powers. Dante's inversion of the figure, making the lower half of the Minotaur the animal part, points to such a moralistic interpretation.[6] Theseus's victory would in this case be a moral one, the triumph of the higher faculties of man over his lower instincts. His victory would thus mark the birth of morals. A political reading is also possible and common. Theseus's victory over Minos is the triumph of political principle over arbitrary rule, of Athens over Crete, the defeat of the old order and the coming of the new. The very abstractness of these readings underscores again the question of singularity, of individuation: Theseus's victory is that of reason, of higher instincts, of political principle. The specificity of the text vanishes as we glide into allegorical abstraction and accept the plurality of potential readings that the myth contains.

The same problematics appear when it becomes evident that Theseus's slaying of the Minotaur displays a series of elements that relates the episode to other myths. The confrontation of Theseus and Minos is the well-known struggle between the old king and the prince; Theseus's journey into the labyrinth, the regressive voyage in search of origins, the slaying of the Minotaur (who is after all also a young prince), the hero's struggle to assert his individuality—all of these elements link the myth to other myths of generation, such as the Oedipus myth. It might be remembered here that Theseus not only defeats Minos, but also, though inadvertently like Oedipus, kills his own father Aegeus by forgetting to change the sails. Moreover, as in the cases of Oedipus and the Minotaur, Theseus's origins are clouded by mystery: it is not clear whether he is the son of Neptune or the son of Aegeus. His journey to the center of the labyrinth, like his earlier journey to Athens, is a journey back to the source to establish (or reestablish) his own beginning. As soon as we insert the Theseus story into a general mythology, it begins to lose its specificity; its own origins begin to recede into infinity or to dissolve and multiply as if in a gallery of mirrors. The thematics of genealogy that pervade the readings of the myth—it represents the birth of reason, of morals, of political principle—perhaps reflect this dialectic that subtends its structure.

What we find in *Los reyes* is then necessarily not a version but a subversion of the myth of Theseus. To begin with, as Cortázar himself has emphasized on many occasions, his Ariadne gives Theseus the clew only in order to free the Minotaur, once the monster has killed the hero. As Alfred MacAdam perceptively notes, *Los reyes* contains a "double tragedy."[7] Instead of a triumph, Cortázar's version offers a mutual defeat: Theseus's quest leads not to heroic distinction, but to indifferentiation. The Minotaur, who would represent such indifferentiation and thus be the victor, is dead. Theseus's pursuit of individuation is thwarted from the start: he constantly recognizes himself in others, not only in the Minotaur, but also in Minos. What is emphasized in Cortázar's version is the violence that Theseus commits against himself in defeating Minos and killing the Minotaur. Instead of the erection of individual presence, Theseus's regressive voyage creates a vacuum at the center; the Minotaur is dead, Theseus has fled. The clash, the violence of conception suggested by the erotic act *contra naturam* by which the Minotaur was conceived, is repeated at the end of Theseus's journey. The blood of Pasiphae has been spilled again. Whereas previously the labyrinth was inhabited by the "lord of games" (the Minotaur),[8] it now stands as an empty gallery of winding walls. Theseus's victory has led to that other labyrinth suggested by Borges: the labyrinth of total indifferentiation, the desert, the white page. The I, the you and the we float in a space without perspectives and dimensions, as interchangeable masks of primeval chaos and apocalypse.

This confrontation of the monster and the hero constitutes the primal scene in Cortázar's mythology of writing: a hegemonic struggle for the center that resolves itself in a mutual cancellation and in the superimposition of beginnings and ends. The very image of man unborn, the Minotaur is the possessor of the immediate but naïve knowledge of man before the Fall. His speech is the incoherent, symbolic language of a savage god. Theseus, on the other hand, is not only a dealer in death, but is the very image of death. His linear, cogent language is temporal, discursive—it is discourse. In his enclosure the Minotaur speaks a perishable language that is not temporal but that is reinvented every day. The words he utters are, even if momentarily, attached to the things they represent:

> Oh, his pained monologues, which the palace guards heard in wonder, without understanding them. His profound recitals of the recurring waves, his taste for celestial nomenclatures and the catalogues of herbs. He ate them pensively, and then gave them names with secret delight, as if the flavor of stems had revealed their names to him . . . He raised the whole enumeration of celestial bodies, and seemed to forget it with the dawn of a new day, as if also in his memory dusk dimmed the stars. And the next night he took delight in inaugurating a new nomenclature, ordering sonorous space with ephemeral constellations.[9]

If in other versions of the myth the birth of reason, morals or politics is at stake, what we have in *Los reyes* is the violent birth of writing. The catalogue of herbs that the Minotaur "tastes" is a series of disconnected words, without syntactical and therefore temporal structure, linked to their individual origin through their "stems." By killing the Minotaur, Theseus attempts to replace the perishable sound of individual words with the linear, durable cogency of discourse, a cogency predicated not on the stems of words but on their declensions, on the particles that link them in a structure whose mode of representation would not be sonorous but spatial—writing. The irony, of course, is that once writing is instituted, Theseus does not gain control of the labyrinth but becomes superfluous and flees. Because writing cannot be dimmed like the stars with each dawn, because it is not a memory whose traces can be erased, Theseus is not needed to reinvent it, as the Minotaur reinvented his nomenclatures every day. Writing is the empty labyrinth from which both the Minotaur and Theseus have been banished.

This primal scene appears with remarkable consistency in Cortázar's writing. I do not mean simply that there are monsters, labyrinths and heroes, but rather that the scene in which a monster and a hero kill each other, cancel each other's claim for the center of the labyrinth, occurs with great frequency, particularly in texts where the nature of writing seems to be more obviously in question. The most superficial consideration of Cortázar's first novel, *The Winners*, will no doubt reveal the existence of the primal scene. But I would like to examine two briefer texts, "All Fires the Fire" and "The Pursuer."

The title of "All Fires the Fire" is drawn from Heraclitus and suggests the indifferentiation obtained when all things return to their primal state and ends and beginnings resolve into one.[10] The story is in fact two stories that reflect each other, being told simultaneously. One is a lover's triangle taking place presumably in contemporary Paris and told for the most part through a telephone conversation. The other also involves a lover's triangle of sorts: it is the story of a gladiator who is made to fight a gigantic black slave by a Roman consul who is jealous of his wife's interest in the gladiator. In the first story (I use first here for the sake of clarity, but there is no hierarchy of this kind in the text) Sonia calls Roland to plead with him and to announce that Irene is on her way to his apartment. Their conversation is made difficult by a bad connection. A mysterious voice in the background keeps reading a series of figures—is it a gambler? These figures, in their stark meaninglessness, are remindful of the Minotaur's "celestial nomenclatures." They oppose the flow of speech, the discursiveness that Roland wants to achieve. The dark depths from which the sounds in the telephone line seem to emerge also evoke the labyrinth and Ariadne's clew. Roland's cool and logical entreaties to Sonia, who finally commits suicide, are Theseus-like in their reasoned discursiveness. There is, furthermore, although very obliquely suggested, a potential monstrosity in Sonia, whose interest in Irene seems to be as strong as her interest in Roland. In the other strand of the story the primal scene is present in much more obvious fashion. The hero-monster confrontation is clear, and there is, moreover, an echo of one of the versions of the Theseus myth offered by Plutarch in which the Minotaur, instead of being a monstrous creature, is a powerful and hateful man named Taurus, whom Theseus defeats in combat at the Cretan games.[11] Although, naturally, some of the details are different in Cortázar's story, the basic situation is essentially the same. The young gladiator has risen from the ranks because of his heroic deeds to become known as an individual, and by competing for the affections of the consul's wife he has also become a potential usurper.

There are other, more direct echoes of the primal scene in the text of the story. When the black giant enters the arena, he does so through the gallery used by the beasts, and the description of the gate through which he passes evokes the act of birth: "They have raised the creaking gates of the dark passage where they have wild animals come out, and Marcus sees the gigantic figure of the Nubian retiarius appear, until then invisible against the background of mossy stone."[12] The labyrinth is evoked in the description of the arena, where it appears sketched on the sand as a trace, "the enormous bronze eye where hoes and palm leaves have sketched their curved paths darkened by traces of preceding fights." It is, of course, at the center of that maze that Marcus and the Nubian retiarius stage their combat.

As in *Los reyes*, there is no victory at the end of "All Fires the Fire," but rather a mutual annihilation. The fight between the Nubian retiarius and the gladiator is resolved when both fall dead upon each other in the sand. The mutual killing and the sand, which suggests the desert, prefigure the fire that kills everyone at the end, the fire that destroys the arena and which also levels the apartment building where, centuries later, Roland and Irene have fallen asleep on each other, like the dead gladiators, after making love. The stories merge at the end, not only on the level of the action but also at a conceptual level; love and war, presumably opposites, mingle to evoke the topic of the *ars amandi, ars bellandi*. Like the two gladiators and the lovers, the two stories have a common end that abolishes their difference and returns the text to the indifferentiation of origins—all texts the text.

In "The Pursuer" the various elements of this mythology are even more directly related to writing. The story tells of the last months in the life of the jazz saxophonist Johnny Carter, as reported by Bruno, a writer who had previously published a biography of the musician. It is rather easy to discern in the story the general outline of the primal scene. Bruno's visit to Johnny as the story opens is reminiscent of Theseus's journey into the labyrinth; the jazzman lives in a small, dark walk-up apartment, a sort of lair, and he is described in animal terms: "But he's making gestures, laughing and coughing at the same time, shivering away under the blanket like a chimpanzee."[13] Johnny is also described as a huge fetus or newborn monster, naked and coiled onto himself and making inarticulate sounds: "And I saw Johnny had thrown off the blanket around him in one motion, and I saw him sitting in the easy chair completely nude, his legs pulled up and the knees underneath his chin, shivering but laughing to himself" (184).

While Johnny appears as a monstrous fetus, Bruno, the writer, stands for order and profit. Bruno wants to "regenerate" Johnny, to make him abandon his intuitive cavils about time, his drugs and his visions. But Bruno's apparent good intentions conceal his desire to kill Johnny, to reduce him to that image of him which he has created in his book. Johnny's death at the end of the story appears to take place in order to round out Bruno's book:

> All this [Johnny's death] happened at the same time that the second edition of my book was published, but luckily I had time to incorporate an obituary note edited under full steam and inserted, along with a newsphoto of the funeral in which many famous jazzmen were identifiable. In that format the biography remained, so to speak, intact and finished. Perhaps it's not right that I say this, but naturally I was speaking from a merely aesthetic point of view. They're already talking of a new translation, into Swedish or Norwegian, I think. My wife is delighted at the news. (220)

The last two sentences, which are the conclusion of the story, indicate the measure in which the death of Johnny also signals Bruno's defeat. The allusion to the translations, and particularly the vagueness of the allusion, shows to what extent the text has already been taken away from Bruno—how, in a sense, he is out of the picture. The laconic last sentence, in its homely triviality, reinforces this notion by showing how the pleasure generated by these new versions of the biography is deflected away from Bruno. Like the labyrinth, the text is empty at the end. The book has become a funeral monument, a tomb.

But in a sense it is the whole story that reveals Bruno's defeat. In spite of his naïve assertion that his book is "intact and finished," "The Pursuer" is a postscript or supplement to that earlier book, and more than the story of Johnny, it is the story of Bruno's futile attempts to commit Johnny to writing. Bruno's writing of "The Pursuer," his return to the book that he had already written, is like Theseus's journey into the labyrinth, the very image of self-reflexiveness. The pursuer is Bruno, not Johnny, who on the contrary is the epitome of hieratic immobility. Johnny lives unreflexively, a sort of inarticulate monster who is more on the side of things than of words—his means of expression, the saxophone, is not verbal. The rivalry between Johnny and Bruno is apparent from the beginning in their playful banter, in which the musician mocks the writer's practical sense. Bruno himself is aware that his relation to Johnny is an exploitative one, that he and all the others who hover around him are "a bunch of egotists": "Under the pretext of watching out for Johnny what we're doing is protecting our idea of him, getting ourselves ready for the pleasure Johnny's going to give us, to reflect the brilliance from the statue we've erected among us all and defend it till the last gasp"(182). Johnny's retaliation is to tell Bruno that his book has missed the point, that the real Johnny is absent from it: " 'Don't get upset, Bruno, it's not important that you forgot to put all that in. But Bruno,' and he lifts a finger that does not shake, 'what you forgot to put in is me' "(212). Bruno winds up writing about himself, subjecting himself to the same operation to which he submits Johnny. The text of the story is in the end Bruno's pursuit of himself, a pursuit that turns into a flight—the vanishing of infinitely receding sequences. "The Pursuer" is a postscript to Bruno's biography of Johnny, but it is also a postscript to the story that it tells, a postscript that can only be a prologue to a further story.

As in the previous texts analyzed, the hero's regressive quest leads not to individuation and difference, but to a notion of indifferentiation: empty labyrinth, desert, fire, the infinite where ends and beginnings merge and dissolve. A reflection of Bruno's brings out, in a metonymical play, this dialectic of ends and beginnings:

> It drags me to think that he's at the beginning of his sax-work, and I'm going along and have to stick it out to the end. He's the mouth and I'm the ear, so as not to say he's the mouth and I'm the . . . Every critic, yeah, is the sad-assed end of something that starts as taste, like the pleasure of biting into something and chewing on it. And the mouth [Johnny] moves again, relishing it, Johnny's big tongue sucks back a little string of saliva from the lips. (167)

We shall have to look at this passage in the original, not only because the translator, Paul Blackburn, got carried away and became too explicit, but because there is in it an anagrammatic clue that is important to note:

> Pienso melancólicamente que él está al principio de su saxo mientras yo vivo obligado a conformarme con el final. El es la boca y yo la oreja, por no decir que él

es la boca y yo . . . Todo crítico, ay, es el triste final de algo que empezó como sabor, como delicia de morder y mascar. Y la boca se mueve otra vez, golosamente la gran lengua de Johnny recoge un chorrito de saliva de los labios.[14]

There is a complex and compelling metonymical and anagrammatic network here that leads to the notion of the mutual cancellation of Johnny and Bruno. If Johnny is the mouth and Bruno the ear, or the anus, they both stand for absences, holes, and what remains between them is the saxophone, a curved gallery of air, or, to continue the physiological metaphor, the labyrinthine digestive track (or the Eustachian tube). This imagery of absence is the same as that in Octavio Paz's poem "La boca habla," incorporated by Severo Sarduy into *Cobra*:

> La cobra
> fabla de la obra
> en la boca del abra
> recobra
> el habla:
> El Vocablo.[15]

It is an imagery of absence conveyed by the repetition of the *o*'s, a figure of the hole, as in "El es la boca y yo la oreja, por no decir que él es la boca y yo . . ." It was not reticence that kept the obvious word out, since it is more conspicuous in its absence, but the desire both to create a gap at the end of the sentence and to stop on "yo." That "yo" is already, by its very orthography, the hole, the void, the last letter of Bruno's name, but also the beginning of Johnny's—"Jo." In fact, by taking the beginning of Johnny's name and the end of Bruno's, by practicing with their names the operation that the sentence quoted suggests, we have "yo no." Ends and beginnings merge, and the result is a negation, a canceling out.

Cortázar plays this philological game, more often than has been suspected, to undermine the notion of individuality. A clear instance of this, but on another level, is Francine in *Libro de Manuel*, who so obviously stands for France and French values that she becomes an ironic abstraction. Not as obvious, though here the literary device is much more traditional, is Andrés, the protagonist of that same novel, whose name means, of course, everyman, or man in general. One might further note in this connection that the *o* plays a key role in the names of many of Cortázar's characters: Nora, Wong, Oliveira, Roland, Romero, Roberto. That *o*, or zero, is the grapheme that designates an absence, a dissolution of individuality, a sphere demarcating nothingness. In chapter 148 of *Hopscotch* Cortázar quotes one of Aulus Gellius's etymologies in which it is suggested that the origin of the word *person* is related to that *o* that occupies its center:

A wise and ingenious explanation, by my lights, that of Gabio Basso, in his treatise *On the Origin of Words*, of the word *person*, mask. He thinks that this word has its origin in the verb *personare*, to retain. This is how he explains his opinion: "Since the mask covers the face completely except for an opening where the mouth is, the voice, instead of scattering in all directions, narrows down to escape through one single opening and therefore acquires a stronger and more penetrating sound. Thus, since the mask makes the human voice more sonorous and firm, it has been given the name *person*, and as a consequence of the formation of this word, the letter *o* as it appears in it is long."[16]

The suggestion that the voice would then be the distinguishing mark is clear; but the voice is no mark at all. In the case of Johnny, where the voice is made firmer and more sonorous by his musical instrument, we would find the mark in the saxophone, not in him.

But if "yo no" is the cryptic message of Cortázar's mythology of writing, what then of our initial question about how to read an author? And if conception denies the possibility of conception, if a cogent and distinguishing theory of literature appears to be foreclosed by the ultimately negative gesture of self-referentiality, how is Cortázar's literary production held together? What can we *retain* as the distinguishing mark of his work?

It is not by accident that Cortázar's mythology of writing, as I have represented it here, should bear a Nietzschean imprint, since it is a Nietzschean problematic that seems to generate it. "Who writes?" is an essentially Nietzschean question. The struggle between the Minotaur and Theseus is analogous to that between Dionysus and Apollo in *The Birth of Tragedy*. In "The Pursuer" this Nietzschean quality is particularly evident. Johnny, whose musical instrument is a direct descendant of the Dionysian *aulos*, exists as if in harmony with the vast forces of the universe—with truth and actuality—and suffers as well as experiences joy for it. Bruno, on the other hand, the Apollonian seeker of light, deals in illusions; his aim is to domesticate Johnny's savage wisdom. The birth of tragedy, according to Nietzsche, is generated by the confrontation of these two figures, a birth that signaled the victory of Dionysus over Apollo, for tragedy could only emerge when the god of reason spoke the language of the god of music. In Nietzsche there remains a vestigial theodicy that confers meaning to the death of the hero. It would be reassuring to be able to say the same about Cortázar. But the analogy between the birth of tragedy and Cortázar's version of the birth of writing can only be carried so far, and beyond that point is where Cortázar emerges. Nietzsche, still the philologist in this early work, traces a curve that represents the birth of tragedy and its gradual decline, a decline provoked by the counteroffensive of Apollonian powers. Not so in Cortázar, where, as we have seen, each confrontation leads to a mutual cancellation, each conception carries with it its concomitant death. Writing in Cortázar must be born anew in each text; the whole of writing must emerge with each word, only to disappear again—not an eternal return, but a convulsive repetition of construction and deconstruction. A formal reflection of this might be found not only in the heterogeneity of Cortázar's longer texts, but also in their reliance on dialogue.[17]

Cortázar emerges, then, at the point of the cancellation, of the negation. He must therefore be read whole, establishing no generic distinctions nor privileging either the fictional or the expository texts. Each text must be read as if it were the totality of Cortázar's production, given that each begins and ends in a question so fundamental as not to be transferable from one to the other, but must rather be repeated in each text and in each reading—a kind of spasmodic eschatology. Only the double thrust of the question can be retained. Holistic criticism is not a process of accumulation whereby details are gathered, stored, to construct with them the image of an author, but instead one where the impossibility of assembling the fragments in a coherent whole can provide a glimpse of totality.

There is an ultimate meaning to Cortázar's mythology of writing that belies its negativity, one that is performative rather than conceptual. What Theseus's self-reflexive quest shows is that literature, in the long run, cannot say anything about itself. The countermodernist position that decries literature's purity, its refusal to signify something other than itself, fails to recognize that, on the contrary, literature is always having to signify something else, and to implicate someone else. And indeed here we are reading, talking, writing about Cortázar, or better yet, reading, talking, writing Cortázar. Minotaur, Theseus, Johnny, Bruno—we as readers also drift into our own textual journeys, to turn reading once more into the ritual confrontation where you and I and we share for one moment, in each other, the illusion of meaning.

[1] See Eugenio Donato, "Structuralism: The Aftermath," *Sub-Stance*, no. 7 (Fall 1973), pp. 9–26. Neither Anglo-American "new criticism" nor French structuralism really ever abandoned the notion of authorship. It is always found, albeit relegated to a self-consciously marginal position, as a rhetorical license that is tolerated but not questioned. It is only in what Donato calls the aftermath of structuralism that the notion of authorship has been subjected to a radical critique.

[2] Paris, Seuil, 1966, pp. 60–61. My translation.

[3] José Ortega y Gasset, *The Dehumanization of Art and Other Essays on Art, Culture and Literature*, Princeton, N.J., Princeton University Press, 1968, pp. 31–32.

[4] Michel Foucault, *The Order of Things. An Archaeology of the Human Sciences*, New York, Pantheon, 1970, pp. 217–21.

[5] Jean Hyppolite, *Genesis and Structure of Hegel's Phenomenology of the Spirit*, Samuel Cherniak, John Heckman, trs., Evanston, Il., Northwestern University Press, 1974, p. 160.

[6] See Borges's commentary in *The Book of Imaginary Beings*, rev. & enl. ed., Norman Thomas di Giovanni, tr., New York, Discus, 1970, pp. 158–59.

[7] *El individuo y el otro. Crítica a los cuentos de Julio Cortázar*, New York, La Librería, 1971, p. 34.

[8] *Los reyes*, Buenos Aires, Sudamericana, 1970, p. 73.

[9] Ibid., p. 49. My translation.

[10] The title may come from fragment 28 of Heraclitus: "There is exchange of all things for fire and of fire for all things, as there is of wares for gold and of gold for wares." Philip Wheelwright, *Heraclitus*, New York, Atheneum, 1971, p. 37.

[11] Plutarch, *The Lives of the Noble Grecians and Romans*, John Dryden, tr., Arthur Hugh Clough, ed., New York, Modern Library, 1932, p. 11.

[12] *All Fires the Fire and Other Stories*, Suzanne Jill Levine, tr., New York, Pantheon, 1973, pp. 116–17.

[13] *Blow-Up and Other Stories*, Paul Blackburn, tr., New York, Collier, 1968, p. 169. Subsequent page numbers refer to this edition.

[14] *Las armas secretas*, Buenos Aires, Sudamericana, 1964, p. 108.

[15] Buenos Aires, Sudamericana, 1972, p. 229.

[16] *Hopscotch*, Gregory Rabassa, tr., New York, Signet, 1967, p. 436. Cortázar takes this excerpt from *Noches Aticas*, Francisco Navarro y Calvo, tr., Madrid, Biblioteca Clásica, 1893, vol. 1, p. 202. The relevance of Gellius's book in relation to Cortázar's novel is greater than might be suspected. In his preface Gellius says the following about the composition of his book: "In the arrangement of the material I have adopted the same haphazard order that I had previously followed in collecting it. For whenever I had taken in hand any Greek or Latin book, or had heard anything worth remembering, I used to jot down whatever took my fancy, of any and every kind, without any definite plan or order; and such notes I would lay away as an aid to my memory, like a kind of literary storehouse, so that when the need arose of a word or a subject which I chanced for the moment to have forgotten, and the books from which I had taken it were not at hand, I could readily find it and produce it." *The Attic Nights of Aulus Gellius*, John C. Rolfe, tr., Cambridge, Ma., Harvard University Press, 1970, p. xxvii. Cortázar has of course followed this same method of composition in the "dispensable" chapters of *Hopscotch*, as well as in *Libro de Manuel*. In fact, just as Ludmilla composes the *Libro* for Manuel's future enlightenment, so did Gellius assemble his "in order that like recreation might be provided for my children, when they should have some respite from business affairs and could unbend and divert their minds."

[17] For further commentary on *The Birth of Tragedy* and "The Pursuer" see Djelal Kadir, "A Mythical Re-enactment: Cortázar's *El perseguidor*," *Latin American Literary Review*, 2 (1973), pp. 63–73.

Doubles, Bridges and Quest for Identity: "Lejana" Revisited

By JAIME ALAZRAKI

> *I have made the journey and*
> *come back, changed but alive.*
> Clancy Sigal

The double as a theme or motif is a subject of far-reaching implications and rich transformations in Cortázar's fiction,[1] but the verification of its presence alone is, at best, a point of departure for the study of his texts and, at worst, a mere label that seemingly resolves everything but that in reality leaves the text untouched. Thus if we say that in "Lejana" (The Distances) the Budapest beggar is the double of Alina Reyes, as has been generally acknowledged, we have still said nothing regarding the character; at most we have defined a literary device without entering into its narrative function. The already abundant commentary devoted to the study of the double in general[2] has shown the variety of uses and functions of this fictional procedure. It can manifest itself as a "mirror image," as a "secret sharer," as an "opposing self," as a "fragmented mind," as "paths of ambivalence," as mere "baroque duplication," as "psychomachia," et cetera.[3] What truly counts is the double's ability to perform certain functions related to the purposes of the narrative. For this task it is necessary to follow a course opposite to the one adopted until now—not so much to explain the text through the double, but to explain the double through the text in which it has been inserted as an answer to questions and problems posed by the text. Albert J. Guerard has pointed out that "no term has been more loosely used by casual critics of modern literature. As almost any character can become a Christ-figure or Devil-archetype, so almost any character can become a Double."[4]

The multitude of possibilities that the theme of the double offers constitutes the foundation of Robert Rogers's book *The Double in Literature*. In spite of the numerous and various categories of definition and classification that Rogers proposes, none represents a precise measure of the specifics of the text. Reading Rogers's book one gets the impression that each text implies a different notion of the concept of the double and that the number of species in his taxonomy requires a similar number of examples taken from world literature. If there are as many types and subtypes of doubles as there are texts, one must conclude, as in the case of any fictional device, that its detection and definition in any narrative represents just a starting point for the study of its function, operativeness and bearings with the rest of the story as a whole. Of the many doubles studied by Rogers, the one which comes closest to "Lejana" is the type defined in the chapter "Fragmentation of the Mind." To illustrate this kind of double, Rogers resorts to examples as variegated as R. L. Stevenson's *Dr. Jekill and Mr. Hyde*, Hesse's *Steppenwolf*, James's *The Portrait of a Lady* and Shakespeare's *Othello*. The selection is so broad as to prevent an encompassing definition of the studied type. The unifying feature would be, according to Rogers, the split of the self into different and sometimes even opposite personalities. Aside from this common trait, each work follows its own specific course.

Alina Reyes's self is also divided, but this division does not coincide with the concepts of id, ego and superego suggested and later abandoned by Freud, who felt dissatisfied with their effectiveness. The split of Alina's self responds to a new notion for describing the structure of human psychology, a notion which Morton Prince defines in his work *The Dissociation of a Personality*: "The mind may be disintegrated in all sorts of ways. It may be divided, subdivided, and still further subdivided. The lines of cleavage may run in all sorts of directions, producing various sorts of combinations of systems of consciousness."[5] Freud, too, in one of the few references to multiple personality, "treats dissociation from a functional point of view, suggesting that it may occur when the ego's various object-identifications come into severe conflict with each other."[6] But the work which analyzes this aspect of the structure of the self more thoroughly and with more substantiating data is R. D. Laing's *The Divided Self* (1960). Laing's study is an "attempt to reconstruct the patient's way of being himself in his world," an approach he calls "existential phenomenology." Its task consists of "articulating what the other's 'world' is and his way of being in it."[7] This new psychiatric approach does not differ in essence from the approach found in a certain type of fiction where the writer, too, attempts to reconstruct the world of his characters through the characters themselves. If the realist novel depicted them through an omniscient narrator and understood them in terms of the narrator's logic, the existential novel, since Dostoevsky, attempts to depict and understand its characters through the logic, or rather lack of logic, of the characters themselves. It is, in summary, an insight from within, in contrast to the external view of the traditional novel: either the character is seen by the author's eyes, or the author consents to let the character see himself with his own eyes. In the first case the characters react to the author's outlook; in the second they establish their own outlook through which they see the world around and inside them. It may be argued that in both cases there is an author who shapes his characters and that to a greater or lesser degree the character's world is subordinated to the writer's will. And so it is. What has changed is the writer's *attitude* toward his characters—from an omniscient attitude to one of impotence. The realist narrator was able to explain everything; the existential narrator, on the other hand, withholds explanations and lets the characters explain themselves through their own limitations and their individualized view of their own selves and their way of being in the world. The approach of the new psychiatry parallels the existential narrator's attitude. The analyst avoids an external understanding of the patient because, explains Laing, "if we look at his actions as 'signs' of a 'disease,' we are already imposing our categories of thought onto the patient, in a manner analogous to the way we may regard him as treating us . . . If one is adopting such an attitude towards a patient, it is hardly possible at the same time to understand what he may be trying to communicate to us" (33).

At this point it could be argued that the psychiatric treatment of a patient is leagues away from the literary treatment of a character and thus the validity of these observations from the field of psychoanalysis vis-à-vis the analysis of a literary character becomes questionable. Yet a close reading of "Lejana" reveals that although Alina Reyes may not represent a clinical case of schizophrenia, she has clear schizoid tendencies, and Cortázar has attempted to understand these tendencies from inside the character in a manner similar to that in which existential phenomenology approaches the patient. The word "patient" might disturb Cortázar's reader, and he would be right in refusing to convert the character into a mental patient; but I am suggesting nothing of this kind.[8] However, it is beyond doubt, as Laing observes, that "it is not always possible to make sharp distinctions between sanity and insanity, between the sane schizoid individual and the psychotic. Sometimes the onset of psychosis is so dramatic and abrupt, and its manifestations are so unequivocal, that there can be no question or doubt about the diagnosis. However, in many cases there is no such sudden apparently qualitative change, but a transition extending over years, at no single point in which may it be at all clear whether any critical point has been passed" (137).

Alina Reyes's relationship toward everything that represents the world of her body (her mother, the tea parties, the concerts, her friends, her fiancé) and toward her interior self (her games: playing anagrams and palindromes, playing a queen, a beginner at a brothel in Jujuy, a maid in Quetzaltenango, a Budapest beggar) brings to mind the schizoid split according to Laing's definition: "The individual experiences his self as being more or less divorced or detached from his body. *The body is felt more as one object among other objects in the world than as the core of the individual's own being.* Instead of being the core of his true self, the body is felt as the core of a *false self*, which a detached, disembodied, inner, 'true' self looks on at with tenderness, amusement, or hatred as the case may be" (69; my stress). There is one Alina Reyes who plays the games of the "grownups"—stereotyped games which Alina plays compelled by convention but without truly participating in them.[9] The one who plays them is not she, but rather her body, which the other Alina observes as if it were "one object among other objects": "Let her suffer. I give a kiss to señora Regules, tea to the boy from the Rivas', and I keep myself for that inner resistance. . . . I only know it's like that, that on one side I'm crossing a bridge at the same instant (but I don't know if it is at the same instant) as the boy from the Rivas' accepts the cup of tea from me and puts on his best spoiled face. And I stand it all right because I'm alone among all these people without sensitivity and I'm not so despondent" (19).[10] But even more revealing is the entry that Alina records in her diary on 25 January; she is surprised to hear what Nora tells her about the concert in which she accompanied her friend at the piano:

> What did I know about acts, I accompanied her as best I could, I remember hearing her as though she were muted. *Votre âme est un paysage choisi* . . . but I watched my hands on the keys and it seemed to me *they were playing* all right, that *they accompanied* Nora decently. . . . Poor little Nora. Let someone else accompany her. (Each time this seems more of *a punishment,* now I know myself *there* only when I'm about to be happy, when I am happy, when Nora is singing Fauré I know myself *there and only the hate is left.*) (20; my stress)

These texts and others indicate clearly enough that Alina perceives the acts of her body, her social behavior, as a *false self* and that, on the other hand, she identifies her *true self* with the other Alina who has found a shelter in a world mentally constructed. "When the self," explains Laing, "partially abandons the body and its acts, and withdraws into mental activity, it experiences itself as an entity perhaps localized somewhere in the body.[11] This withdrawal is in part an effort to preserve its being, since relationship of any kind with others is experienced as a threat to the self's identity. The self feels safe only in hiding, and isolated. Such a self can, of course, be isolated at any time whether other people are present or not" (75–76). The description of the concert on the evening of 28 January is, as a whole, an example of Alina's power of isolation, of her ability to transpose selves as swiftly as she transposes the letters of an anagram: "I saw Elsa Piaggio acclaimed between one Chopin and another Chopin, poor thing, and *my orchestra seat gave directly onto the plaza, with the beginning of the bridge between the most immense columns.* But I was thinking this, notice, it's the same as making the anagram *es la reina y* . . . in place of Alina Reyes, or imagining mama at the Suarez's house instead of beside me" (23; my stress). Alina is fully aware that the world in which she views herself as a queen/beggar is a realm devoid of physical reality, and that although she crosses the Market Bridge in Budapest and walks through Vladas Square in the same city, these events occur in her mind while she is physically seated in a concert hall in Buenos Aires. Yet later on the two levels overlap and intermix in spite of Alina's repeated efforts to distinguish and separate them— at times with a parenthesis: "(This last I was thinking)"; at others, with references to the concert program in progress: " 'Albéniz!' and more applause and 'The Polonaise!' "; and finally with a drop of humor mixed with cynicism: ". . . but let them come tell me that the same thing could have happened to anyone else, that she could have journeyed to Hungary in the middle of the Odeón. Say, that would give anyone the shivers!" (24).

There is nothing abnormal in Alina's behavior, but this normality is the manifestation of her false self through which Alina masks her inner struggle. Laing has observed:

> The "normal" individual, in a situation all can see to be threatening to his being and to offer no real sense of escape, develops a schizoid state in trying to get outside it, if not physically, at least mentally: he becomes a mental observer, who looks on, detached and impassive, at what his body is doing or what is being done to his body. If this is so in the "normal," it is at least possible to suppose that the individual whose abiding mode of being-in-the-world is of this split nature is living in what to him, if not to us, is a world that threatens his being from all sides, and from which there is no exit. For them the world is a prison without bars, a concentration camp without barbed wire. (79)

From the beginning of the story it becomes apparent that the world in which Alina moves and acts is one with which she does not identify, a world which is strange to her and which naturally becomes a threat to her true self. All or almost all the references to that world in Alina's diary have an alienating nuance clear enough to convey that she does not feel part of it: the face of a party friend, Renato Viñes, is described as "a spluttering seal, that picture of Dorian Gray in the last stages" (it should be remembered that Oscar Wilde's novel is the story of an alienation between the protagonist and his picture); her mother is depicted as "an enormous fish and so much not herself;" The Rivas boy has "a dummy's face"; Luis María, her fiancé, gazes at her "with his puppy-look," and further on she calls him "my puppy, my booby"; the music, during the concert, becomes one thing more to tolerate and endure: between "one Chopin and another Chopin," between Albéniz and "The Polonaise," between Julián Aguirre and Carlos Guastavino, Alina remains removed from the concert program.

That world of "happiness" for others but unhappiness for Alina becomes a threat to her self. It is this world, that she sees as foreign, which asks her to be what she is not or refuses to be; and her fear of being "engulfed, enclosed, swallowed up, drowned, eaten up, smothered, stifled" by it forces her to take shelter in that part of her self which others reject but which she recognizes and accepts as unremittingly authentic. At the very beginning of the story, in the first entry of her diary, Alina uses three metaphors for defining herself which attest to her fear of being destroyed by others. She says first that she is "a terrible sounding bell," an image that in a schizoid context alludes to a condition of alienation in which the patient ceases to be himself so as to become a mere "echo" of others. She adds that she is "a wave"— a body of water whose shape and "reality" depends not on itself but on the gravity or the wind that produces it and whose form lacks all permanence and is determined by factors other than itself. Finally, Alina sees herself as "the chain Rex trails all night against the privet hedges"—a compressed account of her drama, since Alina views her true self as a queen (*rēx*, Latin for "king")—but she also knows that she is imprisoned and tied down with "the chain" of her false self, a chain she drags help-lessly and submissively like a well-trained dog (Rex). Other references Alina makes about her alienated self—the cold and the snow coming in through her "broken shoes" —are not plain vagaries of her feverish imagination but define a psychological state by means of a terminology of unequivocal meaning within a schizoid code. Threatened by everything that demands of her to be what she is not, Alina clings to that zone of her self in which she recognizes a genuine being.

Ironically yet understandably, it is this part of her that others consider unwanted and see as the "distant one," the remote Alina they "reject," "beat," "abuse" and "mistreat," the Budapest beggar whose torn shoes let cold and snow in. Alina tolerates this false self up to the point where it threatens to suffocate her true self. When this happens, an imbalance results which forces Alina to turn further away from her false self and to retreat into the other self, the queen/beggar, unreal for others but intensely real for her. It is the world of the others which has lost all reality for Alina. This split between fantasy and reality has been defined by Minkowski as *autism* and is fully described by Laing:

> But the person who does not act in reality and only acts in phantasy *becomes himself unreal.* The actual "world" for that person becomes shrunken and im-poverished. The "reality" of the physical world and other persons ceases to be used as a pabulum for the creative exercise of imagination, and hence comes to have less and less significance in itself. Phantasy, without being either in some measure embodied in reality, or itself enriched by injections of "reality," becomes more and more empty and volatilized. The "self" whose relatedness to reality is already tenuous becomes less and less a reality-self, and more and more phan-tasticized as it becomes more and more engaged in phantastic relationships with its own phantoms (imagos) (85). . . . For the schizoid individual direct par-anticipation "in" life is felt as being at the constant risk of being destroyed by life, for the self's isolation is its effort to preserve itself in the absence of an assured sense of autonomy and integrity. (90)

Alina's ontological division into a false self and a true self is already stated in the first pages of her diary. As one goes further through it, this division deepens and she loses contact with a world which for her has become "senseless," hostile and alien and which induces her to identify fully with those phantoms that she was able to recognize earlier as images of her mind but that now have become her dominant reality. The encounter with the beggar amounts for Alina to a bridge with the other, an ultimate effort to reencounter herself and to reconquer her lost reality: "Easier to go out and look for that bridge, to go out on my own search and find myself" (23). At the end of her diary Alina presents the acute schism of her self in unequivocal terms. The encounter with the beggar unmistakably portrays an act of self-fulfillment: "And it will be the queen's victory over that malignant relationship, that soundless and unlawful encroachment. If I am really I, she will yield, she will join my radiant *zone*, my lovelier and surer life; I have only to go to her side and lay a hand on her shoulder" (26). Alina acknowledges the unreconcilable conflict between her false self and her true self, since the acceptance of the former implies the denial of the latter. Throughout the diary she explores one self (the true one) in the territory of the other (the false one), and the diary is but an exercise of quest for the authentic self threatened and rejected by others. At the end of her diary Alina finds herself at a critical point where the coexistence of her two selves becomes an impossibility: either the false one swallows the true one, which is tantamount, if not to suicide, then to the loss of all reality; or the true one breaks with the false one and totally surrenders itself to those "phantoms" which for Alina represent her most genuine reality. Laing describes this stage of the schizoid development in terms that may shed some light on Alina's development as a character:

> The "true" self, being no longer anchored to the mortal body, becomes "phantasticized," volatilized into a changeable phantom of the individual's own imagining. By the same token, isolated as is the self as a defence against the dangers from without which are felt as a threat to its identity, it loses what precarious identity it already has. Moreover, the withdrawal from reality results in the self's own impoverishment. Its omnipotence is based on impotence. Its freedom operates in a vacuum. Its activity is without life. The self becomes desiccated and dead. (141)

> The individual's apparently normal and successful adjustment and adaptation to ordinary living is coming to be conceived by his "true" self as a more and more shameful and/or ridiculous pretence. *Pari passu* his "self," in its own phantasied relationships, has become more and more volatilized, free from the contingencies and necessities that encumber it as an object among others in the world, where he knows he would be committed to be of this time and this place, subject to life and death, and embedded in this flesh and these bones. If the "self" thus volatilized in phantasy now conceives the desire to escape from its shut-upness, to end the pretence, to be honest, to reveal and declare and let itself be known without equivocation, one may be witness to the onset of an acute psychosis. Such a person though sane outside has been becoming progressively insane inside. (147)

Alina's perception of this developing insanity and her awareness of the fact that "to be honest, to reveal and declare and let her true self be known without equivocation" is equivalent to a break with her false self through which she is identified by others, are clearly indicated in the text: "To say to Luis María, 'We're getting married and you're taking me to Budapest, to a bridge where there's snow and someone.' I say: and if I am? (Because I think all that from the secret vantage point of not seriously believing it. And if I am?) All right, if I am . . . But plain crazy, plain . . . ? What a honeymoon!" (21).

But the story is not a clinical chart, and it is not our task to offer a diagnosis. The purpose of these observations is to study the effectiveness of the narrative as a literary text. In this sense, the first conclusion is that the diary as the narrator's vehicle of information is the most immediate formalistic accomplishment. If it had been narrated in the first person by the same Alina, it would have required a coherence (not of style but of composition) against the grain of the fragmented perception through which the narrator views and registers the conflict between her two selves. The diary, as a literary form, allows for the only coherence to which the narrator's outlook accedes without violating her naturalness—intimacy, fragmentariness and an aura of authenticity which befits and is a condition of the diary form. In "Lejana," as in almost all of his short stories, Cortázar has achieved a naturalness that he himself defines as one of the greatest excellences of a narrative: "What is told in a story should indicate by itself who is speaking, at what distance, from what perspective and according to what type of discourse. The work is not defined so much by the elements of the *fabula* or their ordering as by the modes of the fiction, tangentially indicated by the enunciation proper of the *fabula*."[12]

The division of Alina's self is perceptible through the hesitations, the contradictions and the temperature of the discourse. For a character who sees others as the embodiment of her false self and at the same time as a threat to her true self, the diary is perhaps the only possible form of expression: how could she otherwise "tell" others what is happening to her, when those others represent for her the very negation of what she is experiencing? Alina can only tell herself about the painful process of volatilization of her false self and the no less painful search for a bridge of access to her true self. The only alternative to the diary as an expressive vehicle might have been a psychiatrist's series of patient interviews with the aid of a tape recorder. But such an alternative, as used in phenomenological psychiatry, cannot serve as a model for the short story, which functions according to very different laws and purposes.

With Alina's acceptance of her phantoms as the "embodiment" of her true self, the diary comes to a close. It is here that the most difficult problem of the text surfaces: how does Alina's situation as exposed through the diary resolve itself? In clinical terms? Of course not. The narrative is not the clinical history of a case which, as such, should conclude with the diary's closing, since the analyst purports to understand "the patient's disjunction between the person one is in one's own eyes (one's being-for-oneself), and the person one is in the eyes of the other (one's being-for-the-other)." This understanding is needed to comprehend the meaning of Alina's quest and her urge to fulfill herself through the other, and for this reason the story does not conclude with the diary. The power source that sets the story in motion is the conflict between Alina's false self and true self, between Alina Reyes "her mother's daughter," Nora's friend, Luis María's fiancée, and between the beggar who awaits her on a bridge in Budapest, between the one here and the "distant one."

Lionel Trilling has observed that "one of the most salient characteristics of the culture of our time is the intense, we may say obsessive, concern with authenticity of the personal life as a criterion of art."[13] A good part of Cortázar's work is marked by a similar concern which takes on the form of a search. If *Hopscotch* is the great novel of that search—a quest for a "final island," "a kibbutz of desire," "a center," but in the end, as Cortázar himself has said, a territory "in which man would find himself in a sort of total reconciliation and abrogation of differences"[14]—"Lejana" is perhaps the first expression of that search. Alina Reyes is the first character in that long line of *perseguidores* or "pursuers" who throughout Cortázar's entire work seek and explore a country which is but the territory of the self in search of authenticity. Like Talita in *Hopscotch*, Alina is about to cross "the bridge," knowing that in this act she gambles her bones; for if the danger of the bridge Horacio and Traveler built lies in the fragility of their relationship, embodied as a metaphor *in vivo* in that "crazy" bridge which Talita is to cross as proof of a balance that could be upset at any moment,[15] the danger to which Alina is exposed is also the break of a precarious balance—the two parts of her divided self—that could be shattered into pieces at any moment. But Talita and Alina cross the bridge, sensing that in this act they touch a territory in which the imminence of a reencounter is about to happen.

The bridge that Talita crosses in *Hopscotch* spans the space of absurdity, but she crosses it because, without understanding, she "understands" that "only by living absurdly is it possible to break out of this infinite absurdity."[16] While *Hopscotch* provides an existential answer to Talita's perplexity, "Lejana" resolves Alina's dilemma according to a poetics of the fantastic. In order to bestow literalness on Alina's phantoms the narrative yields the telling of the story to a narrator in third person. We know that Alina's phantoms are the most forceful expression of her true self; but since the fantastic lies, if one follows Todorov's definition, in the hesitation between "the strange" (which does not violate the causal order except through the reader's consciousness) and "the marvelous" (which adds a second order to the order of causality),[17] this hesitation will not occur until the end, as a climactic point at which a subtly built gradation tops off.[18] The second narrator of "Lejana" maintains the everyday order established throughout the diary, ultimately yielding to a magical act through which the imaginary plane breaks into the historical plane. The bridge dreamed so many times by Alina becomes a physical reality in a distant and cold city, but the appearance of "the ragged woman with black straight hair" converts it into a metaphor of that "center" so much sought after and into which Alina enters "complete and absolute." Alina's phantom—her intimate and distant self, the self rejected and beaten by others—is no longer a phantom besieged and harassed by the system of her false self; it assumes the dimension of a reality which returns to Alina her seized happiness: "She surrounded the slender woman feeling her complete and absolute within her arms, with a springing up of happiness equal to a hymn, to loosing a cloud of pigeons, to the river singing" (27).

In the beggar Alina "embraces" (in the double sense of hugging and adopting) her true self and exorcises her false self. The encounter represents "the queen's victory over that soundless and unlawful encroachment." In the embrace the other "joins Alina's radiant zone, her lovelier and surer life"; she, on the other hand, "the very lovely Alina Reyes in her grey blazer," the false one, abandons her as would a stranger. It matters not if in psychiatric terms this transference is equivalent to a psychotic alienation and a break. In literary terms it represents a reconciliation—the acceptance of an authentic self and the rejection of an alienated self—because the point of view of the narrative is Alina's point of view and not that of an "objective narrator" who observes and diagnoses from outside, and also because literature does not aim at "curing" but at understanding.

The division of Alina's self amounts to what in the jargon of the double is known as "decomposition" and "dissociation";[19] but the use of the double in "Lejana" is neither a literary trick which, according to Ralph Tymms, has placed the double "among the facile, and less reputable devices in fiction"[20] nor the history of a crude clinical case which imposes on the reader a distance that removes him, as in the case of Dostoevsky's *The Double*,[21] from the character and hinders him from identifying with the character's plight. Alina's quest, on the other hand, poses questions in which any responsive reader recognizes his/her own dilemmas. If there is a double in "Lejana"—the queen/the beggar—it aims not at shaking or astonishing the reader with an uncanny event, as happens in some stories which toy with the supernatural and profit from the impulse of a literary tradition, thus turning the device into a mere "trick" of the trade. The use of the double in "Lejana" is motivated and justified from within the story. Its function is discernible only if one first understands the character's moving humanism and the complex makeup of her divided self. Then the fantastic event becomes one more dimension of the real, a non-Euclidean geometry which tolerates the intolerable in metric geometry and which acts not as the contradiction of the latter but as its supplement. The fantastic thus becomes not a break with historical reality, although it may seem so from our logic parameters, but the *realization* of what appears to be unreal within our causal contexts, a development similar to the chrysalis of a butterfly which abandons its cocoon/habitat to reach a more advanced stage of its cycle.

Although the structure of "Lejana" is that of a diary plus a coda in indirect style, it has, like the other stories in *Bestiario*, four narrative links: a space (a) in which the characters move (b), generating a conflict (c) which resolves itself in a denouement (d). Yet unlike the other stories, in "Lejana" these links do not form a sequential chain but overlap. From the outset each one of the four units crisscrosses with the others, and the progression of the narrative proceeds not through a successive order in which each unit absorbs and replaces the preceding one, but instead by bringing into one single focus the various structuring units. The first three pages of the story already define the narrative space (the world inside and outside Alina's home), present and place the characters (Alina, mother, Nora, Luis María, mother's friends), introduce the conflict (the images of the bell, the wave and the chain through which Alina views herself) and anticipate the denouement ("let her be anything a Budapest beggar"). But this totality has so far been presented in a rather cryptic way, and the rest of the text functions as a system of telescopic lenses, one unit sliding within the other, which alters the first sketchy picture into a clear and sharply defined image. Like the other stories in *Bestiario*, "Lejana" presents a conflict between a closed order (the system of Alina's false self) and an open order (what has been so far defined as her true self) which is resolved with the absorption of the former by the latter. The struggle between the two selves which dispute Alina's being concludes with a break through which the character suppresses a closed order— in whose space dwells her false self—so as to enter into an open order in whose space the fulfillment of her true self becomes possible.

In *Hopscotch*, in a note from Morelli's notebooks, there is a remark very much apropos of "Lejana": "Man only is in that he searches to be, plans to be, thumbing through words and modes of behavior and joy sprinkled with blood" (363). The motives of Alina's search are in no way different. It matters not if in that search Alina gambles and loses all the cards of her sanity, because that sanity is the very root of a state of alienation that forces her to obliterate herself by renouncing her being or, what amounts to the same thing, by becoming those meaningless roles she is forced to play, by effacing her identity with those empty games she must play. The beggar who meets Alina at the center of a distant bridge is, on the other hand, the only one she recognizes as her "radiant zone," as the projection of her authentic self and as the point of reencounter and reconciliation between her being-for-herself and her being-for-the-other. The bridge Alina crosses is but the same one that in *Hopscotch* is defined as "a bridge from man to man" (267), and after crossing it Alina meets with the other and becomes the other. Without the complexity and plurality of focuses of *Hopscotch*, "Lejana" airs in a germinal stage some of the questions that trigger Horacio Oliveira's search. In "Lejana" there is a fantastic answer to that search, but the fantastic element is not an attempt "to play with the reader's fears."[22] It is, rather, a route of access to that second order through a metaphor which, like "the noises" in "House Taken Over," the tiger in "Bestiary," the *mancuspias* in "Cefalea" or the rabbits in "Letter to a Young Lady in Paris," is not only a mere delusion of the character but an epistemological means of knowing, in poetic terms, layers of reality which escape logical schemes.[23]

[1] Luis Harss correctly defines the double as "a constant in Cortázar's work," and in the same interview Cortázar himself comments on the subject: "The *figuras* are to a degree the culmination of the theme of the double insofar as they show, or try to show, a concatenation, a relationship between different elements which, seen from a logical vantage point, becomes inconceivable" (in Luis Harss, *Los nuestros*, Buenos Aires, Sudamericana, 1966, p. 292). To a greater or lesser degree most of the commentary on Cortázar's fiction touches, directly or indirectly, upon the subject of the double.

[2] Among the more useful book-length studies on the double are the following: Otto Rank, *Der Doppelgänger: Psychoanalytische Studie*, Leipzig, 1925; Wilhelmine Krauss, *Das Doppelgängermotiv in der Romantik*, Berlin, 1930; Ralph Tymms, *Doubles in Literary Psychology*, Cambridge, Eng., 1949; Masao Myoshi, *The Divided Self*, New York, New York University Press, 1969; Robert Rogers, *The Double in Literature: A Psychoanalytic Study*, Detroit, Wayne State University Press, 1970 (includes bibliography); Carl F. Keppler, *The Literature of the Second Self*, Tucson, University of Arizona Press, 1972 (in addition to the bibliography, pp. 229–235, the last chapter offers a critical review of the most important works on the subject); Albert J. Guerard, *Stories of the Double*, New York, 1967.

[3] These definitions correspond to the various chapters of Rogers's study. To these, Keppler adds his own: the second self as "twin brother," "pursuer,"

"tempter," "vision of horror," "saviour" and "the beloved."

[4] Albert J. Guerard, "Editor's Introduction" to a *Daedalus* special issue on "The Perspectives of the Novel," Spring 1963, p. 204. Quoted by Rogers, p. 2.

[5] Morton Prince, *The Dissociation of a Personality*, New York, 1908, p. 75. Quoted by Rogers, p. 91.

[6] Sigmund Freud, *Standard Edition, The Ego and the Id* (London, 1962), vol. 19, pp. 30–31. Quoted by Rogers, p. 92.

[7] R. D. Laing, *The Divided Self*, London, Penguin, 1966. Subsequent quotations indicated by page number of this edition.

[8] To do so would be equal to asking of the character to reason, think and behave according to a realist code, as if one were to ask Gregor Samsa "to stop acting as the gigantic insect he found himself transformed into." "Lejana," like many other of Cortázar's short stories, responds to a type of narrative discourse that has been loosely defined as "fantastic" but that departs considerably from the models set by this genre in the nineteenth century. For a more comprehensive discussion of this aspect of Cortázar's work, see my article "The Fantastic as Surrealist Metaphors in Cortázar's Short Fiction," *Dada/Surrealism*, New York, no. 5, 1975, pp. 28–33.

[9] I have studied the function of game in "Lejana" in my essay "*Homo sapiens* versus *homo ludens* en tres cuentos de Cortázar," *Revista Iberoamericana*, no. 84–85 (July–December 1973), pp. 611–24. See

also Linda Cummings Baxt, "Game in Cortázar," unpublished doctoral dissertation, Yale University, 1974.

10 For the sake of this article's readability I have used Paul Blackburn's English translation of "Lejana" included as "The Distances" in *End of the Game and Other Stories*, New York, Pantheon, 1967. Subsequent quotations are from this edition.

11 Alina makes several references to the cold and snow coming in through her shoes, as if the beggar's presence manifested itself mainly in her feet. It goes without saying that the "mistreated" and "beaten" beggar is a portrayal of how Alina feels in her true self, a metaphor that will break, at the end, into the historical level of the narrative producing the "fantastic" event, thus confounding "the realist project and the ethical project."

12 Julio Cortázar, *La vuelta al día en ochenta mundos*, Mexico City, Siglo XXI, 1967, p. 94 (my translation).

13 Lionel Trilling, "Authenticity and the Modern Unconscious," *Commentary*, vol. 52, no. 3 (September 1971), p. 39. (Included in the same author's volume *Sincerity and Authenticity*, Cambridge, Ma., Harvard University Press, 1972.)

14 In Harss, p. 267.

15 In chapter 43 of *Hopscotch* Talita comments on her crossing the bridge built with boards by Horacio and Traveler and says: "I'm in the middle (of both of you) like that part of the scale that I never know the name of" (Gregory Rabassa, tr., New York, Random House, 1966, p. 265).

16 *Hopscotch*, p. 101.

17 See Tzvetan Todorov, *Introduction à la lit-* *térature fantastique*, Paris, Seuil, 1970, particularly chapter 3, "L'étrange et le merveilleux," pp. 46–62.

18 Unlike Cortázar's other short stories, "Lejana" postpones the appearance of the "fantastic" event until the end. Only in this aspect does it come close to the gradation that characterizes the composition of the fantastic story.

19 See Rogers, pp. 12–13.

20 Tymms, as quoted by Rogers, p. 31.

21 On Dostoevsky's *The Double* Rogers makes the following observation: "Yet in spite of the fascination which Golyadkin exerts over the reader, he can never long forget that this man who sees his double is mad, mad in a clinical sort of way which we are not aware of when we hear the wild and whirling words of a Hamlet or the tempestuous lamentations of a Lear. The reader, therefore, inevitably disengages himself to some extent from Golyadkin and his double, all of the ambiguities of the work notwithstanding, in a manner which does not occur when Dostoyevsky (and other authors) employ the medium of latent decomposition" (p. 39).

22 A definition of the fantastic accepted by most critics who have studied this genre. See Roger Caillois, *Images, images . . .*, Paris, 1966; Louis Vax, *L'art et la littérature fantastiques*, Paris, 1960; H. P. Lovecraft, *Supernatural Horror in Literature*, New York, 1945; Peter Penzoldt, *The Supernatural in Fiction*, New York, 1965.

23 I have discussed at length the concept of "epistemological metaphor" in my essay "Tlön y Asterión: metáforas epistemológicas," included in *Borges: el escritor y la crítica*, Madrid, Taurus, 1976, pp. 173–200.

An Erotics of Liberation: Notes on Transgressive Behavior in *Hopscotch* and *Libro de Manuel*

By MARGERY A. SAFIR

Julio Cortázar has more often expressed admiration for Jules Verne than for the Marquis de Sade. Yet he clearly takes a lesson from both, and what he learns is, surprisingly, the same: the powerful effects of exceptional behavior. In essence, what both Verne and de Sade deal with, and here I quote Susan Sontag, who appears as a character in Cortázar's latest Verne-like work, *Fantomas contra los vampiros multinacionales*,[1] is "fantastic enlargements of human energy."[2] Cortázar's use of expanded energy or extra-ordinary behavior is not random. On the contrary, a clear pattern emerges in his novels in which extreme behavior comes to the fore only in moments of intense anguish in the protagonists' lives, moments which clearly signal a brink, a suspension between one level of consciousness and another. Extreme behavior is for Cortázar, as for de Sade, Lautréamont and Georges Bataille, "a resource for ordeal and for breaking through the limits of consciousness."[3]

I have chosen to examine this type of extreme behavior in *Hopscotch* and *Libro de Manuel* because it is my belief that it has become far too commonplace to speak of *Libro de Manuel* as a radical departure from *Hopscotch*, ignoring the strong structural, linguistic and thematic parallels which run between the two novels. It is my hope that by pointing out one constant pattern of behavior, I might implant the suggestion, at least, that *Libro de Manuel* may represent more of a variation on *Hopscotch* than a reaction against it. In discussing how a pattern of extreme behavior, essentially transgressive in nature, is used in these two novels to pass from crisis to liberation, I have opted to shy away from general statements and to attempt instead a kind of close reading of one decisively important moment of crisis in the life of each novel's protagonist. By looking at what actually constitutes the protagonists' behavior in these moments, I hope to show that there is a significant level of parallel behavior in *Hopscotch* and *Libro de Manuel*, and that although the signifiers may vary from one novel to the next, the signified reached in these decisive moments of the protagonists' existence remains identical.

Horacio Oliveira is embarked upon a search—a search which, as I understand it, is essentially based upon a concept of restitution. It includes not only an impulse to depart toward other dimensions of reality, but also a desire to return to the point of departure, a point which, because of the intervening voyage, would be changed and restored to its original significance. Within the context of this search the common denominator shared by Oliveira's life with La Maga, his approaches to the absurd, his taste for music and alcohol and his participation in Bretonian happenings is, as Oliveira recognizes, the fact that they form "part of a confused series of against-the-grain exercises that had to be performed, approved, left behind."[4] This confused list of exercises attempted by Oliveira at different points in *Hopscotch* is summarized to a large degree in the climactic scene of part one, "From the Other Side." Chapter 36 of *Hopscotch* represents a critical moment in the protagonist's life. La Maga is gone, the Club is dissolved, Oliveira is definitely alone for the first time in the novel. He is at a point where something must happen to determine the course he will take. Within the context of the novel chapter 36 forms a kind of ritual of initiation. It is a "long path marked with pitfalls, obscurities, stops [which] suddenly comes out into the light" and which ends the protagonist's Parisian adventure and propels him across the Atlantic to Buenos Aires.[5] The ritualistic nature of this chapter is explicit. As the chapter opens, Oliveira sees himself enveloped in what he calls a "night of *empusae* and *lamiae,* evil shadows, the end of the great game." "It is written," he adds. The fact that in this scene Oliveira is often not called Oliveira, but rather is referred to as "the newcomer" underscores the intention of ritualistic initiation which permeates the chapter.

It is nighttime when the chapter begins. The time element opens up a series of associations which seems entirely appropriate to the protagonist's situation: night is, of course, the time of dreams, not of wakefulness; darkness suggests the negation of rational illumination, the ascent of the surrealists' dark side of man, and also suggests death. Night is the time of danger for the taboos which govern the day, and it is the time of happenings, as evidenced by the fact that it was also night when the Club met to listen to jazz and drink vodka, when Berthe Trépat gave her concert, when Rocamadour died; it will also be night when Oliveira descends to the basement morgue with Talita and when he begins to construct his labyrinth in the insane asylum in Buenos Aires.

It is not surprising that the type of symbolic association suggested by the temporal element at the beginning of this chapter is carried through in an equally symbolic spatial movement: Oliveira descends to the banks of the Seine beneath a bridge, an architectural structure which in Cortázar's works so often suggests the idea of doubles, passage to other zones or the possible reconciliation of opposites. A background detail which frames Oliveira's movements would seem to heighten the ritualistic nature of his actions and to indicate that his nocturnal descent is a form of rupture and symbolic death. I refer to the bookseller's boxes which border the Seine, boxes which capture Oliveira's attention because they "took on a funereal tone at night, a string of makeshift coffins" (202). I think it is important to recognize that Oliveira's nocturnal descent represents an agreement between means and metaphysics in which to pass to another plane is necessary in order then to return restored and reborn. As such, his movements recall an entire Western tradition of ultimately redemptive descents: Odysseus and Aeneas, who descend to the underworld and emerge closer to the end of their journeys; Christ, who after descending into Hell, later arises resurrected; Dante, who also descends to the Inferno, emerging afterward closer to his final destination, Paradise. In other words, when Oliveira, in a critical moment of his life, descends to the banks of the Seine within a symbolic context which echoes this Western mythological and religious tradition, he is exemplifying Mircea Eliade's observation that in moments of crisis man imitates the acts of his gods or of his ancestors.[6]

Oliveira's spatial descent to the banks of the Seine also has its parallel in a social descent which represents a break with bourgeois society. Oliveira goes toward the world of the *clochards,* or hobos, a marginal social group which, in contrast to other marginal groups, is characterized by its abstinence from work. This detail is important and gives a clue to the nature of the scene which we will witness in this chapter. Twentieth-century anthropological and psychological studies have suggested that work is the activity which separates man from animal and which forms the basis of human society.[7] As the center of society, work is also the source of all repression. Perhaps Georges Bataille is clearest on this point, insisting that all fundamental taboos are born from the necessity to restrict any activity whose free reign would represent a threat to work. Starting from this basis, thus, the only human group which escapes the most basic taboos is what Bataille calls the "underworld," a subculture which, like the *clochards* in *Hopscotch*, exists outside of the exigencies of work.[8] Among the underworld, as among Cortázar's *clochards*, all the limits of normal society disappear, including the rationality associated with the obligations of economic production and the need to repress non-productive explosions of energy. In other words, the descent into the world of the *clochards* is clearly a movement toward "el otro lado," the other side. It is perhaps worth adding that Cortázar's explicit references to Georges Bataille in *Hopscotch* and in various essays show that he is thoroughly familiar with the theory I have just outlined.[9] Given this fact, I think it is fair to see in Cortázar's selection of the *clochards* a signifier of Bataille's underworld and an indication that we are entering a moment in Oliveira's life in which many of the key elements of Bataille's thought may be in evidence.

The particular *clocharde* whom Oliveira encounters in chapter 36 is Emmanuèle, a woman whom he and La Maga had observed and whom La Maga, without Oliveira's knowledge and thus to his great annoyance, had befriended. Despite his familiarity with Emmanuèle, Oliveira does not immediately embrace the *clocharde* and the world she represents. On the contrary, Oliveira's initial reaction is typically bourgeois: he is repulsed by Emmanuèle. He reacts not with liberating exhilaration, but with disgust, and he experiences nausea when confronted with Emmanuèle's filth, the disorder of the underworld and the presence of elements associated with death and decay and thus governed by taboo. Oliveira's sensation of nausea is crucial for the dynamics of the chapter, for it opens up the possibility of seeing his subsequent actions in terms of the interplay between taboo and transgression. This becomes clear when we consider that transgressive activity is not the absence or ignorance of taboo. Rather, there can be transgressive activity only where there is consciousness of taboo.[10] It is Oliveira's nausea which here signifies this consciousness of taboo. His nausea is a prerequisite, something which must exist in order to be consciously overcome, thus achieving movement toward planes beyond habitual limits. This is precisely the phenomenology in evidence in the early part of chapter 36. I quote:

> Untrain the senses, open your mouth and nose wide and take in the worst of smells, human funkiness. One minute, two, three, easier and easier, like any apprenticeship. Keeping his nausea under control, Oliveira grabbed the bottle, even though he couldn't see he knew the neck was anointed with spit and lipstick, the darkness sharpened his sense of smell. Closing his eyes to protect himself against something, he wasn't sure what it was, he downed half a pint of wine in one gulp. Then they started to smoke, shoulder to shoulder, satisfied. The nausea went away, not conquered but humiliated, waiting there with its crooked head, and he could begin to think about anything. (209)

This first step taken, his nausea subdued, Oliveira, now entering into a shared world with Emmanuèle and giving himself over to random thought, is free to pass into more serious zones of violation, to enter a world of hallucinatory visions and of the absurd, a world in which man's most fundamental taboos are challenged and violence and eroticism reign unchecked. My reference is to a vision which now overtakes Oliveira as he contemplates Emmanuèle:

> ... Oliveira saw the spots of dirt on her forehead, her thick lips stained with wine, the triumphal scarf of the Syrian goddess that had been trampled on by some enemy army, a chryselephantine head rolling around in the dust, with spots of blood and gore but keeping all the while the diadem of red and green stripes, the Great Mother stretched out in the dust and trampled on by drunken soldiers who amused themselves by pissing on her mutilated breasts, until the greatest clown among them knelt down to the accolade of all the others, his penis standing out erect above the fallen goddess, masturbating onto the marble and letting the sperm trickle into the eye-holes from which officers' hands had already plucked the precious stones, into the half-open mouth which accepted the humiliation as a final offering before rolling off into oblivion. (209–10)

Although produced perhaps by Oliveira's drunkenness, this vision is not a gratuitous hallucination. The vision is ordered; its order is found in the fact that each oneiric element leads to a signified of either death or eroticism. These signifieds, if taken on a secondary semiological level of meaning, in turn point to an identical concept: transgression. I think it is worth taking a moment to look at the process through which death and eroticism come to share the concept of transgression. Proceeding from the idea of taboo as a consequence of a need to repress activities which threaten productive work, death clearly becomes the primary taboo, for it is the antithesis of production. From this initial taboo others emerge by means of association. For example, death suggests pain and blood. Violence, being associated with these same elements, becomes linked to death and thus, like death, governed by interdiction.[11] Through a similar process of association the taboo on death also extends to eroticism, i.e., to that type of sexual activity which is not directed toward reproduction of the species. This particular association has again been studied most comprehensively by Georges Bataille.[12] Bataille suggests that early man developed a very concrete association between the blood emanating from the body in violent death and the blood flowing from the sexual organs in time of childbirth and menstruation. This same association between death and eroticism, Bataille asserts, also exists on more abstract levels. He notes that individual life represents a discontinuity; i.e., to be an individual is to interrupt the continuous space of humanity. Death, on the other hand, is a continuity, not only because of its permanence, but above all because of the nothingness which comes forth when the identity of each discontinuous being is erased. An erotic act, in reality, is a movement between our precarious discontinuity and continuity. It consists of two individuals, each conscious of his own identity, who then for an instant lose that identity in the moment of erotic activity, and above all, in the moment of orgasm, a moment which in the French vernacular is so aptly called a "petite mort." Erotic behavior thus comes under the realm of taboo, for on both a concrete, visual level and on a more abstract plane it is associated with the primary taboo—death.

These summary references to Bataille's thesis suffice, I think, to explain my interpretation of Oliveira's erotic and violent vision in chapter 36 as a paradigm of transgressive attitudes. It is of significance to this interpretation, moreover, that in Oliveira's vision the object of violence and erotic behavior is a goddess, since within

Western tradition the dynamics of taboo-transgression almost always appear within a religious or quasi-sacred setting.[13] It should be noted as well that parallels could easily be drawn between key elements of Oliveira's vision and certain forms of "regulated" or "permitted" transgressions such as rituals of religious sacrifice characterized by the presence of virgin goddesses and blood rites.

It is following this hallucinatory sequence that Oliveira, still sitting beside Emmanuèle and clutching the bottle of wine, recalls the poem "Tuércele el cuello al cisne" (Wring the Neck of the Swan). There is good reason, I think for this particular work to come to mind at this moment in the chapter, for the specific images used in "Tuércele el cuello al cisne" relate closely to the transgressive vision Oliveira has just had. As in Oliveira's vision, the object of violence in the poem is sacred—the swan being a form assumed by the god Jupiter and also the symbolic goddess of modernism. The swan is possessed of erotic significance as well, a significance born from its mythological role in the rape of Leda and from the phallic value assigned to its powerful neck in modern Freudian terminology. In this poem, moreover, the specific act of violence used against the swan is a type of violent sacrifice in which eroticism is implicit. The sacred swan's neck is wrung; it is strangled, and as Emir Rodríguez Monegal has written, strangulation is a form of violence in which the assassin chokes his victim "with a movement which symbolizes masturbation."[14] Seen in this fashion, the images of "Tuércele el cuello al cisne" echo exactly Oliveira's transgressive vision in which a soldier masturbates over the body of a fallen goddess.

The significance of the appearance of González Martínez's poem does not reside alone in its repetition of imagery, however. The poem also serves as an emblem of Oliveira's behavior in chapter 36 and of what his behavior is revealing to him. The poem represents a rupture. Its theme is a rejection of modernism, a poetic movement which belongs to what Oliveira calls "el buen lado," the good side. What the poem seeks, however, is not a complete break. It seeks to violate the swan of modernism only in order to restore it to its original state. This attempt at redemptive destruction is similar to Oliveira's two-way search, in which death and rupture are sought as a means of restoring full vitality. It is the concept articulated throughout *Hopscotch*, in which destruction and transgression are seen as redemptive forces and in which "in order to save [something which is dying], first it has to be killed or at least given such a blood transfusion that the whole thing will be like a resurrection" (444).

Oliveira's vision and González Martínez's poem having established an atmosphere of mental if not demonstrative violation of taboos, the transgressive behavior in chapter 36 now becomes explicit and externalized: Emmanuèle takes Oliveira's sexual organ into her wine-stained mouth, and Oliveira calmly acquiesces. The transgression here is twofold: it lies in the non-reproductive erotic act of oral sex itself; and it lies in the public and shameless nature of the act, violating bourgeois notions of privacy and the decorum which prescribes that even the permitted sexual act of reproductive intercourse between spouses should be hidden. The transgression is recognized immediately. And appropriately, it is recognized by a signifier of the ordered world from which Oliveira descended at the start of the chapter. A policeman arrives and carries Oliveira and Emmanuèle off.

In the absurd situation of buttoning his pants and entering a police van with

Emmanuèle, Oliveira reaches his maximum lucidity. It is in his drunkenness and so-called perversity that he articulates the lesson of this adventure, that he affirms, calmly and consciously, the liberating powers of the path trod by so many Western heroes before him: one must descend; one must break structures, be they moral, societal or linguistic; one must transgress the limits of society as the only hope for returning to that society restored. In Oliveira's words:

> ... people grabbing at the kaleidoscope from the wrong end, then you had to turn it around with the help of Emmanuèle and Pola and Paris and La Maga and Roca-madour, stretch out on the floor like Emmanuèle and from there begin to look out from the mountain of manure, look at the world through the eye of your asshole and you'll see patterns pretty as can be, the pebble had to pass through the eye of your asshole, kicked along by the tip of your toe, and from Earth to Heaven the squares would be open, the labyrinth would unfold like the spring of a broken clock as it made workmen's time fly off in a thousand pieces, and through the snot and semen and stink of Emmanuèle and the shit of the Obscure one you would come onto the road leading to the kibbutz of desire . . . (215–16)

This is the end of part one of *Hopscotch*, "From the Other Side."

Now that I have pointed out what I consider the key elements of Oliveira's behavioral pattern in chapter 36 of *Hopscotch*, it becomes almost obvious in what ways Andrés's behavior in *Libro de Manuel* represents a fundamental repetition of Oliveira's. A reading of one critical moment in Andrés's life is important, however; for although the signified is identical to that in chapter 36 of *Hopscotch*, the selection of signifiers is sufficiently different so as to indicate a new level of intensity and a more overt adherence by Cortázar to the liberating possibilities of transgressive behavior.

Andrés, like Oliveira an Argentine living in Paris among friends, books and music, and a man also divided between two women who represent two different worlds, is, like his counterpart in *Hopscotch*, embarked upon an obsessive quest. His quest has its origins in a strange dream: Andrés sees himself in a movie theatre which has two screens at right angles. He is there to see a Fritz Lang thriller. Suddenly a messenger arrives and tells him that a Cuban wants to speak with him. Andrés follows the messenger until he enters a room where he sees a figure on a sofa. It is the Cuban. Here the scene is cut. The next thing that Andrés sees is himself, now spectator of and participant in a thriller, leaving the room. Andrés knows that he has spoken to the Cuban and that he now has a mission to fulfill. He has no idea, however, what the mission might be.[15] Andrés's quest is directed toward this: to find the message cut from his dream, a message which will show him the road he should elect between the beloved solitude of his life as an intellectual in Paris and total political commitment.

It is a key moment in Andrés's search which I would now like to consider. *Libro de Manuel* is not divided into numbered chapters. Like a movie—the imagery of film runs throughout the novel—it consists of a montage of scenes, and Andrés's decisive adventure really embraces three different scenes within the text. The first scene places Andrés with Francine in a striptease club (266–70, 278–81); the second places them on a balcony of the Hotel Terrass (286–93). These two scenes form a kind of back-drop to the erotic scene in the Hotel Terrass which represents Andrés's definitive act of rupture and transgression (310–14). There are several important aspects of the two preparatory scenes which should at least be enumerated in order then to go on and closely examine the critical third scene. To begin with, Andrés's presence in a strip-tease club populated by prostitutes at the bar and flies in the whiskey means that his decisive adventure, like Oliveira's in chapter 36 of *Hopscotch*, also begins at night in an atmosphere of drunkenness and in a social setting which is marginal to habitual bourgeois norms. The striptease club episode is followed by another movement toward spaces alien to usual bourgeois centers. I refer to Andrés's insistence on taking Francine to a hotel, which, as he recognizes (286), represents a liberation from all order imposed by the center of bourgeois life, the home. It is significant that Andrés's movement toward the hotel which will be site of his decisive adventure follows a symbolic spatial pattern already established by Oliveira: he crosses a bridge. It is also important to note that the two preparatory scenes establish a total consciousness on Andrés's part of the significance of what he recognizes as transgressive actions. Unlike Oliveira, who was, at the beginning of his adventure, more wandering than consciously seeking, Andrés from the start *elects* the road of descent and transgression as a possible means of liberation. From the beginning he looks for taboos to violate in order to force the death or the affirmation of a petit bourgeois, the lifting or the envelopment of the "mancha negra"—the black spot—from his dream (292–93). And he chooses the Hotel Terrass, insisting on a balcony, because the Hotel Terrass, situated beside a cemetery, forces the confrontation with man's most prohibited reality: death. Andrés knows what his role will be and what Francine's will be; the only thing he does not know is the end result of the ritual. I quote Andrés:

> Let's say . . . it's precisely the end of the ceremony, time to know if it's heads or tails, little one; I can't search any more through reason, I need to descend these stairs of cognac with you and see whether there's an answer in the basement, whether you'll help me break out of the black spot, whether you'll kick old Lang in the belly so that he'll cough up the combination to the safe. Come on, it's time now. (292)

Andrés's reference to "the end of the ceremony" ("el término de la ceremonia") clearly recalls Oliveira's reference to his nocturnal descent as "the end of the great game" ("final del gran juego"). Andrés's language also establishes a relationship with another nocturnal descent which is critical for Oliveira in *Hopscotch*. I refer, of course, to the nocturnal descent with Talita to the basement of the insane aslyum in Buenos Aires which precedes Oliveira's construction of his defensive labyrinth in the final chapters of part two, "From This Side." There, in the basement morgue, Oliveira and Talita, in betrayal of Traveler, kiss beside resting cadavers, just as here Andrés and Francine make a symbolic descent which will culminate in erotic transgression in front of a cemetery.

Having made these few comments on the background scenes, we arrive at center stage for the ritual of initiation which Andrés has designed—the hotel room at the Terrass in which Andrés, between cognac and the cemetery below, forces Francine to perform anal intercourse with him. As was true in the case of Oliveira in chapter 36, the transgression here is preceded by an initial and essential recognition of taboo. Unlike the preparatory scenes, where it was Andrés who displayed a consciousness of the taboos which would be violated, here in the hotel room at the Terrass it is Francine who asserts the existence of taboo. Her refusal to perform anal intercourse and her continuous words of negation are, like Oliveira's nausea in chapter 36, the prerequisite that makes transgression possible. Francine's reluctance is, in reality, part of her necessary role in the ritual, and it is closely related to the traditional role of Western woman in the rite of sexual initiation. As Bataille explains (p. 134):

> A man cannot usually feel that a law is violated in his own person and that is why he expects a woman to feel confused, even if she only pretends to do so; otherwise he would be unaware of any violation. Shame, real or pretended, is a woman's way of accepting the taboo that makes a human being out of her. The time comes when she must break the taboo, but then she has to signify by being ashamed that the taboo is not forgotten, that the infringement takes place in spite of the taboo, in full consciousness of the taboo.

Although I feel the validity of this aspect of Bataille's analysis is limited to societies more traditional than our own, the scheme does function in the case of Andrés and Francine. It is Andrés himself who recognizes the necessity of Francine's negations in order for the full impact of the transgression to be felt. He states it plainly: "My pleasure ended at the point where hers began" (313).

If the presence of Francine's negations signifies the existence of taboo, the persistence and the force of those negations underscore the high degree of interdiction which surrounds the particular erotic act Andrés seeks to perform.[16] In anal intercourse two acts which the system of erotic taboos would classify as perverse—an "unnatural" sexual act and sadism—are implicitly embraced. Like the sexual acts present in chapter 36 of *Hopscotch*, anal intercourse is an erotic act par excellence, for physiologically it has no possibility of resulting in conception. Anal intercourse is governed, moreover, by especially deep-seated taboos, since it suggests homosexual relations and since it also affirms a relationship which societal decorum prefers to ignore—the relationship between genitalia and excreta.[17] Andrés's transgression upon seeking to perform anal intercourse lies in part in his affirmation of these sensitive connections.

It is also the erotic sadism inherent in anal intercourse which classifies Andrés's actions in this scene as an extreme level of transgression. In speaking of erotic sadism, I do not refer to Andrés's forcing Francine to commit an act which she negates, for as I have explained, I feel the primary function of Francine's negations is not at all in opposition to Andrés's need for transgression. It is rather in Andrés's attitude of objectification that sadism enters the scene. Maurice Blanchot has noted that de Sade's morality is "founded on absolute solitude as a first given fact."[18] As a result, de Sade's heroes are "uniquely self-centered; the partners are denied any rights at all." This same idea that the key to de Sade's system consists of making the partner into an object has been stressed by Emir Rodríguez Monegal, who outlines what he calls a "sadistic configuration" in which "the glance immobilizes, fixes upon the Other in his condition as an object, it transforms the person into a thing, in order thus to free the sadist."[19] And Jacques Lacan also echoes this thought, asserting that sadism lacks a subject; it is pure quest of an object.[20] This type of sadistic objectification is implicit in the sexual act which Andrés performs with Francine: Francine is restrained, placed mouth down, positioned in such a way that her equal physical participation is precluded. As in certain configurations of violent religious sacrifice, Francine here is physically *acted upon* by Andrés; she is his object, not his partner.

Andrés's sadistic attitude of objectification can also be perceived in the narrative form employed in this scene. It is Andrés who narrates the scene. As narrator, Andrés is a spectator; he divorces himself from the action, making an object of his partner and of himself. The role which Andrés adopts here is identical to that which he plays in his dream, where he is both a spectator of and a participant in the action. A parallel is thus developed between the dream and an erotic attitude in which sadistic voyeurism is critical, for in both experiences spectator and participant are inevitably and simultaneously the same. (This relationship extends to the reader as well, since, given the montage structure of the novel, he must be an accomplice, a participant in constructing the text, while at the same time a spectator of the events presented.)

These aspects of the erotic act which Andrés performs with Francine are important because they show to what extent Oliveira's actions in chapter 36 of *Hopscotch* are repeated in the Hotel Terrass scene of *Libro de Manuel*. In *Hopscotch* there is an oneiric vision of a passive female figure, a fallen goddess. She is violated through a non-reproductive and non-heterosexual erotic act. The vision also involves the linking of excreta with eroticism through the figure of a soldier urinating on the fallen goddess. In *Libro de Manuel* Oliveira's oneiric transgression becomes Andrés's real transgression. A passive female figure, Francine, is used as a sacrificial object, is ritualistically violated through another non-reproductive sexual act which is associated with homosexual activity. And once again excretion, this time through the sexual act itself, is linked with eroticism.

Linguistic violence plays a critical role in both *Hopscotch* and *Libro de Manuel*.[21] Because of this, I think it should be mentioned that the entire dynamics of the transgressive scene in the Hotel Terrass can really be seen in linguistic terms. In particular, it is possible to see the dynamics of the scene being played out between two basic groups of signifiers: one group, using words such as "censorship," "shame" and Francine's negations, identifies "el lado de acá," this side of the "black spot," the point of departure (311–12); the second group of signifiers, employing words such as "metamorphosis," phrases such as "life on other sides" and the imagery from Andrés's dream, signifies "el otro lado," the other side, which is the desired goal of the transgressive act (311). The means of transport between these two groups of signifiers is made up of words which signify spatial movement and words which signify movement against the taboos of eroticism, violence and death. The presence of a group of spatial signifiers is a constant in Cortázar's work. And here the words used by Andrés to convey this signified are almost identical to those used by Oliveira: "between two banks," for example, or "to go beyond" or "to have arrived at the outer edge" (310–11). The spatial words in this scene are of particular interest because they are intimately related to the words which signify violence against erotic taboos. In fact, most of the erotic signifiers in the scene also imply spatial movement: "throwing her backward" or "advancing toward the depths" (312), for example. In schematic form, then, the interplay among these groups of signifiers reveals the dynamics of the transgressive scene at the Hotel Terrass: society's taboos are established as the point of departure, and there is then movement in space and in violation of these taboos in order to reach another dimension of reality in which the "black spot" will disappear.

Pointing out the interplay among these groups of signifiers as a skeleton model of the dynamics of this scene should not suggest that the reality of the scene is so simple. It clearly is not. And while a close examination of the intermediate zones in play is beyond the scope of this paper, two factors should at least be pointed out briefly. First, while the language of the scene reveals the signified of the scene, language itself is treated in an ambiguous way throughout the ritual. On the one hand, language, if taken mainly as Francine's negations, signifies the point of departure to be overcome. It is essentially negative and false, divorced from the very real and involuntary contractions of Francine's body. On the other hand, however, language is also related to the desired extra-dimension of reality, for it is a message in *words* which the "black spot" hides—words which remain hidden until Andrés and the reader are ready to hear their true meaning. Language, therefore, is both the point of departure and the goal in this ritual. It fulfills an ambiguous function which parallels precisely Cortázar's concept of restitution, in which the end brings us back to the beginning, but to a beginning which is no longer the same.

The second ambivalent way in which language functions within this scene is related to the transgression of the taboo on violence. The scene is, I believe, inherently violent; and yet it does not contain words whose signified is violence. There are words which connote force, of course—"I compelled her" or "throwing her," et cetera—but even within the context of the scene these are not words of clear violence. The component parts of the scene simply do not contain the strong sense of real violence which the scene as a whole communicates. This apparent dilemma is resolved, I think, by an understanding of the nature of violence. It is a silence.[22] Violent words can never connote violence; they can only show rational man, civilized and thus verbal man, speaking *about* violence. This is the flaw in de Sade: the language of violence is silence, and he attempts to achieve violence through spoken language.[23] Cortázar, on the other hand, respects the essential nature of violence, which "never declares either its own existence or its right to exist, it simply exists."[24] In short, it is precisely the *absence* of words whose signified is violence in this scene which permits the total transgressive violence of the acts to be felt. This is why, moreover, the scene is, in my opinion, more fundamentally violent than erotic. For the erotic is also essentially silent; it too belongs to man's instinctual self. The truly erotic, like the truly violent, cannot be put into words. As a result, there is an inherent irony in this scene: it is *not* erotic because it narrates eroticism; it *is* violent because it avoids violent language. The essence of the scene—its violence—is linguistically an absence, in the same way that the essence of Andrés's dream is both verbal and absent.

The scene at the Hotel Terrass, which, like chapter 36 of *Hopscotch*, commenced in a moment of intense crisis for the protagonist, has its end result, as in *Hopscotch*, in a form of liberation. If it is the transgressive experience with Emmanuèle which frees Oliveira to go toward "other sides," it is the remarkably similar Hotel Terrass scene which catapults Andrés toward knowledge of the other side of the "black spot" and toward a break with his solipsistic intellectual life. For all the zigzag of scenes which occurs between Andrés's violation of Francine and his discovery of the words "Wake up," it is clear from the moment of transgression that Andrés will wake up, that he cannot go backward, that he will irremediably march toward the Joda (356).

For Andrés, as for Oliveira before him, a brink situation will have been dealt with through erotic transgression and will lead to a liberation from habitual perspectives and norms.

In discussing eroticism in *Hopscotch* and *Libro de Manuel*, I have tried to relate it to the entire system of Western taboos and especially to the death taboo. I have done this because I believe that Cortázar is not interested simply in eroticism for its own sake. Rather, I think that what Susan Sontag has said of Georges Bataille can be paraphrased and said here of Cortázar: His scenes make such a strong and upsetting impression because he understands clearly that what eroticism is really about, ultimately, is not sex, but death.[25] This is very important, because understanding Cortázar's use of eroticism in this way suggests that the erotic acts in *Hopscotch* and *Libro de Manuel* are only one of many signifiers which could have been used to point to a radical rupture with life's habitual limits. In other words, the importance of the erotic transgressions in these novels is not their eroticism per se, but rather their fundamental repetition of the Western tradition of descent, death and resurrection, in which Oliveira's going to the banks of the Seine and Andrés's going to the Hotel Terrass are essentially identical to Dante's going to the Inferno in order to rise to newer heights after the voyage below.

Having established the fundamental identity between the protagonists' actions in *Hopscotch* and *Libro de Manuel*, I would like, in concluding, to look briefly at one of the important changes from *Hopscotch* to *Libro de Manuel*. Oliveira's acts of transgression are performed within a purely individual context. Andrés's acts of transgression, in contrast, closely bear upon contemporary society as a whole. Here the newspaper clippings in *Libro de Manuel* play the significant role. It is known that in many ancient societies the death of the king often unleashed violent and transgressive behavior on the part of the individual members of the society.[26] In other words, death, a transgression on the part of the guarantor of social order, represented the disintegration of that order; and during the time that the royal flesh decayed on the bone, transgression on all levels was let loose and tolerated. In *Libro de Manuel* a similar pattern exists, since the newspaper clippings, documenting violence and transgressive activity on the part of governments, represent a disintegration of order in contemporary society like that set off by the death and corporal decay of the king in ancient societies. What runs through *Libro de Manuel*, then, are parallel levels of transgression. There is the transgression by governing bodies which sets off and justifies the transgressions of the novel's characters. The governmental transgressions are presented through a series of newspaper clippings; and these same clippings which document transgression are *themselves* a form of transgression, since they physically and visually violate the novelistic space, while at the same time attacking the fictitious world with a violence which is real and present.

Finally, a word should be said about how the actions of the protagonists of *Hopscotch* and *Libro de Manuel* extend to the writing of the novels themselves. Cortázar has commented many times that he writes when he finds himself haunted by an obsession which reaches crisis levels.[27] In this sense, the author's stance in the moment of writing parallels his protagonists' stance in their moment of transgression.

Cortázar's writing, moreover, is closely related to his protagonists' transgressing. The relationship can be drawn on several levels, but perhaps the most important is that which has been studied by Bataille and Severo Sarduy.[28] I refer to the idea that, together with the taboos of death and eroticism, certain types of writing are themselves a taboo of bourgeois society. The type of literature which is transgressive is that literature which does not write *about* something, but rather actually *is* something.[29] This is certainly the case of chapter 36 of *Hopscotch* and of the scene examined in *Libro de Manuel*. There the writing is not merely a discussion of certain transgressions but is itself a transgression; it is as clear an affirmation of eroticism and death as are the actions of Oliveira or of Andrés. Interestingly, the word chosen by Bataille to describe the meaning of this type of consciously transgressive literature is "awakening," a variation on the same word which in *Libro de Manuel* is the final message hidden behind the "black spot" and delivered by the Cuban to Andrés.

Writing is related to transgression in other ways as well. Life is movement, and to write is to stop this movement and to impose a static formation. In this sense, writing violates life; the violation is, of course, redemptive since it ultimately bestows a more permanent form of existence. The text itself represents still another kind of transgression. Each individual element of the text is like an individual discontinuous life. The text, however, can only exist when the individuality of each element is destroyed and the continuity of the whole is freed and allowed to reveal itself. The text, thus, in the writing and in the reading, represents a liberating "petite mort" similar to that found in the transgressive erotic act. Cortázar recognizes this relationship. In speaking of the scene in *Libro de Manuel* which has been examined here, he repeats the vocabulary and the configuration of transgression-liberation: "That erotic scene," he commented in an interview in *Le Monde*, "arose from a need on my part of total transgression of Latin American taboos. I had to write that scene if I wanted to reach my goal of liberating language."[30] For the author, then, as for his protagonists, there is a need and then a conscious movement toward recognized transgression, and there is a concept of erotics inevitably related to ultimate liberation.

This concept of the liberating potential of erotic and transgressive forces is, in conclusion, a key link between *Hopscotch* and *Libro de Manuel*. *Hopscotch* repeats a strong tradition of redemptive descents in order to seek the protagonist's liberation; its ending suggests that the liberation has been found, but it is nonetheless an ambiguous conclusion. Ten years later *Libro de Manuel* appears. The tradition of descent is now more deliberately pursued; the descent is now to further depths of transgression in the actions and in the writing. And here clearer heights of illumination are reached. The process is completed. Ascension and conversion plainly occur. There is no ambiguity. What is important here is both the basic identity and the change in intensity. The identity is, in my opinion, fundamental enough to make superficial many of the differences which have been commonly cited between the two novels. The change in intensity makes necessary the order of the books, for *Libro de Manuel* is not a repetition of *Hopscotch*, but a continuation which necessarily builds upon the earlier novel and goes beyond what was established there; it is not a reiteration of the earlier novel, but an outgrowth of it, an inevitable and desirable Volume II of *Hopscotch*.

1 Mexico City, Excelsior, 1975.

2 Susan Sontag, *Styles of Radical Will*, New York, Farrar, Straus & Giroux, 1969, p. 46.

3 Ibid., p. 58.

4 Julio Cortázar, *Hopscotch*, Gregory Rabassa, tr., New York, Pantheon, 1966, p. 207. All subsequent references in English are to this edition. References in Spanish are to Sudamericana's 9th edition of *Rayuela*, Buenos Aires, 1968.

5 Roland Barthes, *S/Z*, Richard Miller, tr., New York, Hill & Wang, 1974, p. 76.

6 Mircea Eliade, *Le mythe de l'éternel retour*, Paris, Gallimard, 1949, pp. 44–80, especially 45–46.

7 Particularly lucid expositions of this theory can be found in Georges Bataille, *Death and Sensuality*, New York, 1962 (original French: *L'érotisme*, Paris, Minuit, 1957); and Herbert Marcuse, *Eros and Civilization*, Boston, Beacon, 1955.

8 Bataille, pp. 30–31, 40–42, 149–63. Bataille's thought is developed and refined throughout the entirety of *Death and Sensuality*. As a result, it is somewhat misleading to cite specific pages, as if the whole of Bataille's exposition on a given subject were contained in them. I therefore ask the reader to accept the pages cited as only a general guide and to keep in mind that a study of the entire text is necessary for any real comprehension of the thought.

9 For example, *Rayuela*, p. 544. Also, Julio Cortázar, "que sepa abrir la puerta para ir a jugar," *Ultimo round*, Mexico City, Siglo XXI, 1969, pp. 141–54; or Julio Cortázar, "Ciclismo en Grignan," *Ultimo round*, pp. 70, 75.

10 Bataille, pp. 37–38, 67–68.

11 Ibid., pp. 42, 45–48.

12 Ibid., pp. 49–62. This reference serves for the entire discussion of the relationship between death and eroticism on this page.

13 Ibid., pp. 71–94, 109–40, 221–52.

14 Emir Rodríguez Monegal, "Le fantôme de Lautréamont," *Narradores de esta América*, vol. 2, Buenos Aires, Alfa Argentina, 1974, p. 170.

15 Julio Cortázar, *Libro de Manuel*, Buenos Aires, Sudamericana, 1973, pp. 101–104. Subsequent references are to this edition. Translations are my own.

16 For a fuller discussion of anality and taboos see Norman O. Brown, "Studies in Anality," *Life Against Death*, Middletown, Cn., Wesleyan University Press, 1959, pp. 179–307, especially his discussion of Jonathan Swift's works in "The Excremental Vision," pp. 179–202.

17 Bataille, pp. 57–58, 65–66.

18 Ibid., p. 167. See also Maurice Blanchot, *Lautréamont et Sade*, Paris, Minuit, 1949.

19 Rodríguez Monegal, p. 170.

20 Severo Sarduy, "Del Ying al Yang," *Mundo Nuevo*, 13 (July 1967), p. 6. See also "The French Freud," *Yale French Studies*, 48 (1972).

21 For a discussion of the functions of linguistic violence see Bataille, pp. 137–39, and Manuel Durán's fine article, "Inside the Glass Cage: Poetry and 'Normal' Language," *New Literary History*, 4 (1972–73).

22 Bataille, pp. 186–87.

23 Ibid., pp. 187–93.

24 Ibid., p. 188.

25 Sontag, p. 60.

26 Bataille, pp. 65–70. See also Roger Caillois, *L'homme et le sacré*, Paris, Gallimard, 1950.

27 This idea has been expressed by Cortázar in numerous essays and interviews, including "Del cuento breve y sus alrededores," *Ultimo round*, pp. 35–45.

28 See Bataille, *Les larmes d'éros*, Paris, Pauvert, 1961; Sarduy, "Del Ying al Yang"; Octavio Paz, *El arco y la lira*, Mexico City, Fondo de Cultura Económica, 1956; and Monegal, "Le fantôme de Lautréamont," pp. 164–67.

29 Sarduy, p. 8.

30 Françoise Wagener, "Entretien avec Julio Cortázar," *Le Monde*, 20 September 1974, p. 26. See also Julio Cortázar, "que sepa abrir la puerta para ir a jugar," *Ultimo round*, pp. 141–54.

31 I am grateful to Professor Juan Bruce-Novoa of Yale University for the time spent with me discussing the works of Georges Bataille, Juan García Ponce, Maurice Blanchot and others who have studied the nature of taboo.

Eros ludens: Games, Love and Humor in Hopscotch

By SAÚL YURKIEVICH

By changing the initially forecast title, "Mandala," to the definitive one, *Hopscotch*, Julio Cortázar relieved his novel of ritual excess and made explicit that playful axis which generates and completely permeates the text. Naming the novel *Hopscotch* heightens the idea of the game over that of the rite of initiation; it draws the narrative space toward an immediate boundary, one more tied to ordinary experience. Therefore the mythic transmutation and symbolic capitalization will operate from the basis of a more trivial image but with greater empirical concretion, with less power of alienation but with greater sympathetic weight, at once becoming more existential and vivid. Cortázar replaces the supreme center or circle, symbol of the universe and receptacle of the divine; he replaces the magic domain—the pantheon, the holy mountain, the concentrated, nuclear space suitable for prayer and meditation, epi-theophanic space, the world axis that communicates with cosmogonic energy. For this temple, *imago mundis*, he substitutes his degraded and easily understood version: hopscotch. He changes the semantic vector in order to imprint the novel with another circulation of meaning. Instead of the center or original space, the spatialization of the extra-spatial, image and means of spiritual ascent, the return of the ego to original oneness and concentration of the multiple within the original unity, he proposes a child's game played without guile, unaware that he is dealing with the image of the Christian basilica, itself a substitution for other, more remote diagrams, for other labyrinths.

The rectangle of the game, equivalent to the earth, represents the atrium; the transept, originally in seven parts (the days of the week or the celestial spheres) unfolds through the nave to end in the half-moon of paradise or the apse. According to the text only the simple—La Maga, children or madmen—installed without knowing it in innocent plenitude, those who perceive elemental truth directly by non-speculative identification, through precodified, precategorical, prelogical contact with sensible concretion in its supreme immediacy, only those who possess that knowledge by sympathetic consubstantiation, those who exist without knowing it, maintain the ability to overcome all the obstacles of the stormy course that hopscotch imposes. Only they have access to the sacred zone, to the kibbutz of desire, to completion, to plenitude of contact with the axial.

Cortázar discards the name "Mandala"—too remote and charged with eschatological weight, because it overemphasizes the theodicial aspect of the novel. He chooses "hopscotch," a term which belongs to common knowledge, and he transfers to it the allegorical weight of the mandala, of the representation of the universe, of the initiatory journey marked by purifying deeds of increasing difficulty in order to reach heaven, of maximum ontological consistence, revelation, clairvoyance and plenary communion. Traversing the hopscotch diagram will be compared with traversing human existence; the game consists, like destiny, of the conjunction of skill and luck.

Paradoxically, hopscotch appears as a metaphor before it does as an anecdote. In the novel there are two kinds of hopscotch. That kind "from the other side" does not intervene directly in the action; it is a referent of discourse, a figure of speech, metaphoric hopscotch that progressively takes on transcendental value; and it is with all that semantic weight, with that fiduciary richness, that it enters the action "on this side" to convert itself into real hopscotch (one unreal, the other real, or both real and unreal?), gifted with the transmuting power of a mandala and capable of carrying out the transformation of Talita into La Maga. In *Hopscotch* the space where action takes place is always positively or negatively symbolic, differentiated as weak space (territory) or as strong (zone, opening, bridge or passage). Even the reference to Paris, a site verifiable with extratextual existence, means here a labyrinth, a hopscotch, a mandala, a center, a magic ball, a place of rabdomancy, of geomancy, a way of reaching the noumenon: "Paris is a center, you understand, a mandala through which one must pass without dialectics, a labyrinth where pragmatic formulas are of no use except to get lost in. Then a *cogito* which may be a kind of breathing Paris in, getting into it by letting it get into you, *pneuma* and not *logos*."[1] In *Hopscotch* all places are symbolic; the text establishes space and its meaning as go-betweens, as mediators; it configures and validates space.

Hopscotch is a game, a bridge or a passage at the same time; in other words, it is a bridge or passage as well as a game. The novel *Hopscotch* is a metaphorical trick, a lyrical toy, a novelistic toyshop, a sleight of hand against occidental reason, against the "blind alley at the service of the Great Idealist-Realist-Spiritualist-Materialist-Infatuation of the West, Inc." (447). A swarm of intentions and absurdities in pursuit of an "anthrophany," it is "the imperfect and desperate condemnation of the literary establishment, the mirror and reflection of the other establishment which is cybernetically and carefully making of Adam that which his name spells when read backwards: nothing."[2] Faced with the crisis of the traditional belief in homo sapiens, given the failure of our inaccurate mechanism of understanding, *Hopscotch* configures the change in a man who looks for catalysts to provoke naked and unfiltered contact with a reality not mediated by the "interposition of myths, religions, systems and reticulations."

The antidotes against ego- and logocentric totalitarianism, against technological absolutism, against the logic of domination, against a one-dimensional, castrating, disembodying, repressive logos, the means to correct the distorted evolution of Western thought, the outlets for a new metaphysical beginning or the entry into the recuperation of initial wholeness—everything which Cortázar calls bridges or passages is both negative and positive. One negative triad—misconduct, thumbing one's nose at society, madness—is complemented by another positive one: eros, games and humor.

Misconduct inevitably goes against the established order; it consists of practicing the most hardened marginalization in order to reach the reverse of the obverse, of leaving behind not only conventional ways of knowing but also the habitual recourse to buses and to history, to the notebook of enrollment, to the actions and vocabulary of the tribe, to the social scene, to any physical or moral imposition; it consists of isolating oneself from the species, of being a monkey, a dog or a fish among men in order to eliminate through regression any residue of false humanity. Misconduct implies unpigeonholing oneself, unlabeling oneself, declassifying oneself, uncategorizing oneself, removing one's strings, provoking disorder with mindlessness: ". . . something tells him that the seed lies in brainlessness, that the bark of a dog is closer to the omega than a thesis on the gerund in Tirso de Molina" (495). Opening up and phenomenal porosity restore the fluency and mutability to reality. The two parts of the novel end in maximum misconduct: the nauseating traffic with the *clocharde* Emmanuèle, and Oliveira's entrapment within a web of strings and a pit of basins. Misconduct determines the action as well as speech; *Hopscotch* can be considered an attempt to unwrite the novel, to unseduce oneself literarily so that language may bloom again, delving deeply into reality: "From being to speech, not from speech to being" (442).

Misconduct is above all a social attitude, a counterattack to arrest Grand Custom. Its interior correlative, within the level of perception, is thumbing one's nose, removing oneself, not being there or being half there: "the feeling of not being completely within any of the structures, the webs that life weaves in which we are simultaneously the spider and the fly."[3] Oliveira exercises "attentive disattention" in order to escape utilitarian vision; he tries laterally to become receptive and open to attain paravision, that instantaneous confronting of the absolute in which everything becomes extrapolative and intervallic. Oliveira practices interstitial vision to detect the fissures in appearance and to glimpse through them the world in itself. This tendency toward leaving himself, toward non-concentration and toward alienation, this desire to reach the psychic bottom, to transpose the prevailing absurd by forcing it to the limit, to reach the greatest naturalness through deliberate transgression—these imply an approach, an admiring connection with the radical absurdity that is madness, madness identified with the inscrutable divine order, as if by human madness one could arrive at cosmic reason.

These interceding bridges, these potential passages intersect, converge in multiple textual crossroads; they touch, intrigue and catapult; conjunctions plot their skirmishes, their subversions of different levels, from antics to the most radical derangement. Dancing to the same piper, they simultaneously operate at all levels, determining the means of representation as well as that which is represented, conditioning the imagery as much as reflection, the message as much as its support. In counterpoint to the negative bridges or passages are those that permit access to a liberated zone. Three basic zones—games, love and humor—are fused in the Cortazarian emblem of *eros ludens*.

The game, a rupture in the normal continuum, being exempt from external constraint, fractures the order of pragmatic realism. A festive interregnum, it transports one to an exceptional zone in which free will is recovered. It permits escape from the imperious satisfaction of immediate necessities and allows one to enter another sphere of activities that have their own direction and regulation. If it is accepted, the game acquires a positive character, instigating a code whose violation can entail unforeseeable damage. Games establish their own progression, their own concatenation. They can begin, like the episode of the bridge of boards, with the trivial entertainment of straightening nails without knowing why. An apparently aleatoric dynamic, capricious but accepted as a motivating purpose, determines an even more absorbing, riskier, more decisive and more transcendental advance. The game, once one embarks within its specific realm, admits neither revision of its rules nor opposition to its mandate. Freedom of options is fused with an extreme fixity. The game absolves one from the restrictions of the empirically real and, on transporting one to a different space and time and restoring a community apart within a separate domain, it makes possible an extraordinary contact with reality. It implies a derangement inclined toward ritualization by its proximity to the mythical, the liturgical and the esoteric. It provokes passage from cultural to cult. When it takes on the weight of metaphorical richness and symbolic plenitude, as it does in *Hopscotch,* it becomes a link between esthetic, mystic—which is to say, alogical or analogical—and playful perception. The game is converted into a bridge to cosmic solidarity.[4]

The figurative conjunction of love and the game is perfected, for example, in chapter 21, where La Maga figuratively becomes a "vertiginous hopscotch":

> Why shouldn't I love La Maga and possess her beneath all those ceilings purchased for six hundred francs, in beds with musty and unraveled spreads, for in that crazy hopscotch, in that race of moneybags I recognized myself and called myself by name, finally and until I would escape from time and all its labeled monkey-cages, where from its show windows Omega Electron Girard Perregaud Vacheron & Constantin marked the hours and the minutes of sacrosanct castrating obligations, into an atmosphere where the last bonds were being loosed and pleasure was a mirror of reconciliation, a mirror for larks but a mirror, something like a sacrament from one being to another, a dance around the altar, a coming on of sleep with mouth to mouth, sometimes without untangling ourselves, our sexes warmly joined, our necks like twining vegetative signposts, our hands determinedly caressing thigh and neck . . . (94–95)

Love with La Maga becomes a numinous encounter, an axial contact with the center that transforms their miserable den into Eden. Recognition, true understanding of the self, permits access to a name, abolishing all distance between the sign and the signified. The way of unity, triumph of the pleasure principle over the reality principle, annihilates horizontal biography, chronology and topology and invalidates mutilating separation. In love, life denudes and unties itself joyfully in order to recover original plenitude and integrity. The solidarity of love is reconciliation, the freest alliance with substantial reality without deforming or distancing filters (social and cognitive conventions and stereotyping language). "A sacrament from one being to another, a dance around the altar" indicate transfiguration; they project one into primordial time and space; they announce a natural epiphany, connected with Adamic nudity, not stained by clothes, the signs of historical time; they announce the harmonious reintegration of that compound person with that integral multiplicity which is the universe.

There is in *Hopscotch* an amorous bipolarity between the game and sacrifice, which tends to be radicalized, to convert itself into the extreme opposition between love and death. On one hand, games become sacred; they become vectors of supreme meaning, transports into the sacred zone; they ritualize themselves, becoming hierophantic ceremonies; they seek to become sacrifice, like the transmutation of La Maga into Pasiphaë and of Horacio into the Cretan bull. On the other hand, there is a counteroffensive to "avoid like the plague any sacralization of games," of impeding polarization or loss of control. When falling into panicky delirium and the absorption of the lovers in erotic pathos take place, the game and humor combined function as an anticlimax, as elements of a desacralizing, demythifying and dispassionate distancing.

Among the initiatory games tending to ritualize themselves, connected to the erotic sphere, imbued with mysterious relationships (myth, magic, liturgy, sacrament), with cosmological symbology, like hopscotch and the kaleidoscope, we encounter ambulatory rabdomancy and the fishbowl game. Ambulatory rabdomancy postulates fated encounters through astral attraction or telepathic communication. It is at the same time playful manipulation, traffic with occult powers and going against conventional practices; it means placing oneself in an exceptional state of availability. It consists of making an appointment vaguely in a neighborhood at a certain time and wandering through the Parisian labyrinth until the meeting occurs through presentiment or magnetization. For Oliveira this wandering guided by remote control invalidates his "ordinary logical motives" and destroys his "librarian's prejudices." The magnet Love, with its game of attraction and rejection, operates as the cause or, without causal reason, as the concerting/disconcerting conductor of encounters and misencounters. *Hopscotch*, a novel marked by the idea and action of searching, originates from one of many such encounters.[5]

The fishbowl game is also a passage from a territory to a zone, leaving the street and floating into a fluid world, abolishing the compartments which obstruct free circulation between all levels of reality. The fishbowl game reestablishes guilty intervalency (the lovers are fish, red and black birds, butterflies, Giotto, jade dogs, a purple cloud) and unanimous communication. An orgy of metaphors and analogies, immersion in the mythic waters permits omnimodal and omnivorous imagination to exercise its connecting eros, to go through the walls of the fishbowl and to reintegrate itself sporadically in frank, paradisiacal solidarity. Eroticism establishes the realm of unrestricted, unconditional, irresponsible, homological convergence. A fusing and effusive high tide, it imposes the imaginative proliferation of figurative meaning on the restrained, objective world. Imprisoned in copulative passion, all is swept away by the metaphorical flood, yoked together by a universal pairing.

The game of love implies bodily contact, a progression which culminates in copulation, a simultaneous absorbing of each other, mutual dissolution of the daylight individual, nocturnal fusion and confusion, a joining together that masculine-feminines the lovers into a single being within sexual death. It can begin with a playful caress, like exploring La Maga's mouth with the fingertips, or with the cyclops game: staring into each other's eyes, drawing closer and closer until mouths come together, bite each other and explore each other. Here the game is connected with animalized man, with regenerative involution, with time out of mind, with the dark descent into formlessness, with naturalizing fragments of myths which reestablish cosmic solidarity. The game is transformed by desire into an embodied struggle, into love's war.

The fifth chapter of *Hopscotch* presents the culmination of an erotic climax, the hallucinatory metamorphosis of Horacio into a bull and of La Maga into Pasiphaë, the transport of transgressing love that makes possible, by means of a barbarous ascesis, through sexual saturation, the leap into otherness. La Maga desperately holds on to moments of climax; for her, orgasmic progression "was like waking up and knowing her true name"; copulation grants her maximum ontological consistency, reveals her true identity and gives her the most substantial sense of self. The motor that activates the sequence is that of erotic euphoria over against the depression of the crepuscular biographical zone; the memories that bloom and the distress are vectors of deflation: frustration, the mutilation of a strained wholeness, the spoiling of one's true nature, a cold, hostile darkness: entropy.

Burning, resplendent love, shining within vertical time which it connects with the center, struggles against profane time, that of irreversible interest, darkness and tearing down. The pair persists between communion and divorce. Oliveira's function is to excite La Maga in order to prevent her falling into darkness and depression. Excitement begins with erotic play to provoke through the game the passage from the order ruled by the reality principle to that of the pleasure principle, to leap over the wall of psychophysical restrictions from the world of obligations in order to force her to escape herself, to cause the surrender which makes possible the transfiguring trance, submersion through disorder or excess in prehistory or transhistory, that is, radical truth.

"Then he would have to kiss her deeply, incite her to new play, and the other woman, the reconciled one, would grow beneath him pull him down . . ." (28). Ecstasy, orgiastic intoxication, removes restrictions, separation and boundaries; it implies the temporary loss of binding individuality so carefully constructed in the world of consciousness and categorical classifications, the world culturally and historically determined by speech superimposed upon the dense indifferentiation of the species. Frenetic love implies alienation, confusion of individualities, annihilation of opposites and of sexual heterogeneity; it brings back androgynous fusion, provokes the momentary death of egocentrism and of the censoring consciousness; it returns one to undifferentiated natural continuity, to that genesic and generic self which forms the species. Ever vigilant consciousness (analytic thought, discursive succession, abstract elevation) is opposed to panic rapture, the realm of the instinctive, materializing imagination, of the abolition of biography, of the return to ancestral memory, of the passage from cosmos to chaos, of the fall into the formless, into the protoplasmic state prior to emergence, into consolidation, into the difference between pure forms, the fall into the lower realm, into a dark mixture, into the forest of the flesh, into deep confusion: ". . . she would surrender then like a frantic animal, her eyes lost, her hands twisted inward, mythical and terrible, like a statue rolling down a mountainside, clutching time with her nails, with a gurgling sound and a moaning growl that lasted interminably."

Regressive ecstasy catastrophically liberates one from unidimensional reality, from generalizing, categorical thought, from illusory cognitive neutrality; it is satori or a mental cataclysm that sets up easy contact with the materiality of the not-I, with the other and otherness through transubstantiation; it is the height of devastating reality that destroys the ego's defenses, an atrocious giving-in to original plenitude, an agonizing return to primordial integrity. The delirious casting aside of abstract thought, volatizer of the sensorial and leveler of the qualitative, animal frenzy reestablishes immersed, participating, precodified, prelogical and precategorical perception: not logos but pneuma, not *sema* but *soma*, semen.

Sexual paroxysm involves the abolition of lineal discourse; it puts an end to inferential coherence, to superficial causal order, to ordered succession, to progressive, univocal unfolding; it produces the irruption of ambiguous confusion and promiscuity; it cancels the distance between words and things, between subject and object, between inside and outside, body and mind, causes and effect, the thing in itself and phenomena, being and nonbeing; it abolishes the dualism of thought, of enlightenment (enlightment versus obscuration, lucidity versus confusion, clairvoyance versus clouded vision). Astonishment, passion, effusive descent—"like a statue rolling down a mountainside, clutching time with her nails"—descent to corporal discourse. The word made flesh recovers its profound dimension; it becomes consubstantial, capable of incorporating the other person, the beloved and the lover, into itself, capable of entering, penetrating and penetrated, capable of ingurgitating, of absorbing everything within its own matter. The libidinous, pulsating word, the vigorous struggle between ingestion and expulsion, between the instinct of conservation and the desire for death.

The return to the mythic state transforms horizontal, profane time, with its irreversible, vectorial succession of daily deaths through inanition and weakness, into a time of catastrophic epiphany, a vertical time that combines itself with the regenerating center, a reversible time that returns to the beginning, a circular time of present eternity, of reintegration with genesic cycles. It implies escaping oneself, not controlling oneself in order to retrace evolution, disaculturating oneself in order to escape history: "One night she sank her teeth into him, bit him in the shoulder until the blood came, because he had fallen to one side, a little forgetful already and there was a confused and wordless pact" (28). It is the return to the beginning, a regression to unembarrassed instinct not distorted by logos without eros. The recuperation of libidinous energy, it avoids substituting words for the experience that precedes, characterizes and hides being (the verb without the thing itself).

The return to the confusion of the depths and of the origin is equivalent to death: "Oliveira felt that La Maga wanted death from him, something in her which was not her awakened self, a dark form demanding annihilation, a slow wound which on its back breaks the stars at night and gives space back to questions and terrors." Sexual plethora projects one beyond oneself; the violence of copulation takes the ego back to its elemental state; it destroys words, shatters Apollonian order, eliminates the waking self, catapults one into cosmic disorder and buries one in the maternal night, pulsing with copulations that engender and destroy. Oliveira, "off center like a mythical matador for whom killing is returning the bull to the sea and the sea to the heavens," consummates by sacrifice the restitution of the victim to the nether world; his descent is to the receiving and bestowing center. The sacrifice starts an interchange of energies, life for life, in order to reestablish communication with the powers of origin.

Possessed by the orgiastic ritual, Oliveira metamorphoses into a bull, the primordial titan, paradigm of virile potency, archetype of the inseminator; he changes into the Cretan bull, the incarnation of Zeus, the fecundator, the model of masculine fertility, the promiscuous deity of multiple marriages. Within the paroxysm of vital tension, in the ritual of barbarous opulence, sexual fury provokes through its overflowing the convergence of the human orgy with natural excess, with the lustful overabundance of nature. The sacrifice breaks down any holding back; it goes beyond all limits, it "return[s] the bull to the sea and the sea to the heavens." It reinstalls one within the cosmic environment; it implies a universal shuddering, the cataclysm that goes back to materia prima in order to make possible a new creation.

Oliveira, the bull that reconciles the human order with the animal through natural excess, that makes germinal power flourish frenetically, transforms La Maga into Pasiphaë, mother of the Minotaur, and subjects her to complete disorder of the senses, to maximum outrage, to expiatory contravention of regulated conduct, to the overwhelming invasion of bodily excess. This excess of materiality, of gross, confused and dense matter, disrupts the vigilant consciousness that only accepts those doses of reality allowed by its control. This plethora frees itself with terror; it combines with primitive, titanic order, with terrible strength and with abysmal depth. The whirlpool of outrage represents the possession of ecstatics by nature through joy and agony and culminates in the traumatic restoration of unity, the cataclysmic cancellation of the principle of reason or individualization. The orgy transports one to illogical time- and spacelessness; it dismantles the intelligible order; it exasperates, terrifies and bewilders La Maga ("Terribly mistreated that night, opened up to an absorbent space that beats and expands . . ."); it makes the participants phenomenological sponges, opening them to the axial. The sacrifice, a ritual death, responds to the desire to keep oneself within that opening, to make definitive the transitory entrance into the paradise of elemental communication. Love the transgressor constitutes that violent ascesis, that chaotic epiphany that achieves the return to the womb. Sexual saturation is the *via unitiva*, the sacrament that transports one suddenly into the realm of solid intercommunication; within the orgy love becomes the intervallic nexus; it is transformed into "a passport-love, a mountain pass-love, a key-love, a revolver-love, a love that will give him the thousand eyes of Argos, ubiquity, the silence out of which music is possible, the root out of which a language can be woven." (425)

Love is connected with the death and resurrection of the phoenix; it is a flood, a phenomenal destruction, apocalypse, the union of heaven and earth reduced to a confused mass, to the primordial, chaotic situation in order to make a new generation possible. Through cyclical dissolution and reconstitution, one succumbs in order to be reborn through a virginal emergence with all one's powers intact: "Only the pleasure in its final wingbeat is the same; before and after, the world has broken into pieces and it will be necessary to rename it, finger by finger, lip by lip, shadow by shadow" (423).

Love is configured as an aquatic ritual, navigation, a marine immersion: "to stick [one's] head into the crest of a wave and pass through the fabulous crash of [the] blood" (422). Changing from La Maga to Pola is diving into "a new ocean, a different set of waves." In the cyclops game buccal connection, the unification of breath, the mutual absorption of saliva, is imaged as diving into fecundating water: "And if we bite each other the pain is sweet, and if we smother each other in a brief and terrible sucking in together of our breaths, that momentary death is beautiful. And there is but one saliva and one flavor of ripe fruit, and I feel you tremble against me like a moon on the water" (33). Sexual fusion is the entrance to a liquid universe in which images proliferate, beginning with the identification of water with woman and sea with mother. Woman, as a grinding agent, softens and liquifies everything; possessing her implies diving in, dissolving oneself. The feminine is presented as albuminoid and protoplasmic; it becomes the germinal liquid, an embryonic world.

The passages of maximum eroticism are presided over by liquification and shot through with aquatic isotopes that correlate the female with the warm darkness of the depths of the sea. Coitus is the equivalent of regressing to the abysmal unconscious through immersion in the intrauterine world. The water images swarm, animated by an incestuous dynamic of living penetration, symbolized by the correlation between the feminine womb and the depths of the sea and by the reabsorption in the ocean of origin, the source of fertility. The calm of the maternal waters is agitated by the uproar of the seminal fluid. This crystalline, lustrous water becomes stormy and dense; it turns into muddy plasma, the germinal clay.

The pubic smells and the secretions of La Maga's body are associated with sticky substances: "You smell of royal jelly, of honey in a tobacco pouch, of seaweed even though the place might make it topical. There are so many kinds of seaweed, La Maga smelled of fresh seaweed, pulled up by the sea's last surf. Of the wave itself" (542). Oral eroticism moistens everything and provokes an interchange of essential liquids; licking, auscultation and vaginal penetration reestablish the circulation of primordial liquids, and they initiate again the movement of the "wheel of origin." Entrance into the "viscous cave," the cosmic grotto, the universal matrix, provokes maximum communication and conciliation of all the natural orders. The genital and excremental become cosmic: organic excretions become homologous with astral constellations; they turn into initial and final figures of a unanimous configuration. The body—the distance between mouth and anus, the internal cosmos—corresponds to the space between heaven and earth, the external cosmos. The body is a cosmic map. The traversing of the body-mandala is transformed into a voyage in search of origins and of a body not inscribed by perverting history or by submission to the unhealthy machine of society. Through excrement, through the excremental canal, who can arrive at the center of Edenic brilliance and fall through "[the skin's] abysses with the roll of emerald dice, gadflies and phoenixes and craters . . . ." (543).[6] The visceral microcosm, with its injections, swallowing, irrigation, its ebb and flow, with its effervescence, agitation and bustle, is identified with the depths of the sea, with germinative plasma, with the vermicular, with the embryonic swarming of the oceanic night, that which precedes cosmic birth:

A liquid cosmos, fluid, in nocturnal gestation, plasmas rising and falling, the opaque and slow mechanism moving around grudgingly, and suddenly a rumbling, a mad race almost against the skin, a flight and a gurgling of contention or leaking, Pola's stomach a black sky with fat and slow stars, glowing comets, a tumbling of immense vociferant planets, the sea like whispering plankton, its Medusa murmurings, Pola the microcosm, Pola the summing up of universal night in her small fermented night . . . . (457)

Cortázar struggles to descend to the corporal depths. To the extent that his rejection of rhetorical discourse and generalizing abstraction increases, to the degree that he distances himself from overbearing logomachy, from the ethic of sublimation, from spirituality and from transparency, to that extent his vision and language are incarnate: they become flesh and lubricate each other; they become more vibrant and libidinous, and they reintegrate themselves within the fluidity, instability and mutability of substance itself. Discourse descends to the boiling, qualitative richness of the world of matter. Freed from the dictatorship of propositions, syntactic models and grammatical submission, language, restored to things themselves, increases its perceptible concretion through contact with the crass and gross, with the digestive, the genital, and the fecal. The *clocharde* Emmanuèle incarnates maximum fecality, the fecality which is reversible and can be transformed into gold. Through her dirt and foulness, Oliveira attempts to go beyond the limit of normal tolerance, the boundary between the licit and the illicit, the customary and the extraordinary, so that everything becomes acceptable. He puts into practice the last lesson of Heraclitus, buried up to his neck in a mountain of dung: descend to filth, lower oneself, contradict one's urges, go against false decency:

> . . . you had to . . . stretch out on the floor like Emmanuèle and from there begin to look out from the mountain of manure, look at the world through the eye of your asshole and you'll see patterns pretty as can be, the pebble had to pass through the eye of your asshole, kicked along by the tip of your toe, and from Earth to Heaven the squares would be open, the labyrinth would unfold like the spring of a broken clock as it made the workmen's time fly off in a thousand pieces, and through the snot and semen and stink of Emmanuèle and the shit of the Obscure one you would come onto the road leading to the kibbutz of desire . . . ." (215–16).

Against sublime discourse, fecal discourse. Against religions, systems and rules Cortázar offers direct and impudent contact with visceral reality, gross contact, beyond all grace, without mythopoeic mediation. Writing is ripping the skin away from language, reeducating the senses, opening oneself up to the nauseating, "to be in dung up to the neck." To write is to strip oneself of literary garb, to remove investiture; to write is to unwrite oneself. Writing: putting one's hand into the viscera, penetrating the desired and desiring heart, descending in order to inhabit the body and reconcile the word with organic functioning and productivity.

Oliveira demands a radical love which would provide "the root out of which a language can be woven." Love acts as a catalyst as much at the level of the story as at that of discourse; it transforms the representation as well as its support. Erotic and verbal imagination combine into one narrative impulse where the vehicle is as vigorous as its vision or where vision is above all a linguistic invention: aphrodisiac language. Erotic ecstasy produces a sweeping expansion of the word; erotic frenzy provokes a metaphoric saturation which overflows any realistic retention. The verbal whirlpool obliterates normal distributions, and selection is exiled by a hallucinated combination. Lyrical climax is made concrete by means of an imperious, all-inclusive metaphorization which becomes more and more radical. In chapter 64 love takes possession of the chalk drawings on the Parisian sidewalks and expands them imaginatively until it takes possession of the city itself:

> The Rue Dauphine in gray chalk, the stairway carefully done in tones of brown chalk, the room with its lines of flight astutely drawn in bright green chalk, the curtains in white chalk, the bed with its serape where all the chalks ¡*Viva Mexico!*, love, its chalks yearning for the fixative that would keep them in the present, love in perfumed chalk, mouth in orange chalk, sadness and surfeit of colorless chalks

spinning around in imperceptible dust, settling on the sleeping faces, on the exhausted chalk of the bodies. (366)

Within this erotic-metaphoric saturation words copulate according to an independent game of attraction and rejection. Cortázar opens the floodgates to an overflow, to a conjunctive superabundance in which relationing and figurative eros sets up its incentives and its vast, diverse constellations. When the lexicon at hand proves inadequate for his invading voracity, it is substituted by Gliglish, an emollient, albuminoid language, by a verbal magma in which words become soft and dissolve; they acquire a plasticity and a fluidity proper to the embryonic state. No other language would be more appropriate for the expression of eroticism than this ooze, this turgid protoverb, this slippery jelly:

> No sooner had they cofeathered than something like a ulucord encrestored them, extrajuxted them, and paramoved them, suddenly it was the clinon, the sterfurous convulcant of matericks, the slobberdigging raimouth of the orgumion, the sproemes of the merpasm in one superhumitic agopause. Evohé! Evohé! Volposited on the crest of a murelium, they felt themselves being balparammed, perline and marulous. (373)

Oliveira wants to avoid alienating sacralization, the turning of his games into sacrifice. Against Dionysian exaltation, against the cosmic projection of sexual frenzy, against euphoric transfiguration, against lyrico-erotic amplification, against the fervid, devastating expansion of desire and against the orgasmic climax Cortázar proposes the burlesque correction of Emmanuèle's horrible smells and scabs, the profanation of the trampled Great Mother, spotted with the urine and sperm of drunken soldiers (chapter 36) or the "hair-raising vision of raving maniacs in nightshirts chasing [Talita] with razors and grabbing stools and bed-legs, vomiting on their temperature charts and masturbating ritually" (285). Over against exalting sacrality, insulting sacrilege; over against erotic enthusiasm, playfully humorous anticlimax.

Games and humor constitute techniques of withdrawal, cooling off, distancing, and distention; they intervene between the sentimental whirlwind and frenetic vanity as a desacralizing antidote. They restore language to the surface; they dismiss Apollonian rhetoric and bring to the surface the Dionysian language of the visceral depths. Against the possessive introduction of passion, erotic delirium and oneiric wandering, the unsubmissive, irreverent games and humor produce a lucid break, an ironic splitting, a liberating separation.

Games, humor and irony become possible when existential urgency abates. They diminish the pressure; they relax compulsion in order to restore independence. They entail a conscious practice of detachment, which Oliveira/Cortázar exercises to preserve his voluntary displacement as an outsider. Oliveira leaps into an alter ego with his ruptures, irruptions and surprising disruptions; with his confusion of hierarchies that makes the worthless transcendental and the supremely important almost worthless; with his black humor that suspends moral norms and emotional imperatives; with his exercises in profanation, his reductions to absurdity, his references to the ridiculous, his recourse to the outlandish, his absurd associations, his juxtapositions in the majestic with the popular or vulgar, his parodic mobility, his puns, his verbal irreverence, his word games, his burlesque language games, kicking himself with polyglot insults, his orthographic humor, his joking homophony and his street language inserted into passages of metaphysical inquiry or into decisive passages. His humor and irony impose a margin of absence; they entail indifference, leisure, intelligent aloofness from threatening demands, a detaching of himself from his identity, a willingness to pay the price of sacrilege and impiety.

To humorize, to ironize is to strike a kind of balance, to oppose all despotic hegemony, to keep within bounds that massive plenitude, that absolute momentaneity that is instinct, to turn away from the trembling bog, to escape the black hole. Humor is negative freedom, the power to turn around tragic irreversability, to discredit greatness, to hold back in the face of an impulsive inundation, a way to combat sentimental imperialism and to restrain cancerous excitement. Humor is the art of the superficial, the tangential and the ductile. A vaccine against the oppression of intransigent pathos, humor reestablishes indetermination, uncertainty, the appreciation of the nomadic; it breaks up magnetization, the polarization of ecstasy, entrancement, reverence, delirium and the compulsive vectorality of passion.

[1] Julio Cortázar, *Hopscotch*, Gregory Rabassa, tr., New York, Pantheon, 1966, p. 427. All quotations are from this edition.

[2] Julio Cortázar, *La vuelta al día en ochenta mundos*, Mexico City, Siglo XXI, 1967, p. 26. The *Adán/nada* reversal is lost in English.

[3] Ibid., p. 21.

[4] Play is a basic component of *Hopscotch*; it intervenes in a determining way in the process of producing the text, and it acts on all levels of the text. Games enter into the story with variable amounts of interference, with distinct factual importance, with greater or lesser narrative function (maximum development of the narrative aspect appears in the scene of the boards and of Oliveira's defense with strings and pans). There are games that take place at the level of meaning and those that affect the language, that work on a specifically linguistic level: they are strictly verbal, like the cemetery game, the game of balancing questions, the invention of newspaper headlines and the creation of outlandish metaphors in unknown languages. There is also the meta-narrative game, that of the mirror relationship with Morelli's book, the open structure, the elective or aleatory reading, the multiplication of the operating possibilities—all are effects of of the playful attitude of the author, who wants to overwhelm his reader so that the latter undertakes *Hopscotch* playfully, so that he reproduces it by playing.

[5] The search marks the entire tale. *Hopscotch* begins with the question: "Would I find La Maga?" Oliveira, a prospective seeker (for La Maga and Eden) and a retrospective one (in the game of recovering the insignificant, the unostentatious, the perished), defines himself as such: "It was about that time I realized that searching was my symbol, the emblem of those who go out at night with nothing in mind, the motives of a destroyer of compasses" (7). La Maga is also fascinated by searching: "All things considered, it's not easy to talk about La Maga, who right now must certainly be walking around Belleville or Pantin, carefully looking at the ground until she finds a piece of red cloth. If she doesn't find it she'll go on like that all night. She'll rummage in garbage cans, her eyes glassy, convinced that something horrible will happen to her if she doesn't find that piece of ransom, that sign of forgiveness or postponement" (8).

[6] See Roberto Echavarren-Walker, *Le monde romanesque de Julio Cortázar*, Ph.D. Dissertation (University of Paris), 1974.

Vampires and Vampiresses: A Reading of 62

By ANA MARÍA HERNÁNDEZ

Cortázar has always shown a keen interest in the Gothic aspects of vampirism. He is thoroughly acquainted with the numerous *nosferati* preceding and following Bram Stoker's darkly illustrious Count and jokingly refers to himself as one of the "undead," since he is allergic to garlic and preserves an oddly youthful appearance at sixty-two years of age. His interest in vampirism might have been reawakened by the many publications on the theme immediately preceding the writing of *62: A Model Kit*: Valentin Penrose's *Erszebet Báthory, la comtesse sanglante* (Paris, 1962); Roger Vadim, Ornella Volta and Valeria Riva's *The Vampire: An Anthology* (London, 1963); Tony Faivre's *Les vampires* (Paris, 1963); and Ornella Volta's *Le vampire, la mort, le sang, la peur* (Paris, 1962).

62 works with a very complex system of cross-references and allusions, functioning on different levels but with the central theme of vampirism as a common basis. The novel's major "keys" are presented in the first paragraph. The words spoken by the fat client ("Je voudrais un chateau saignant") refer to a raw Chateaubriand, but also to the "blood castle" at Csejthe (near the town of Fagaraş in Romanian Transylvania) where Erszebet Báthory (the "Blood Countess") performed the deeds that made her famous in the early seventeenth century. The restaurant Polidor alludes to Juan's namesake, Dr. John William Polidori (private physician to Lord Byron), who conceived his novel *The Vampyre* during the memorable soirée at the Villa Diodati in Switzerland (15 June 1816) at which Mary Shelley's *Frankenstein* was born. The Byron circle, inspired by Byron's own dramatic recitation of Coleridge's "Christabel," had gathered to create horror stories. At one point in the reading Shelley ran away shrieking; later, they found him, pale as death, leaning against a fireplace. After Polidori revived him with ether, he confessed he had envisioned a woman with eyes in place of nipples.[1] "Vision," as we shall see, is one of the main motifs in 62.

Polidori's own novel deals with the destructive effects of an uncontrolled, boundless egoism. Lord Ruthven, the vampire in question, is a transparent allusion to Byron. "Christabel," on the other hand, deals with *female* vampirism and has distinct lesbian overtones. The book Juan bought, as we are told later in the paragraph, is by Michel Butor, whose last name is partially homophonous to the Countess's. It also sounds like *vautour* (vulture), a traditionally sinister bird of prey which feeds on the young and the weak, like Lord Ruthven, Christabel, Juan and Hélène—and, of course, the Countess.

Upon entering the restaurant Polidor, Juan decides to sit facing a mirror; immediately we are reminded that vampires, according to folklore, have no reflection. Even though we are not told whether Juan sees his reflection or not, his mental confusion at this point shows that he lacks mental "reflection." Loss of reflection or of the "shadow" is a rather common occurrence in tales of supernatural horror; in most cases, this phenomenon is associated with some kind of diabolical pact or ceremony performed in one of the magical vespers. In "A New Year's Eve Adventure" E. T. A. Hoffmann presented Adalbert von Chamisso's character Peter Schlemihl, who had sold his "shadow" to the devil. The loss of the shadow—Jungian symbol for the repressed, true self—implies a loss of the soul or a loss of virility. Most importantly, it implies the loss of the capacity to establish lasting human relations.[2] A man without a "shadow" is, like Melmoth, a wanderer. Like the hero in Hoffmann's tale, Juan performs his ritual (entering the restaurant Polidor, buying the book, sitting in front of the mirror) on a magical vesper, Christmas Eve. Christmas Eve marks the birth of a Divine Child, likewise a Jungian symbol for the true self. But this child will be condemned to death by men's spiritual "blindness." Similarly, the young patient who represents Juan's true self is condemned to death by Juan's own spiritual blindness and egoism. Juan deliberately looks for loneliness and degradation in the magical vesper associated with love and hope; and as a result of his diabolical rite, he will lose his soul at the end of the novel. The mirror also alludes to the incantatory spells celebrated by Countess Báthory in order to preserve her youthful appearance. She celebrated these rituals at dawn, facing a mirror.

Another "key" is provided by the bottle of Sylvaner that Juan orders. The first letters of its name contain a reference to "las sílabas centrales de la palabra donde latía a su vez el centro geográfico de un oscuro terror ancestral"—that is, Transylvania, Cradle of Vampires. Throughout the novel Cortázar alludes to "the Countess" in connection with the Hotel of the King of Hungary but does not mention her by name. Countess Báthory, a native of Hungarian Transylvania, was walled in as a punishment for her crimes. However, neither the crimes nor the punishment took place in Vienna. Critics who have traced the allusions to the Blood Countess have skipped a second set of mirror images: those associating the Viennese Frau Marta with Erszebet Báthory's Aunt Klara, who initiated her niece in the sadistic practices that made her famous. Erszebet's "amusements" had started when her husband, Count Nadasdy, left her for long periods of time to fight the Turks:

> During his [Count Nadasdy's, Erszebet's husband] long absences his bride paid frequent visits to her aunt, the Countess Klara Báthory, a well-known lesbian, who raped most of her ladies-in-waiting, and whose amorous advances to soldiers on guard duty and washerwomen at her castle had made her the talk of Vienna. Her procuress, well provided with funds, had provided a steady stream of attractive and easy-going girls for her lesbian orgies. Countess Elizabeth must have been very much attracted to the sexual perversions devised by her aunt's fertile mind, to judge by her frequent visits.[3]

As Juan and Tell wander around the Blutgasse (a street named after a Mayor Blut, but interpreted by Juan as "the street of blood") expecting to find the spirit of Countess Erszebet, the narrator says "sabiendo muy bien que no iban a encontrarla a esa hora, aunque más no fuera porque la condesa debía rondar otras ruinas" (81).[4] They *know* Erszebet's ghost is not there. Is it, then, Klara's ghost they are searching for? Significantly, Clara is the name of the heroine of Cortázar's first, unpublished novel, "El examen." She was married *to a character named Juan.* Does Cortázar include Klara Báthory (Frau Marta) in the novel because he sees her as his own sweet Clara twenty years later? Does he blame Juan for her metamorphosis?

A further key is provided by Tell, who reads a novel by Joseph Sheridan Le Fanu. The novel is, most probably, "Carmilla," reputedly the best vampire story ever written. In this novel, as in "Christabel," the vampire is a woman and a lesbian. She is also eternal, successively reincarnated under anagrams of the same name: Millarca, Mircalla, Carmilla. The novel provided the theme for Carl Theodor Dreyer's movie masterpiece, *Vampyr*, well known to Cortázar. In the novel we find a play of mirrors involving an older, sinister vampiress (Countess Mircalla Karnstein) and a younger, seductive one (Carmilla) who captivates the young heroine with her fatal charms. The theme of lesbianism plays a central role in Cortázar's works. This aberration, openly admitted in the case of Hélène, is subtly suggested in most other feminine characters. Paula forms a strange liaison with the homosexual Raúl; Paula/Raúl, as their names indicate, seem to be two sides of the same personality. During Horacio's conversation with the *clocharde* the latter hints at a possible relationship between herself and La Maga. Ludmilla, Andrés Fava's mistress in *Libro de Manuel*, has a lesbian past as well. Gabriel Ronay observes that in exploring the psychology of lesbian aberrations—one of which is vampirism—the link between love and pain, the most fundamental in the whole range of sexual psychology, is of crucial importance. Women have a natural penchant for rituals involving blood, since the shedding of blood is inseparable from the female's rites of passage (menstruation, defloration, childbirth, et cetera). The lesbian aberrations are often accompanied by a regression to "primitive" courtship rituals wherein the shedding of blood occupies a central place.[5]

Cortázar's male characters often express the primitive's dread for those "women's societies" in which strange rituals beyond the comprehension of men are performed ("El ídolo de las Cícladas," "Las ménades," Oscar's dream of the moonstruck girls in *Libro de Manuel*, Dina [Diana] the black Artemis in "Cuello de gatito negro"). But the theme has other implications as well. Homosexuality involves a failure to grow beyond the early narcissistic stage and come to terms with the "otherness" of the opposite sex.[6] Cortázar's self-centered, narcissistic heroes are bound to look for women who resemble them as much as possible, so that in loving them they would still be loving themselves. Likewise, in possessing them they would really be possessing themselves. Juan and Hélène are two manifestations of the same personality. A relationship which originates in a failure to deal with "the Other" and in a desire to "recover oneself" must be, in essence, vampiristic.

By dealing with its psychological implications we discover the very essence of Cortázar's vampirism, which is—in spite of the many references to Gothic novels—essentially psychological, like Poe's. Rather than Sheridan Le Fanu's "locked room" situation (briefly parodied in the episode of Frau Marta and the English girl), what we have here is a set of relationships like those uniting Ligeia to her husband or Madeline Usher to her brother. Juan's obsession with the remote, cold and cruel Hélène is as metaphysical as that of the typical Poe hero. For Juan, as for Morella's or Ligeia's husband, "the fires were not of Eros." He really wants to possess Hélène's essence, not her body. He cannot even approach her, and when he does, he does not "see" her. He makes love to "Hélène Arp, Hélène Brancusi, Hélène dama de Elche." Nor does he "see" Tell, on whom he projects his ideal vision of Hélène, too ("doncel de Elche, fría astuta indiferente crueldad cortés," p. 77). Tell is cast in the role of the physical Lady Rowena whom Ligeia's husband employs in order to bring back his celestial, defunct wife. Tell is indeed nothing more than a "thing" on which Juan "feeds" ("te cosifico," p. 67). The rest of the characters, too, are vampires or are vampirized in their turn: Nicole and Marrast by each other, Celia and Austin by their respective parents, Austin by Nicole, Nicole by Calac (aspiring), "la gorda" by Polanco.

Hélène, the most evident vampiress, is branded by the pin she wears, which has the form of a basilisk: "The basilisk has such a dreadful stare that birds at which it merely glances fall down and are devoured."[7] The vampire, likewise, fixes and petrifies its victim with its stare. "Vision" is Hélène's terrible attribute. Her vision, however, is no different from Juan's "blindness." Hélène does not look at the other in order to see him; she looks at him in order to immobilize and devour him. Neither she nor Juan will be able to break the spell that hangs over them, for they are incapable of understanding the symbolic events of which they are part.

These events start when Hélène's patient dies. From the moment she sees him, Hélène will identify her young patient with Juan. After he dies, she falls into a trance during which she associates him with past memories and vague anticipations regarding herself and Juan. The patient becomes a link between her past and her future. While thinking of him, she centers her attention on the advertisement of "the girl who loves Babybel cheese"; her eyes appear like tunnels leading to something she needs to discover—or recover. Then, as if by chance, she meets Celia, the exact opposite of the young man who has died. Celia has just broken away from *las escolopendras*, her family, and confronts life like a young mythological heroine, a Psyche. To Hélène, she appears as overwhelming as the girl in the ad. Hélène, rather than breaking away from her own *escolopendras*, misunderstands the message and tries to reach "the other side of the tunnel" through Celia, whom she associates with the doll she has just received from Tell. The doll is Hélène herself: a petrified figure hiding an undefined or perverted sexuality. Celia, on the other hand, appears as the promise of deliverance. But like the hero in Hoffmann's "The Sandman," Hélène must *see* through the doll. She does not. Instead, she tries to "fix" Celia, to absorb her life and turn her, too, into a doll or a vampiress. She loses her first chance of deliverance when she kills the young patient. He was Juan's soul and, as such, the reckless young hero who could have killed "the basilisk" and delivered the maiden hidden inside herself. She misses her second chance when, having failed to recover her own soul and live her own life, she tries to absorb Celia's. She reenacts the fate of Countess Erszebet, who, having wasted her life waiting for a perennially absent husband, attempted, after his death, to steal from others the youth she had lost forever:

> The death of her husband in 1604 had a shattering effect on Countess Elizabeth, and played an important role in the loosening of the last vestiges of control over her bloodlust . . . she resolved to bathe regularly in virgins' blood. She took these baths at the magic hour of 4 a.m., when the dark forces of night were already powerless and the first nascent rays of light heralded the birth of a new day.[8]

Celia, however, understands the ceremony when she breaks the doll by accident. The doll was her own motionless and lifeless existence as an undefined adolescent; she breaks the bisexual doll, thereby breaking the homosexual spell Hélène had tried to place on her.

Hélène seems somehow to hold Juan responsible for the course the events have taken. Indeed, if she had to decipher the doll's and the patient's message, he had to decipher at the same time the meaning of the scene between Frau Marta and the English girl. Yet at the decisive point, when Frau Marta is about to possess the girl, Juan fails to understand what these actions mean: "Things have taken place in a different way, maybe because of us, because of something I was on the point of understanding and didn't understand."[9] When Parsifal fails to ask about the mysteries in the Grail Castle, castle, king, Grail and attendants all disappear and the Waste Lands remain sterile. Only the eye of consciousness can break the spell. Likewise, Juan fails to ask the meaning of the scene he witnesses. As the result of this failure Hélène's life remains waste.

In their studies of the theme of vampirism in Poe's works Allen Tate and D. H. Lawrence agree that Poe's heroines are turned into vampires through a man's inability to awaken them to womanhood: "D. H. Lawrence was no doubt right in describing as vampires [Poe's] women characters; the men, soon to join them as 'undead,' have, by some defect of the moral will, made them so."[10] The same can be said of Hélène. When Juan finally visits her apartment, he fails to kill the Gorgon in her by symbolically piercing her with his sword (phallus), because he has not subjugated her first with the eye of consciousness. She retaliates by "petrifying" him, symbolically castrating him. After a night of love, she mocks his very manhood, laughing in his face and telling him "lo mismo me da Celia que tú" (261). Indeed, there is no difference between him and Celia, except that Celia succeeds in outgrowing her adolescent vagueness after she leaves Hélène's apartment. Juan chooses not to: "I lost myself in analogies and bottles of white wine. I got to the brink and preferred not to know. I consented to not knowing, even though I could have."[11] He does not want to know because he does not want her reality to interfere with his own selfish vision of her. But by petrifying her, he becomes, paradoxically, her victim. As Esther Harding observes, love for an ideal vision is a sin against the Moon Goddess, against life.[12] Juan sees Hélène as Diana, himself as Acteon (235); he is right when he fears, in his nightmare, "el Perro's" revenge. Diana's dogs (34, 238) represent her "terrible" side, unleashed in order to destroy and dismember Acteon, who looked at her body without *seeing* her. His inability to see Hélène makes Juan cling to her, vampire-fashion—or like a child to its mother—expecting her to satisfy his needs and conform to his ideal of her. But this expectation robs him of his manhood: "It is, as the ancient myth puts it, a castration to the mother . . . not the initiation ordeal voluntarily taken with a religious motive. It is an involuntary sacrifice to the mother, which brings no renewal."[13]

Austin's meeting and falling in love with Celia stands out as one of the most idyllic love scenes in the whole of Cortázar's writings. In this scene Austin and Celia "look"—literally and symbolically—at one another. Open, honest love between man and woman breaks the spell of the vampire. Through their act of love Austin and Celia, now free, are cleansed from their former "perverse" entanglements; they take the "bath" Juan and Hélène were always unable to take in their nightmare. Juan and Hélène, on the other hand, experience a blind, negative and mutually destructive encounter. Imprisoned in their respective egos, they act out a grotesque parody of the act of love.

Austin, described as "Parsifal" and later as "Gallahad" and "Saint George," acts the part of the mythological hero, slaying the Dragon he has first "seen." But Juan, who has lost his shadow, will be cursed with the repetition of that one event he did not understand in the Hotel of the King of Hungary. In the scene where Austin kills Hélène we read that "Someone, perhaps a woman, cried out in the bed, one single time." Later, after Hélène has been killed, we read that "Someone cried out again, fleeing through a door in the back of the room. Face up, Hélène's eyes were open."[14] That "someone" is Nicole, in whom the slain vampiress's spirit becomes reincarnated in order to haunt Juan. When he leaves the apartment after finding Hélène's corpse, he sees Nicole on a boat, sailing toward the sunset, about to jump into the water. He prepares to jump after her, but it is too late—Frau Marta (Klara Báthory) takes her by the arm, whispers in her ear, takes her to a certain hotel. Nicole is, in reality, a mirror image of Hélène, just as Marrast and Calac are mirror images of Juan. The latter's spiritual impotence is reflected in Marrast's statue (sculpted on an "oilcloth stone" and, as such, "soft") and in Calac's "failure." Juan/Marrast/Calac fail Hélène/Nicole through their deliberate blindness and softness, and the latter retaliate by turning into vampires and haunting them. At the end of the novel Juan cannot participate in Feuille Morte's "rescue." He is a victim of his own monster.

[1] E. F. Bleiler, ed., *Three Gothic Novels*, New York, Dover, 1966, p. xxxv.

[2] E. F. Bleiler, ed., *The Best Tales of Hoffmann*, New York, Dover, 1968, p. xxiii. The vampire in Hoffmann's story is called Julia.

[3] Gabriel Ronay, *The Truth About Dracula*, New York, Stein & Day, 1970, p. 102.

[4] Page numbers refer to the Sudamericana edition of *62: Modelo para armar*, Buenos Aires, 1968.

[5] Ronay, p. 106.

[6] "The stage of development from which paranoids regress to their original narcissism is sublimated homosexuality . . . they reduce the chief pursuer to the ego itself, the person formerly loved most of all . . . the homosexual love object was originally chosen with a narcissistic attitude towards one's own image." Otto Rank, *The Double: A Psychoanalytic Study*, Chapel Hill, N.C., University of North Carolina Press, 1970, p. 74. Also R. D. Laing,

The Divided Self, New York, Pantheon, 1969, pp. 146–47.

[7] Bram Stoker, *The Annotated Dracula*, Leonard Wolf, ed., New York, Potter, 1975, p. 54, note 16.

[8] Ronay, pp. 116–18.

[9] *62: A Model Kit*, Gregory Rabassa, tr., New York, Pantheon, 1972, p. 187.

[10] Allen Tate, "Our Cousin, Mr. Poe," *Poe: A Collection of Critical Essays*, Robert Regan, ed., Englewood Cliffs, N.J., Prentice-Hall, 1967, p. 42; D. H. Lawrence, "Edgar Allan Poe," *Selected Literary Criticism*, Anthony Beal, ed., New York, Viking, 1956, pp. 330–46.

[11] *62: A Model Kit*, pp. 273–74.

[12] M. Esther Harding, *Woman's Mysteries: Ancient & Modern*, New York, Putnam, 1970, pp. 196–97.

[13] Ibid., p. 202.

[14] *62: A Model Kit*, p. 278.

Octaedro: Eight Phases of Despair

By EVELYN PICON GARFIELD

It took me many months to read *Octaedro*, mainly because the book distressed me and I had to abandon it several times. When I finally finished reading this last collection of short stories written by Julio Cortázar, I was disturbed by my reaction to the book, for Cortázar had communicated his despair to me in those pages. In many ways these eight short stories seemed to be a continuation of his other works; nevertheless, an indefinable difference existed. These new stories echo the Cortázar with whom I am familiar. In "Verano" (Summertime) a couple's daily routine is interrupted by an unexpected threat; in "Liliana llorando" (Liliana Weeping) and "Los pasos en las huellas" (Footsteps in the Tracks) a hidden dimension of everyday reality is discovered and accepted by the protagonists; in "Manuscrito hallado en un bolsillo" (Manuscript Found in a Pocket) there is a game of chance; in "Lugar llamado Kindberg" (A Place Called Kindberg) and "Cuello de gatito negro" (Neck of the Little Black Cat) there are fortuitous encounters; in "Las fases de Severo" (The Phases of Severo) the strange atmosphere of the story reminds us of the family that lived on Humboldt Street in *Historias de cronopios y de famas* (1962); and finally, obsessive visions of hands and of dreams that haunt one's vigilant hours are found in "Cuello de gatito negro" and "Ahí pero dónde, cómo" (Over There But Where, How). However, in spite of all that was familiar to me in these stories, I could sense an important difference that was difficult to define at first and that I propose to uncover and explain here.

In Cortázar's short stories we expect to encounter a multifaceted reality. By depicting a normal setting and conventional characters Cortázar gains our confidence and puts us at ease with his tales. Innocently reading on, we suddenly find ourselves trapped by a strange and sometimes unreal situation, an oneiric and even fantastic turn of events. In this way we are exposed to and at times threatened by another possible but illogical dimension of the apparently routine reality set forth in the stories. From "Casa tomada" (The House Taken Over) and "Lejana" (The Distances) in *Bestiario* (1951) to "El otro cielo" (The Other Heaven) in *Todos los fuegos el fuego* (1966) Cortázar has presented us with a view of reality riddled with holes, what I like to call a "Swiss cheese" reality.[1] One of his most famous characters, Johnny of "El perseguidor" (The Pursuer) describes this reality:

> "That made me jumpy, Bruno, *that they felt sure of themselves*. Sure of what, tell me what now, when a poor devil like me with more plagues than the devil under his skin had enough awareness to feel that everything was like a jelly, that everything was very shaky everywhere, you only had to concentrate a little, feel a little, be quiet for a little bit, to find the holes. In the door, in the bed: holes. In the hand, in the newspaper, in time, in the air: everything full of holes, everything spongy, like a colander straining itself..."[2]

Through those same holes the unexplained danger of "Casa tomada" filters throughout the house. In that story a strange noise takes over the rooms and forces the sister and brother to abandon their home. In "Lejana" of the same collection (*Bestiario*), by means of a "sponge-like" reality, the protagonist Alina Reyes establishes a strange psychic relationship with an old beggar-woman in Budapest. She dreams about her and finally feels compelled to travel to Budapest to seek her out. When the two women meet on the bridge and embrace, a surprising transmigration of souls occurs. "Alina's soul lodges in the beggar-woman's body while the beggar-woman's soul takes over Alina's body and so the beggar-woman is really the victorious one."[3] In that way Alina's dream world overtakes her everyday existence in a completely illogical way, contrary to our laws of space and time.

In a more recent tale, "El otro cielo," the "colander-reality" serves as a passageway for the protagonist to partake of two lives in distinct places and epochs: twentieth-century Argentina and Paris in the 1870s. Unlike "Casa tomada" and "Lejana," where the characters succumb to a facet of reality which they either imagine or dream, in "El otro cielo" the protagonist finally abandons his exciting life in the Paris of bygone days to return to a routine existence in Buenos Aires. Hardly a threat, Parisian life was a coveted adventure which materialized by means of the protagonist's desire but which ultimately vanished forever.

In the newest collection, *Octaedro*, we once again glimpse the daily existence of a couple as they are threatened by inexplicable forces in the form of a little girl and a mysterious white horse. The setting of the short story "Verano" is clearly auto-biographical—the house, "the path full of ruts and loose stones," the hills, the swallows, the flight from the capital to a countryside which evokes Saignon, where Cortázar spends his summers. Whereas in "Casa tomada" the brother narrates the life which he and his sister lead and thus allows us to share directly in the couple's most trivial pastimes, in "Verano" the third-person narrator observes and comments on Zulma and Mariano's life together. Their routine existence is filled with "nimias delicadas cere-monias convencionales" in the country during the summertime as well as in the city during the rest of the year: "It was all coming full circle again, everything in time and a time for everything, except for the girl who suddenly and gently unhinged the scheme."[4] Cortázar's sentiments about the routine nature of existence surface again here as they did in previous works: *Historias de cronopios y de famas* (1962), *Rayuela* (1963), *La vuelta al día en ochenta mundos* (1967) and *Ultimo round* (1969). In those books the author alluded to domesticated life and custom in pejorative terms, describing them as a nightmare, an absurdity and as "un lugar donde estamos muertos."[5] Ever since *Las armas secretas* (1958) the exceptional departures from routine life and the glimpses of an illogical and provocative facet of everyday reality seem to have become gradually surpressed by the heavy and relentless hand of custom. Routine seems to reestablish itself more and more in Cortázar's stories, despite the author's clear protests in his volumes of miscellaneous excerpts. Even in "El perseguidor" the jazz critic Bruno sought refuge in his customary life in order to protect himself from the provocative reality that Johnny perceived and described through his music. Neither did the protagonist of "El otro cielo" return to the mysterious galleries of Paris, but instead he remained in Buenos Aires, subjected to a conventional life.

Of all the stories published before *Octaedro*, "La autopista del sur" (The Southern Throughway) best exemplifies the definitive victory of routine over a desired and exceptional reality. In that story Cortázar is true to his view of the fantastic as "la alteración momentánea dentro de la regularidad."[6] In "La autopista del sur" some travelers find themselves immobilized in a traffic jam. This common situation achieves unrealistic proportions when the traffic jam lasts months. As the seasons rapidly progress, the people organize a societal nucleus among the stationary cars and eventually embrace a new routine as inhabitants of the highway, until suddenly the cars once again begin to move toward the capital. Even in the face of a fantastic and bizarre situation such as a traffic jam which lasts months, custom reestablishes its sovereignty.

Whereas in "La autopista del sur" the narrative prose communicates a rhythm of routine existence and of implacable time, in "Verano" the narration is more in the nature of a commentary about the weariness of existence between man and woman. Zulma and Mariano's "ready-made" life together is described in the following manner: "One more month of expected repetitions, as if rehearsed, and the jeep loaded to the brim would take them back to the apartment in the capital, to the life that was identical but for its visible gestures" (79). This mild protest against custom and the realization of all that is humdrum in the coexistence of man and woman has a counterpoint in the story. Zulma reminds Mariano that he too has his own routine obsessions—for instance, he always places his bottle of cologne on the left and his razor on the right. It is precisely at that moment that Mariano admits that custom has a reason for being: "But they weren't manias, Mariano thought, but more like a defense against death and nothingness, to order things and hours, to establish rites and passages against a confusion filled with holes and stains" (81). To Mariano custom is a defense against the unknown, whereas for the musician Johnny of "El perseguidor" custom was hateful. His critic Bruno was attracted to the vision of another mysterious and exceptional facet of reality that Johnny seemed capable of experiencing through his music, but Bruno also sensed a protective order in his own routine life. On the other hand, Mariano reaches beyond Bruno's intuition of a protective routine to justify custom, to accept tradition and to defend daily habit. The mild protests which Mariano expresses against humdrum life and his defense of custom as a weapon against death and nothingness seem very different and distant from the protest made by Cortázar in the following passage about another jazz musician, Clifford Brown, in *La vuelta al día* (p. 73): "And afterward routine returns, where he and so many more of us are dead."

In "Verano" Zulma and Mariano's tranquil existence is interrupted when a friend leaves his little girl with them overnight and during that same night a white horse tries to break into the house. An interesting comparison can be made between the threat to this couple's house and life and similar dangers in the first stories of *Bestiario*. In "Casa tomada," a story which was motivated by a nightmare that Cortázar had, a threateningly mysterious noise invades the house from within and forces the couple to abandon it. In another tale, "Cefalea" (from *Bestiario*), Cortázar describes the migraine headaches that plagued him. The *mancuspias* in "Cefalea" are strange animals which surround the house in which their caretakers live. Actually, the house and the caretakers' minds, both besieged by the animals, are synonymous. Above all, the dual menace of the girl and the horse in "Verano" recalls the situation found in the title story of the first collection, "Bestiario." That story was the result of a hallucination that Cortázar experienced when he was ill with an extreme fever. In the story a young girl, Isabel, who is visiting her relatives, the Funes family, becomes accustomed to the presence of a tiger that roams at will through the rooms. The family has devised a system of warnings so that no one will enter the particular room where the tiger happens to be. Isabel is very fond of her Aunt Rema and consequently senses that Rema's brother-in-law Nene is cruel to her. As if Isabel controlled the dangerous animal, she lies to Nene concerning the tiger's whereabouts, with the result that Nene enters the library and is attacked by the animal.

In "Verano" Zulma discerns a strange complicity between the girl who is visiting them for the night and the horse crashing against the window, a liaison which had been developed earlier between Isabel and the tiger in "Bestiario." Zulma insists that the girl will open the door to let the horse in, and, in fact, the next morning the door to the garden is wide open. Unlike the disquieting invasions found in the short stories of *Bestiario*, in "Verano" the unusual provocation to daily routine materializes in the form of a horse, a less oneiric danger than an inexplicable noise, a less fantastic threat than some fabulous *mancuspias* and a more realistic intrusion that that of a tiger roaming through a house. In addition, the ephemeral presence of the horse and child does not threaten to destroy permanently the couple's ordered daily coexistence. In fact, at the end of the story a long sentence rhythmically embodies the implacable return of routine:

> . . . if everything was in order, if the watch kept on measuring the morning and after Florencio came to get the little girl perhaps around 12 o'clock the mailman would arrive whistling from afar, leaving the letters on the garden table where he or Zulma would pick them up silently, just before deciding together what they felt like having for lunch. (90)

We still have to ask Cortázar about the genesis of this story. As with those in *Bestiario*, is it the result of a nightmare, a hallucination, a headache caused by a particularly difficult period in his life? What is the significance of Zulma's terrified reaction to the child and the horse? One critic suggests that Zulma fears Mariano's erotic advances, which she has been avoiding all summer.[7] This is an interesting interpretation which would certainly have a precedent in the short story "El río" (The River). Other critics have viewed her horror as a result of the couple's lack of communication, for the white horse symbolizes and illuminates the estranged relationship between man and woman.[8] Neither of these interpretations attributes enough importance to the role of the young girl, a role which I consider to be fundamental to understanding the story. She is an intruder whose childlike innocence is echoed in the whiteness of the horse and who may represent the daughter that Zulma does not have or does not want to have, a child whose presence would upset the tranquil albeit stagnant life that the couple leads.

Keeping in mind the extreme reaction of fear that Zulma experiences because of the dual presence of the girl and the animal, let us suggest still another rendering based on the traditional sexual symbolism of the horse and the specific eroticism which one encounters in other girls and, by extension, in dolls, that appear in Cortázar's works such as "Silvia," "Siestas" and "La muñeca rota" (The Broken Doll) in *Ultimo round*, and in the novel *62: Modelo para armar*. Perhaps the young girl is an intruder in the established liaison between man and woman, or perhaps she acts as a catalyst by awakening the dormant erotic conjugal relationship. The young girl completes a triangle necessary to the recovery of lost eroticism, an eroticism which always possesses a certain amount of sadism, according to Cortázar—that is, the terror that Zulma feels. In the tradition of his previous stories, Cortázar encourages us to interpret "Verano" in many different ways. On the other hand, unlike the characters in his earlier stories, Zulma and Mariano seem to have become more accustomed to the involuntary intrusions upon their lives. Rather than abandon routine existence, they quickly recover from the mysterious invasion and, with the toothpaste of the following morning's routine, calmly plug up the holes communicating with the exceptionally provocative event of the previous night.

Despite the persistence of routine, dreams, obsessions and imagination prevail in *Octaedro*—with a notable difference. In these stories Cortázar speaks more directly to the reader. He is not content to suggest that there is another side to apparent reality, for he not only imagines and dreams about "otherness" but also takes pains to define that exceptional zone for us. In the story "Liliana llorando" a young man who is fatally ill tries to keep the news from his wife. In order to forget his pain, he keeps a diary of his thoughts and assures the reader that he can "think about anything at all as long as I can write it down immediately" (10). Like the protagonist, Cortázar himself has written stories and even novels to exorcise the obsessions created by his imagination. While the protagonist envisions the sadness his wife will feel when he dies, he plots his own despair, for he dreams of his wife's being consoled by Alfred, a family friend. Near the end of the story, although the patient seems to be regaining his health, he still intends to keep Liliana from knowing of his recovery, for in his dreams she is happy in the arms of another. His dreams have become reality.

Cortázar often develops an interesting relationship between scientific women and the men they betray. One should remember the painful relationship between the adolescent boy and the nurse in "La señorita Cora" (Nurse Cora) and between the anesthetist Hélène and Juan, or his double the dead boy, in *62*. One day Cortázar mentioned to me that certain sadomasochistic attractions exist for him in these relationships between male patients and the women who care for them and at times cause them much pain. Liliana, in this new story, is a chemist, and although she does not directly take care of her husband, in his imagination and finally in reality she deceives him. The protagonist in "Liliana llorando" creates his own reality and transcribes it. Unlike Cortázar, who wrote down his nightmares and obsessions in the short stories of *Bestiario* in order to free himself of them, the patient in this story does not achieve the same exorcism. Instead of ridding himself of these obsessive thoughts, he establishes them as a clear truth which he finally accepts.

Even more painful is the situation of the narrator in "Ahí pero dónde, cómo." In that story Cortázar himself is the protagonist who shares with the reader a recurrent dream about the death of his friend Paco. Throughout the story Cortázar relives the last days before Paco's death in an incessant succession of painfully realistic scenes. In previous stories like "La noche boca arriba" (The Night Face Up) or "El río" the protagonist's dreams persist in and even fuse with wakefulness at the end of each tale. On the other hand, "Ahí pero dónde, cómo" is hardly a short story, but rather an attempt on Cortázar's part to isolate the illogical sensation of dream-wakefulness, to contemplate himself in this agonizing state and to communicate it to us by means of the printed page. In an earlier story, "Las babas del diablo" (translated as "Blow-Up"), the protagonist Michel struggled to describe a difficult situation in his life. Now Cortázar proposes to recount the persistence of a dream that is more real to him than the phenomenological reality that surrounds him. Cortázar once told me of a similar situation: "It's one thing to have an abstract idea that doesn't penetrate your veins, your marrow, but there are those ideas that are almost hallucinatory, that torment you because they are made of flesh and blood, they are more real than the other ideas." Cortázar urges us to recall similar experiences so that he need not feel so alone while he tries in vain to communicate his own anguish to us:

> I probably haven't been able to make you feel that way, but I'm writing it anyhow for you who are reading me because it's a way of breaking the cycle, of asking that you search within yourself to see if you, too, have one of those cats, one of those who are dead, whom you loved and who are over there in a place that I am desperately trying to name with paper words. (105)

The story is clearly autobiographical—Geneva, translators, Chile—to the extent that the author winks at us when he says, "And you the reader probably think that I'm inventing all this; so what, for a long time now people have been calling imaginary those events that I've really lived, and vice versa" (104). Actually, in the story there are many references to his other books. He alludes to *62* and to the city that he writes about in that novel, a city that he has dreamt about since he was twenty years old. Although he wrote a poem and then an entire novel in order to exorcise that nightmare, Cortázar still dreams of that strange city. He described it to me in this way: "When I wrote the poem, I thought, all right, this is an exorcism, I'm not going to dream about the city again; but when I finished it, a few weeks later, I went down there again and I've gone down there several times since." Nevertheless in "Ahí pero dónde, cómo" he informs us that the recurrent dream about Paco has nothing to do with his dream of the city; Paco is another matter entirely. As in previous works, Cortázar's predilection for surrealist painters[9] continues in the dedication to this story, where he names René Magritte's famous painting of a pipe ironically entitled "Esto no es una pipa." During our interview, as Cortázar described his enthusiasm for surrealist paintings, he referred to that very painting:

> If you look at a Matisse you don't need to find any story behind it, only plastic values count; the same with a Braque or a Jackson Pollock. On the other hand, you can't look at a Dalí or a Magritte without knowing what it's called because even though the title has no apparent connection with the painting, it does have something to do with it. When Magritte, I don't know if it is Magritte or Man Ray, paints a huge pipe and calls the painting "This is not a pipe," there is an entire system of thought and metaphor that comes into play there.

In a similar fashion by means of the short story Cortázar tries to make us share an experience which logic tells us is only a recurrent dream but which Cortázar knows is more real than reality itself. Like Magritte, he assures us, "Esto no es un sueño."

Even when dreams and fecund imagination do not openly and defiantly subvert apparent reality, Cortázar insists on revealing the hypocritical acceptance of a false reality to which man so readily succumbs. In his works pursuers such as Johnny and Oliveira recognize the spurious nature of the lives they lead, while other characters

such as Madame Francinet in "Los buenos servicios" (At Your Service) never identify
more than the surface reality of a complex situation. In *Octaedro* this theme is dealt
with in "Los pasos en las huellas" when the critic Fraga thinks that he is writing the
poet Romero's true biography. It is not long before Fraga realizes that he has hypo-
critically chosen to emphasize the poet's greatness while ignoring his baseness. In
order to achieve fame, Fraga has created his own selective biography. Realizing his
complicity in support of a legend about the poet, Fraga decides to expose the false
myth and, consequently, his own hypocrisy. The critic Bruno in the story "El perseguidor" also infuses his book about Johnny's music with his own feelings and
thoughts about jazz. He falsifies the soul of Johnny's music, and the musician be-
rates him on that account. Unlike Bruno, Fraga realizes his error, recognizes the
infamous side of the poet's nature and intends to make his discovery public, thus
risking his own career.

If one takes as a point of departure "Los pasos en las huellas" and "Liliana
llorando," it is possible to see that *Octaedro* is also concerned with the process of
writing, a preoccupation which first appeared as a theme in the stories of *Las armas
secretas*. Aside from the reference to Poe's story "MS Found in a Bottle," the title
"Manuscrito hallado en un bolsillo" reminds us of Cortázar's own manuscripts which
he had misplaced, later found and finally published as "El perseguidor" and "Estación
de la mano" (Season of the Hand). In "Manuscrito hallado en un bolsillo" Cortázar
once again demonstrates his predilection for games of chance. The story reminds us
of the graffiti found on the walls of the University in Paris, a message which Cortázar
reprinted for us in "Noticias del mes de mayo" (News for the Month of May; *Ultimo
round*). The ironic explanation proclaims the following: "HAY QUE EXPLORAR
SISTEMATICAMENTE EL AZAR"—"One must systematically explore chance."
And that is precisely what the protagonist in "Manuscrito hallado en un bolsillo"
does. He takes the subway and adheres to an itinerary, all the while hoping that some
other passenger's travel plans will coincide with his own: "That was the rule of the
game, a smile reflected in the window and the right to follow a woman and desperately
hope that her next move would coincide with the one that I had decided on before
the trip began" (62). The protagonist dictates the rules of the game in which Marie-
Claude finally participates. This underground search differs considerably from Cortázar's earlier games in that it is not as dangerous nor as metaphysical nor even as
humorous as the games that La Maga and Oliveira used to play in *Rayuela*. In spite
of the possible existential interpretation of man's life as a journey fraught with chance
encounters, the protagonist's adventure lacks the requisite anguish and in fact seems
to be more a gratuitous pastime, despite the story's last suspense-filled moments.

In this story, as in "Lugar llamado Kindberg" and "Cuello de gatito negro,"
Cortázar continues to be fascinated with trains and railroad schedules as well as with
fortuitous encounters, a predilection manifest in his novels *Los premios* and *62*. In these
three new short stories chance meetings form the focal point of the plots. During our
interview Cortázar spoke to me of water as a symbolic element of communication
between individuals and of bridges and trains:

You know that I have other places for rites of passage and I don't think they're very Jungian. For example, streetcars or trains obsess me terribly. . . . It's sort of like a projection of the bridge idea. A streetcar or a train is a bridge that moves, besides they frequently pass over actual bridges. But inside, they themselves are a "no-man's land," because steetcars and buses are strange. In them a bunch of people who don't know each other are thrown together and are moved along in space and time. This creates a kind of unity separated from all else. Then that situation seems to me to be able to determine the function of certain unknown laws; certain things can happen there that do not occur outside.

The idea of "figures" has intrigued Cortázar for quite some time now. He gave Luis Harss the following explanation: "I'm constantly sensing the possibility of certain links, of circuits that close around us, interconnecting us in a way that defies all rational explanation and has nothing to do with the ordinary human bonds that join people."[10] In the novel *Los premios* Persio is the first to mention the concept of figures, and later Cortázar himself was to describe accidental coincidences that occurred in his own life and works in "De otra máquina célibe" (Of Another Celibate Machine) and "Encuentros a deshora" (Inopportune Encounters) from *La vuelta al día* and in "Marcelo del Campo o más encuentros a deshora" and "La muñeca rota" from *Ultimo round*. Many of his short stories such as "La noche boca arriba," "Las armas secretas" and "Todos los fuegos el fuego" (All Fires the Fire) and his novel *Rayuela* also reveal these seemingly fortuitous bonds between people, places and events. In fact, Cortázar creates an entire novel, *62: Modelo para armar*, based on a great web of destinies in which characters' paths cross by chance in a series of accidental and purposeful meetings, which when viewed in their totality must represent a "figure."[11] Each character forms a star in a vast constellation unknown to him.

In the three short stories under discussion—"Manuscrito hallado en un bolsillo," "Cuello de gatito negro" and "Lugar llamado Kindberg"—the man who is traveling in the subway or on the highway meets a woman by chance. At the end of each story there is always a definitive break in the very short-lived relationship between man and woman. In fact, with the conclusion of each story the man faces death as a fact or as an implied presence, whereas the woman continues on her way. These women are always described in paternalistic terms as little girls or small animals, especially when they are crying, and they almost always have occasion to weep. When she discovers that she is a coparticipant in a game of chance, Marie-Claude cries "like a wounded little animal" in "Manuscrito hallado en un bolsillo"; the mulatto Dina in "Cuello de gatito negro" is "crying, mewing like a wounded cat"; and the young hitchhiker Lina in "Lugar llamado Kindberg" is described as a "childlike little bear cub" and a "girl-scout cub." One could refer to other women in these stories: Liliana, who weeps a lot, is also described as having "slow feline movements," and she smiles "almost like a little girl"; Severo's wife cries in "Las fases de Severo"; and Fraga's lover Ofelia weeps silently in "Los pasos en las huellas." (Incidentally, in "Manuscrito hallado en un bolsillo" and "Los pasos en las huellas" Cortázar uses his sister's name for the first time in his short stories and perhaps in his entire works. Another critic once pointed out the incestuous relationship between brother and sister in the short story "Casa tomada." Many years ago Cortázar mentioned this interpretation to me and then spoke of his sister Ofelia:

I have only one sister. What's curious is that on a conscious level my sister and I have nothing in common. We've never understood each other. We're like night and day; we've even come to hate each other. Now with time, since we don't see each other, a more cordial relationship exists. But there's a great difference between us. Nevertheless in dreams many times I've awakened astounded because I've gone to bed with my sister in my dreams.

These three short stories and the three female characters in them echo familiar themes and types in Cortázar's works. In "Manuscrito hallado en un bolsillo" the protagonist desires Marie-Claude as if she were "an end, like the truly final stop of the last subway of life" (70). This statement recalls Oliveira's desire in *Rayuela* that love be a key to the absolute: "a passport-love, a mountain pass-love, a key-love, a revolver-love."[12] In the short story woman and love are still viewed as bridges to total being: "the possibility that everything would coincide at once" (62).

In "Cuello de gatito negro" Cortázar juxtaposes his "totemic" animal, the cat, and his constant obsession with hands. In this story the mulatto Dina finds herself compelled to touch and play with strangers' hands in the subway. That is precisely the way in which she meets the protagonist of the story, who accompanies her home. The plot reaches its peak in a terrifying scene of passion when Dina uncontrollably scratches her lover as if she were a cat and he defends himself by seizing her by the neck. Well before *Octaedro*, in the story "No se culpa a nadie" (No One Is To Be Blamed), Cortázar had described a hand which attacked its owner as he attempted to put on a blue pullover sweater. When I asked the author why he and some of his most famous characters such as Oliveira of *Rayuela* and Juan of *62* were so interested in hands, he spoke of his obsession:

Hands have always obsessed me since I was very young. In the first things I wrote, hands played a very important role. I was very young when I wrote that text which I later put into *Ultimo round*, the one that's called "The Season of the Hand." It's the story of a man who sees a hand enter the house, walk around and become his friend. Until one day the hand senses that the man is afraid of it, and then it leaves and never returns. I have an obsession that is somewhat morbid. You know, when I'm alone at home and there's a pair of gloves, mine or someone else's, men's or women's, on top of a table, I never go to sleep without putting them in a drawer or placing some heavy object on top of them, because I'm not able to sleep knowing that these gloves have been left alone in the house. I have the feeling that something is going to bring them to life at any moment.

Cortázar spoke to me of childhood traumas occasioned by tales of strangulations and by horror films like *The Hands of Horlack* with Peter Lorre. He then added: "You know that for a somewhat morbid imagination like mine there is a whole cycle of hands that come and go in my books." And so his obsession with hands appears once again in "Cuello de gatito negro." (For further discussion on the hand in Cortázar's fiction see pp. 595–99 of this issue—Ed.)

As in *Libro de Manuel*, in "Lugar llamado Kindberg" the protagonist is attracted to young people—especially to women—who hold "a world view that had perhaps also once been his own" (113). These are Marcelo's thoughts as he observes the hitchhiker Lina. In Cortázar's latest novel, *Libro de Manuel*, there are letters from a hippy named Sara, who reminds us of Lina in "Lugar llamado Kindberg." A very interesting albeit partial interchange of the traditional roles attributed to man and woman occurs in this story. Unlike the independent and unconventional Oliveira or the men in

Libro de Manuel, the protagonist Marcelo is characterized as a "salesman of pre-fabricated materials," an inhabitant of a "protective bourgeois bubble." He realizes that Lina belongs to a younger generation and refers to her in jazz terminology (another constant in Cortázar's works): "es una osita Shepp, ya no tango, che" (111). Lina travels along with her possessions in a backpack, the way Cortázar likes to travel, like a snail. One might recall the snail Osvaldo in *62* and the observatories of Jai Singh in *Prosa del observatorio*. Cortázar himself describes his affection for this small animal: "The snail lives the way I like to live, sort of self-sufficiently; he moves through life with all his possessions. He carries along his own house." In the short story Lina reproaches Marcelo for his conventional life. "I never arrange anything, why should I? The backpack is like me and this trip and politics, all mixed together and so what?" (113). As if he were her father, she calls him "doctor y papá" and feels at ease by his side because he has long since experienced much of life. As if embodying a maternalistic counterpoint to Lina's sentiments, this evokes in Marcelo memories of a schoolteacher with whom he had fallen in love at the age of twelve. In this manner their personalities and lives are established and fixed: a man weighed down by the ballast of a traditional and comfortable bourgeois existence, a prefabricated life interrupted once in a while by an amorous adventure, and the liberated young woman who feels comfortably lulled by the presence of the "father" figure.

Another interesting twist to the traditional feminine-masculine role is found in an altered yet familiar image. In this story the well-known metaphor that is usually expressed by a male figure to describe Paris as his lover is replaced by Lina's allusion to Copenhagen: "And I told you I don't want to tie myself down, IdontwanttoIdontwantto, Copenhagen is like a man you meet and leave (ah)" (118). The free-spirited Lina is much more akin to the active character of Ludmilla in *Libro de Manuel* than to the famous and intuitive La Maga in *Rayuela,* although both women serve their men as mere bridges in the desired search for complete experience and a grasp of significant and total reality.[13] Despite their superficially free lives, Ludmilla and Lina are not at all independent and, in fact, are defined in part by their respective desires for Marcos and Marcelo.

There are also some limited parallels between the men, between Andrés in *Libro de Manuel* and Marcelo. The former decides to participate in the kidnapping scheme after much hesitation unknown to other Cortázar heroes like Oliveira, while the latter rejects the continued adventure with Lina. Marcelo met her by chance and saw his own abandoned youth reflected in her: "Love didn't even abolish that mirror reflecting the past, the old portrait of himself as a young man that Lina placed before him" (123). At the end of the story he leaves her and speeds away down the road, where he crashes into a tree "at 160 with his face smashed up against the steering wheel, the way Lina used to lower her head because that's how bear cubs eat sugar" (125). Lina is spontaneous jazz, freedom adrift in the world, love that seeks no ties; and he is a "corredor de materiales prefabricados," who rejects Lina on his way to death.

Perhaps it is the presence of death and tears that exasperates me as I read *Octaedro*. Nevertheless, death is constantly a part of almost all of Cortázar's works. As he himself pointed out, "death is a very important and omnipresent element in all I have written." Perhaps my reaction to these stories is influenced in part by Cortázar's last novel, *Libro de Manuel*, published a year before *Octaedro*. In that book, as before in *Rayuela*, the author juxtaposes playful and humorous situations with serious ones and adds a new political emphasis. I miss the homo ludens so apparent in Lonstein's language, in the scenes concerning the strange mushroom, the fantastic turquoise penguins or the absurd protests unleashed in the restaurant. By now, however, I should be quite accustomed to the obvious lack of humor in Cortázar's short stories. Since *Historias de cronopios y de famas*, perhaps his most surrealistic book from the perspective of a playful atmosphere reminiscent of paintings by Joan Miró, the short stories have continued to be devoid of the humor found in the novels. It was, in fact, Calac and Polanco's ridiculous adventures which at moments saved the novel *62* from its abysmal cynicism. Are there any such playful and humorous elements which deliver *Octaedro* from the weary despair and sadness which penetrate every page?

In *Octaedro* there are mere suggestions of the strange mixture of black humor and Alfred Jarry's pataphysics that surround the family living on Humboldt Street in the pages of *Historias de cronopios y de famas*. In "Las fases de Severo" the protagonist-narrator and Severo's other friends and relatives attend a strange ritual in which they observe Severo as he is stricken by a series of involuntary and illogical "phases." Amid drinks and sobs the spectators spend the night watching Severo as if he were the bewitched focus of a "happening," a ritual played out previously; for as the narrator tells us, "that evening everything seemed to happen more quickly" (132).[14] The story describes the successive "phases" that Severo experiences: perspiring, jumping, having his face covered by moths, mysteriously assigning numbers to relatives and friends and finally commanding the spectators to set their watches ahead or back. As Severo passes through his phases like the moon through its own, the atmosphere is filled with the suggestive symbolism of a fantastic albeit possible situation, viewed by sympathetic friends and family. Moving in and out of his bedroom, they converse and drink as if they were engaged in a normal experience, a situation which reminds us of the wake described in *Historias de cronopios y de famas*. Despite the fantastic nature of Severo's "phases," his experiences do not terrify us.

Graciela Coulson and Pedro Lastra offer an interesting biblical interpretation of Severo's phases as a metaphor of the passion and death of man.[15] Despite the originality of this rendering, I prefer to approach the story from a surrealistic perspective for two reasons: first, Cortázar has rarely exhibited interest in Christian symbolism, unless one remembers his brief description of the saxophonist Johnny Carter on his knees like a Christ on the cross; and second, the short story's dedication to a Mexican painter, Remedios Varo, reinforces the author's predilection for those who capture the atmosphere of surrealist art and philosophy, as he has done himself in earlier works, especially in *Historias de cronopios y de famas*, perhaps the best precursor of "Las fases de Severo."

Let us first take as a point of departure a description that Cortázar gave me of surrealist art, and then let us seek correspondences:

The literary content of surrealist painting, Dalí's, Magritte's, for example, Tanguy's, is obvious. They are paintings that have an exclusively esthetic pictorial value on the one hand, but that also have content, a background of an anecdotal, symbolic, psychoanalytical nature—as in Dalí's case—which is important and which you cannot separate from the painting itself.

In the paintings of Remedios Varo the figures have very similar faces, almost as if they were all the same person in different and strange scenes or phases. Nevertheless, they are always surrounded by normal and realistic objects, as in the story about Severo. The fantastic atmosphere that surrounds Remedios's characters as well as Cortázar's Severo is based on their situation, their fantastic use of everyday reality. Ida Rodriquez Prampolini describes Remedios's paintings in her book entitled *El surrealismo y el arte fantástico de México*. That very description could easily apply to Cortázar's short story "Las fases de Severo":

> The juxtaposition of the real and the fantastic comes about naturally, with obvious "tenderness," with surprising enthusiasm, but it never becomes evil, horrifying. . . . The characters are always busy at marvelous chores. . . . Whenever horror does exist, it provokes curiosity, it is not destructive.[16]

There are also similarities between the situation in which Severo, friends and family find themselves and the adventures undertaken by the family on Humboldt Street in *Historias de cronopios y de famas*. However, there is an important difference: all humor has vanished. In "Ocupaciones raras," while the sisters practice howling like wolves, the family builds a scaffold with gallows and a rack in the patio in front of the house, where they finally sit down to dine surrounded by horrified neighbors. In another episode the family takes over the post office, where they give out colored balloons, drinks and snacks along with the stamps. In these anecdotes there is a playful atmosphere of gratuitous absurdity and even black humor which makes us laugh. This is no longer so in "Las fases de Severo," despite the words spoken between the narrator and Severo's child after the last phase:

> —Aren't they playing anymore?—Severo's son asked me, as he was falling asleep but still hanging on with a child's stubbornness.
> —No, now it's time to go to sleep—I told him. —Your mom is going to put you to bed; get inside, it's cold.
> —It was a game. Wasn't it, Jules?
> —Sure, kid, it was a game. Go to bed now. (142)

I should have believed Cortázar when he said that *Historias de cronopios y de famas* is a book which should only be written once. He categorized it as his most playful book, "really a game, a very fascinating game, lots of fun, almost like a tennis match, sort of like that." Then he cautioned me that it was necessary to distinguish between the ingenuous joy of that collection and the humor which he planned to conserve in the rest of his books. Nevertheless, in *Octaedro* he has hardly preserved humor in any form.

Traditionally humor had not played an important role in Cortázar's short stories, nor does it now. Instead, the primary characteristics of his short stories have been the constant threat of an illogical and mysterious force to man in his daily existence and the subsequent defeat of that apparent reality by the unknown. *Octaedro* continues the short story tradition established by Cortázar, for it, too, haunts us with nightmares, obsessions and disconcerting provocations which menace everyday existence. But there is a serious and sad divergence from previous tales. The strange zone which Cortázar continues to describe no longer implacably terrifies nor intrigues the protagonists, nor the reader nor even Cortázar himself, as much as it produces despair. The author tries to describe this other illogical facet of reality in more realistic terms than was done in previous stories. It seems that the terror once experienced in the face of the unknown has now given way to a compromise won over many years. As Cortázar himself says in "Las fases de Severo": "It is always surprising to see how sudden lapses into normalcy, so to speak, distract and even deceive us" (135).

The different atmospheres that prevail in Cortázar's novels and short stories have become more obvious in these last few years. In the short stories man is as impotent as ever when faced with the exceptional in life, although at times he still seeks it out and plays to discover it. He now more easily accepts fleeting chance encounters and momentary outbursts of terror, after which he almost always returns in despair to accept routine life or to face death. In the novels, on the other hand, the author's joyful imagination fights to survive by means of unusual adventures, ingeniously playful language and political optimism. For instance, despite the descriptions of political torture, *Libro de Manuel* saves Cortázar's fiction from wallowing in the cynicism of the previous novel, *62*. As with *Rayuela*, *Libro de Manuel* embodies possible searches; and in opposition to the pervasive and definitive presence of death at the end of *62*, death in the final scenes of *Libro de Manuel* promises regeneration.

It is important to note that love continues to fail completely in the last two novels, for Juan and his friends in *62* as well as for Andrés in *Libro de Manuel*. Nevertheless, in the latter novel the pessimism generated by the absence of unselfish love between man and woman in the individual, personal sphere is diminished by optimism in the political and ideological sphere. *Octaedro* is very different from that latest novel, for these short stories are laden with death, tears, fleeting love affairs and impossible explanations. The pessimism that prevails on the personal level of love between man and woman is but one element of the human destinies that are ultimately altered very little by exceptional events and discoveries glimpsed through dreams, obsessions, dangerous provocations and even chance. *Octaedro* is a continuation of the Cortázar that we know, but there is a difference: Julio is finally accustomed to viewing the other zone of reality. He knows it is there. He experiences it. He tries to share it with us. But he finally must return from it to his everyday reality in despair.

[1] For a discussion of the "other reality" in Cortázar's works see the chapter "Swiss Cheese Reality" in *Julio Cortázar* by Evelyn Picon Garfield, New York, Ungar, 1975, pp. 11–76, and the chapter "La realidad dual" in *¿Es Julio Cortázar un surrealista?* by Evelyn Picon Garfield, Madrid, Gredos, 1975, pp. 13–72.

[2] *Blow-Up and Other Stories*, Paul Blackburn, tr., New York, Collier, 1963, pp. 190–91.

[3] Unpublished interview with Julio Cortázar by Evelyn Picon Garfield in July 1973. Subsequent personal comments by Cortázar are from this interview unless otherwise noted. The translations are my own.

[4] *Octaedro*, Buenos Aires, Sudamericana, 1975, pp. 78–79. Future references to this edition will be made in the text by citing the page number in parentheses directly after the passage. The translations are my own.

[5] Respectively: *La vuelta al día en ochenta mundos*, Mexico City, Siglo XXI, 1967, p. 68; *Rayuela*, Buenos Aires, Sudamericana, 1963, p. 197; *La vuelta al día*, p. 73.

[6] *Ultimo round*, Mexico City, Siglo XXI, 1969, pp. 44–45.

[7] Rosario Ferré, "Ocho caras del miedo," *Zona de carga y descarga*, Puerto Rico, 1975, pp. 11, 31.

[8] Pedro Lastra, Graciela Coulson, "El motivo del horror en *Octaedro*," *Nueva narrativa hispanoamericana*, 5 (1975), pp. 7–16.

[9] For a discussion of the influence of surrealist art on Cortázar's works see *¿Es Julio Cortázar un surrealista?*

[10] Luis Harss, Barbara Dohmann, *Into the Mainstream*, New York, Harper & Row, 1967, p. 227.

[11] For a discussion of "figures," chance and magnetic fields in Cortázar's works see *¿Es Julio Cortázar un surrealista?*, pp. 139–44, 167–73.

[12] *Hopscotch*, Gregory Rabassa, tr., New York, Pantheon, 1966, p. 425.

[13] For a discussion of "El amor y la mujer" in Cortázar's works see *¿Es Julio Cortázar un surrealista?*, pp. 96–118.

[14] For a discussion of the "happening" in Cortázar's works see *¿Es Julio Cortázar un surrealista?*, pp. 154–61.

[15] "El motivo del horror in *Octaedro*," pp. 13–14.

[16] Mexico City, Instituto de Investigaciones Estéticas, 1969, p. 77.

The Ambivalence of the Hand in Cortázar's Fiction

By MALVA E. FILER

Hands are of particular significance in Cortázar's fiction. We can notice their early appearance in "Estación de la mano" (Season of the Hand), a youthful short story included in *La vuelta al día en ochenta mundos*, their return in "No se culpe a nadie" (No One Is To Be Blamed) from *Final del juego*, chapters of *Rayuela* and *62: Modelo para armar* and, more recently, in "Cuello de gatito negro" (Neck of the Little Black Cat) from *Octaedro*. The recurrence of the theme is, by itself, meaningful. And after reading Cortázar's statement concerning his dreams and fears of "hands . . . capable of independent life,"[1] one is led to believe that the subject is important enough to deserve attention.

Hands are the members of the human body most actively involved in the individual's psychological and emotional life. They are a source and instrument of pleasure; they can give love and affection. They can also, however, hurt and kill. Within the individual, popular tradition has identified the right hand with the rational, the left with the irrational or instinctive aspects of the psyche. From there it is a short step to having a hand represent one of the conflicting forces that strive to achieve control of the self. The literary possibilities of this inner conflict, as a subject, are without boundaries, for this is the main preoccupation of any human being. And Cortázar has found many imaginative and daring ways of expressing this conflict in his fiction. I will not make any attempt to explain Cortázar's creations from the point of view of an exclusive psychoanalytic theory. Rather, I would like to relate the role he gives to hands to some attitudes or psychological problems, as shown particularly by his main characters.

Before touching on possible psychological connotations of our subject, however, I should point out that the image of autonomous hands is frequent in fantastic tales, especially in the nineteenth century. Authors such as Gérard de Nerval, Maupassant and Sheridan Le Fanu, to name just a few, made this theme popular and were followed by many others well into this century.[2] In "La estación de la mano" Cortázar mentions the "Étude de mains" by Gautier.[3] This is a very interesting reference, for Gautier's poems, under the respective titles "Impéria" and "Lacenaire," describe two different hands representing completely opposite values. Impéria, an Italian courtesan of the sixteenth century famous for her beauty and spiritual qualities, inspired some other French writers, among them Balzac.[4] Impéria's hand is described by Gautier as a delicate and beautiful jewel: "Comme une blanche poésie / S'épanouissait sa beauté." The poet associates it with images of luxury and sensuality, impossible dreams and bohemia. By contrast, Lacenaire was a murderer who, after a sensational trial, was executed in Paris in 1836. According to a statement made by Gautier, his friend Maxime du Camp had preserved the murderer's hand, and it was in his home that the poet saw it. The adjectives used in the poem make of this hand a symbol of evil.

In Cortázar's story the hand is introduced as a pleasant, affectionate presence, even though it is not described physically in detail. Its attributes are referred to indirectly, by its actions or by association: "The hand was light and it climbed up to its place effortlessly, its nimble fingers looking loose and distracted. Not at all demanding, it was like a bird or a dry leaf."[5] It happily blended with nature and freely moved about the room. The narrator and the hand, to which he gave the name Dg, lived in harmony for a while, until his curiosity and analytic spirit started to undermine this beautiful relationship. (When reading this page one is tempted to think of Dg as an early incarnation of La Maga.) The end is caused by suspicion and fear, as symbolized by the dream of Dg (a right hand) cutting the narrator's left hand. This marks the withdrawal of the hand and an end to the escape from the demands of reality.

By its mere undemanding presence Dg had transformed the life of the narrator. It had introduced beauty and love and a poetic feeling of mystery. Dg had rescued and liberated him from the limitations of life, with its duties and family relations. Without the hand there was nothing to do but put his finances in order, get dressed and walk through the city, the image of a correct and hopelessly average citizen. It is possible that in this early story, whose merits Cortázar has tried to dismiss,[6] we find an anticipation of a subject that is of significant importance in Cortázar's later works: the character's inability to enjoy love and beauty without analyzing it and destroying it in the process—a longing to liberate himself from routine and convention, and yet a lack of trust in that which is not rational. If not in the Manichean way of "Étude de mains," Cortázar shows nevertheless an obvious ambivalence in his feelings toward the hand.

Returning for a moment to Gautier, it is interesting to note that in one of his poems, "Cauchemar,"[7] there appears the image of the severed hand, its five contracted fingers threatening the self in much the same manner as we find in Cortázar's "No se culpe a nadie." The poem starts as follows:

> Avec ses nerfs rompus, une main écorchée
> Qui marche sans le corps dont elle est arrachée,
> Crispe ses doigts crochus armée d'ongles de fer
> Pour me saisir.

And yet the nightmare described by Gautier in horrifying, infernal terms is the expression of a soul who, terrorized as he might be by the image of death, can still face it from the fortress of an unquestioned, undivided self. However, the horror is compounded when, as in Cortázar's story, man becomes his own enemy and the self is turned into a battlefield for warring forces.

Among the many authors who have studied the psychological elements involved in a split of self and body,[8] R. D. Laing is perhaps the most illuminating. In his book *The Divided Self* he describes and documents cases of schizophrenia of various degrees of severity, where the illness occurs in response to the impossibility of keeping a unified sense of self-identity. In the schizoid condition, he finds, "There is a persistent scission between the self and the body. . . . The individual's being is cleft in two, producing a disembodied self and a body that is a thing that the self looks at, regarding it at times as though it were just another thing in the world."[9]

As we read "No se culpe a nadie," we find from the beginning the symptoms of such a schizoid condition in Cortázar's character. He looks at his hand (later on we find out that it is his right hand) as if it were not on his own. The only finger emerging from inside the pullover's sleeve looks wrinkled, contracted and has a pointed black nail. While reading this peculiar description at the beginning of the story, one gets an immediate hint of something uncanny, a feeling that rapidly increases to culminate in unmitigated horror. For the hand, no longer subject to its owner's will, scratches and pinches him, and finally the character's head emerges from the asphyxiating pullover, only to face five black nails striking against his eyes and pushing him into death.

What kind of inner conflict could be represented by this nightmare of having a part of the character's own body attack and destroy him? One wonders if the man with the blue pullover was not suffering from the restrictions of a very conventional life-style and the split was not a rebellion against that part of the self that had submitted to the tyranny of domestic and social duties. After all, the character had reluctantly moved to get dressed only because his wife would be waiting for him in a store, where they had to select a wedding gift. He had to put on the blue pullover, because it matched his gray suit. In Spanish, this last remark is made in the impersonal form: "hay que ponerse el pulóver azul, cualquier cosa que vaya bien con el traje gris,"[10] which sounds as if this was an unquestionable rule that the character would not even consider challenging. And yet putting on and taking off those acceptable clothes throughout the winter made him feel he was becoming increasingly withdrawn and alienated.

In Cortázar's fictional world this kind of routine life is the great scandal against which every individual must rebel with all his strength. And if he is not able or willing to do so, extraordinary elements are usually summoned to force him out of this despicable and abject comfort. In this respect it would be enough to recall "Casa tomada" (The House Taken Over) or "Carta a una señorita en París" (Letter to a Young Lady in Paris) from *Bestiario*. On the other hand, "Tema para San Jorge" (Theme for Saint George) from *La vuelta al día* shows his contempt and hatred for routine. In *Historias de cronopios y de famas* Cortázar expresses his rebellion against the objects and persons that make up our everyday life and the mechanical ways by which we relate to them. At the same time, he cannot help admitting that it is very tempting to accept this world, already organized for us, and to respect the established function of each one of its objects.[11] The five fingers that destroy the man with the blue pullover seem to perform a role equivalent to the materialized obsessions or doubles in his other stories. What is attacked is the imprisoned, mechanized or overly domesticated self. Only here the attacker is a part of the individual's own body, and the punishment is nothing less than total destruction.

Hands are very noticeable in Cortázar's novels, especially *Rayuela* and *62*. The hand, for Oliveira, would intercede to provide an escape from the limits of reason and find access to the "center," the object of his desperate search. "The arrival through illusions to a plane, a zone impossible to imagine, useless to attempt conception of because all thought destroyed it as soon as it attempted to isolate it. A hand of smoke took his hand, started him downward, if it was downward, showed him a center, if it was a center, . . . some sort of infinitely beautiful and desperate illusion which some time back he had called immortality."[12] Chapter 76 of *Rayuela* makes insistent reference to Pola's hands. Oliveira had not had a chance to find out her name, when Pola's hands were already the object of his obsessive attention. In fact, Oliveira meets Pola through her hands. And here again we find the idea of the hand as intercessor: "You moved that hand as if you were touching a limit, and after that a world against the grain began."

The introduction of Frau Marta in *62* is also made through references to her hands: "From an early stage our attention had been fixed on Frau Marta's hands, just as Tell, that morning at the Capricorno, had been caught by the arachnoid way in which Frau Marta had verbally entangled the English girl so as to win the right to go up to her table. Those hands had ended up by obsessing us."[13] There is a similarity between the description of Frau Marta's hands "riffling through an ancient black purse" and Pola's opening her purse, which gives Oliveira "the feeling that the clasp is guarding against an entry into a sign of the zodiac."[14] In both cases the hands symbolically open the way to some kind of mystical experience. But whereas Pola's hands, and hands generally in *Rayuela*, are never threatening, Frau Marta's hands are related to her "arachnoid ways" and altogether sinister appearance. They have "something of an owl about them, of blackish claws"; looking at them, Juan "ended up feeling . . . the emission of an incomprehensible language."[15]

The obsession with hands, clearly stated in *62*, finds a new expression in "Cuello de gatito negro." The situation includes, however, some significant new elements. The inner conflict is seen from outside, through the main character, whose only role is that of a catalytic agent. This time it is a woman who presents us with a split self. Her hands move on their own, totally free of any control or inhibition, causing her extreme anguish and embarrassment. The action starts on the subway, where the man finds himself in the unusual position of having a woman's fingers provocatively climbing over his own hand. Despite her claims of not being able to control her hands, the man feels encouraged into "pursuing the adventure and carrying it to the predictable sexual experience. However, the woman, fearful of yielding at first, soon loses any remnant of self-control. Her hands, turned into gaffs, viciously attack him, trying to castrate him, and her nails leave his face bleeding from his eyes and lips. The savage attack, which the desperate woman cannot prevent, comes after intensive sexual gratification and is as much aggressive toward the man as it is self-destructive. From this point of view "Cuello de gatito negro" brings back to the reader memories of "Circe" from *Bestiario*. For in the two stories the man makes the gesture to strangle the woman but does not complete the act that in both situations would seem more compassionate than leaving her a prey of her own self-destructive impulses.

If we try to summarize the different roles that hands play in Cortázar's fiction, we find that they seem to symbolize instinct, intuition, imagination and, in general, the irrational. Their presence is connected with different attempts at liberating the individual from the limitations of reason, moral convention and the mechanization by routine. However, the liberation of instincts which the author's characters have rationally advocated, particularly in *Libro de Manuel*, is nevertheless a source of anxiety at a deeper level. In fact, there seems to be sufficient reason to believe that Cortázar's characters are torn between the conscious desire to free their repressed instincts and the intensive fear and distrust of anything instinctive and irrational. They want to break the bars built by reason and morals but are at the same time extremely fearful of doing so. The struggle within the self often leads, as is shown above, to different degrees of aggression and self-destruction. If the interpretation proposed here were to be accepted as correct, it would help us to understand why the hand in Cortázar's fiction is an ambivalent if not altogether threatening presence.

[1] Evelyn Picon Garfield, *Julio Cortázar*, New York, Ungar, 1975, p. 145.

[2] The theme of the severed hand appears in Gérard de Nerval, "La main enchantée," in *La bohème galante*, Paris, Hilsum, 1932; Guy de Maupassant, "La main," of which there is an English version in *Short Stories*, New York, Dutton, 1967; Joseph Sheridan Le Fanu, *The House by the Church-Yard*, London, Blond, 1968, chapter 12; and among later authors, William F. Harvey, *The Beast with Five Fingers. Twenty Tales of the Uncanny*, New York, Dutton, 1947, and Maurice Sandoz, "The Hairy Hand," in *Fantastic Memories* (English version of *Souvenirs fantastiques*), New York, Doubleday, 1945.

[3] Théophile Gautier, *Poésies complètes*, Paris, Nizet, 1970. "Étude de mains" is part of *Émaux et camées*.

[4] Honoré de Balzac, "La belle Impéria" and "La belle Impéria mariée," in *Contes drolatiques*, vols. 36 and 37 of the *Oeuvres complètes*, Paris, Conrad, 1912–32.

[5] Julio Cortázar, *La vuelta al día en ochenta mundos*, Mexico City, Siglo XXI, 1967, p. 167. The translation is my own.

[6] In a marginal note added to the story by the author he uses words such as "silly," "pretentious" and "naïve" to describe its quality. However, tenderness and nostalgia are also evoked by this product of a younger period. One wonders if Cortázar's rating of his own work is really as negative as the derogatory adjectives just quoted seem to indicate.

[7] *Poésies complètes*, p. 18. The epigraph, taken from Nerval's *La main de gloire*, is also meaningful, for it gives the image of nails as sharp claws waiting to devour their victim and throw him into the mouth of the abyss—that is, death.

[8] In his essay on "The Uncanny" (The Standard Edition of the Complete Psychological Works, London, 1955, vol. 17) Sigmund Freud links the uncanniness of dismembered limbs, such as a severed head or a hand cut off at the wrist, and particularly when they prove capable of independent activity, to the castration complex. Karl Menninger studies the implications of different cases and degrees of self-mutilation in *Man Against Himself*, New York, Harcourt Brace & World, 1938.

[9] London, Penguin, 1975, pp. 78, 162.

[10] *Final de Juego*, Buenos Aires, Sudamericana, 1964, p. 13.

[11] *Historias de cronopios y de famas*, Buenos Aires, Minotauro, 1966, pp. 11–12.

[12] *Hopscotch*, Gregory Rabassa, tr., New York, Pantheon, 1966, p. 49.

[13] *62: A Model Kit*, Gregory Rabassa, tr., New York, Pantheon, 1972, pp. 79–80.

[14] *Hopscotch*, p. 389.

[15] *62: A Model Kit*, pp. 80–81.

The New Man (But Not the New Woman)

By MARTHA PALEY FRANCESCATO

Persio, Oliveira, Juan, Andrés and Marcos are some of the characters that stand out most, that are most discussed in the work of Julio Cortázar. Who is responsible for the excessive attention that is concentrated on the masculine characters: the critic or the writer? On numerous occasions, critics have emphasized the role of such characters. The writer's literary work offers the opportunities that the critics have used well. But it is Cortázar himself who constructs the bridges. It is not my intention to censure that attitude, nor do I want to condone it. In these necessarily limited pages I will try to focus on the world of fiction in which the most important characters act, and I will try to concentrate on the relationship between man and woman, which is one of the basic relationships of that literary world. The initial question arose from a previous article in which I analyzed the trajectory of the new man in the stories of Cortázar. In concluding it, I asked myself: yes, the new man. But what about the woman?

It is always Oliveira, Juan, Andrés that we hear about. Why not La Maga, Hélène, Ludmilla? Or is the reader supposed to accept the term "man" as meaning "human being," which would also include woman? I don't think so. When Cortázar refers to the "new man" he means precisely that: man. And the term does not include the woman, although Cortázar himself has insisted he refers to both the man and the woman. On the other hand, why *not* only "new man"? A writer—a man—who writes in a world dominated by men, does not have to give woman equal importance. Or should he? In the course of the following discussion, I propose that we forget Cortázar the man. All references will be to Cortázar the writer. And in Cortázar's fictional world, I want to try to understand, to emphasize, the actions and relationships of the characters, men and women—and children. Yes, we must not forget the latter: there is also Manuel, whom everybody wants to help get into a different cycle, at the same time salvaging for him some remains of the total shipwreck. Manuel—the newest new man.

As for La Maga, it is not in her head that her center lies; she is always clumsy and absentminded: "Even Perico Romero had to admit that, for a female, La Maga really took the cake." For a female. On the one hand, the treatment given to her is condescending; on the other hand, Horacio frankly admires her. Horacio's search cannot exist without her, in the same way that he later needs Talita. Although the two women act as Horacio's Vergil, the protagonist, the axis and center of the action is still Dante, Horacio, *the man*.

There is condescension, again, in the need to explain that women could also be "my paredros" in *62: A Model Kit*. It is so difficult to break through the barriers, through the beliefs imposed by society, by an ancestral tradition. "Oh, the pride of the male," Tell cannot help but answer after listening to Juan try to explain his conduct:

> There are times when I feel like a cynic, when the taboos of the race throw me their claws; then I think that I do you wrong, that I objectify you, if you'll allow the expression, that I abuse your happiness, that I put you there and push you

away, . . . that I take you with me only to let you fall later when it is time to be sad or alone. And you, on the other hand, have never made an object of me, unless deep down you pity me and keep me as a daily good deed, your Girl Scout merit badge or something like that.[1]

In response, Tell puts on a maternal attitude, which is at the same time somewhat sarcastic: "But I don't pity you, my child, an object can't pity a man." Juan defends himself:

—You're not an object. I didn't mean that, Tell.
—You didn't mean it but you did say it.
—In any case I said it as a reproach, accusing myself.
—Oh, poor little man, poor little man . . . (67)

Poor man, no one understands him! He is an involuntary victim of his own beliefs, of his desires to overcome the taboos imposed upon him by society.

Hélène, on the surface, is similar to Tell: emancipated, sure of herself, admirable. When the Tell-Juan-Hélène triangle is completed, she too becomes an object, and incredibly, she is happy in that role: "I felt him trembling against me, I offered him my mouth, dirty with words, thanking him for making me be silent, for turning me into an obedient object in his arms" (238). An obedient object. Is it possible that, deep down, Hélène wishes a man to put her in her role as an object, which—who knows?— makes her feel more of a woman? And this woman is precisely the one who is apparently stronger, more independent, less insecure and more decided.

While Juan "objectifies" his two women, perhaps helping them, in his way, the other masculine characters of *62* give us other visions of women: " 'Women are always bloodthirsty,' said Calac with a background of grunts of approval from Polanco and my paredros"; or " 'There is nothing like women,' says Marrast, 'whether a heart is beating or not, the only thing they see is a gold lock.' " On this occasion "my paredros" offers, instead of an approving grunt, a recrimination: "Don't be misogynistic." Marrast himself, at the time Nicole leaves him to go to bed with Austin, bursts out with a description of the incident to Tell, simultaneously revealing his idea of women:

> If I returned to the hotel now I'd kill her
> the chestnut tree dirty with birds hurts me here, Tell, all of you
> bitches all with birds all of you bitches and I am Tell
> with his outrage saving his sex a true man
> my poor bitch poor poor little bitch
> a man safe with his bitch inside
> a man because of bitch
> only because of that
> and then bitch and then bitch and then bitch
> I believe because it's absurd. (198)

It's all right: Marrast is drunk; he is a Frenchman. Nicole, in love with Juan, goes to bed with Austin so that Marrast may have a good excuse to leave her with no scruples or conscience. But why "bitch"? Why are *all* women bitches? Just because he is drunk, sad, in anguish? The fact of *being*, of *being a man*, implies that the woman is a bitch: "a man because of bitch only because of that . . ."

Medrano, Horacio, Juan, Johnny Carter—all are men who live searching for something. La Maga, without knowing it, already has it. She has already found it.

Hélène also goes out searching; she suffers with the package she carries, which gets heavier all the time, but which at the end falls, together with her. And Andrés, especially Andrés, the prototype of the new man. This discovery of the new man, an idea which is so basic and vital in the work of Cortázar, is developed in his writings until it reaches a decisive moment in *Libro de Manuel*. In "The Island at Noon" the protagonist, in whom the struggle between the old man and the new man is concentrated, suffers a defeat. But is it really a defeat? The fact that he has faced the problem and that he has been able to enjoy his existence as "new man," although briefly, makes that defeat only a partial one. Marini struggles and is conscious of that struggle. The people that surround him—and in this case they are men as well as women—do not understand what he is looking for, do not share his vision of the journey to the island.

This journey is an introduction to another journey, the one Andrés undertakes in *Libro de Manuel*. His decision signifies the triumph of the new man, although even this triumph may not be considered complete. Andrés doubts whether his involvement in the "Joda" is because he really wants to participate, or because he thinks Ludmilla will be there. Parallel to this, Ludmilla's journey is explained in her dialogue with Susana: " 'Now I really understand why you are here,' Susana said, although she had understood since the beginning. 'You are one of those who stake their lives for their men when the situation arises.' 'I want to be wherever he is, and besides the theatre is closed today.' "[2]

Ludmilla gets involved in "La Joda" gradually until, because of her relationship with Marcos, she finally decides to join. Andrés is torn by doubt from the beginning, and his internal struggle is constant and heartbreaking, full of anguish, fear, hesitation, questions: "How can you know why the hell, through what craze, because of what black spot of the bitchy mother he goes on walking along this road which leads to a forest, to that other black spot getting closer and closer?" (352–53) Through several pages Andrés reasons out and establishes the possibilities until he makes a decision. We only know about Ludmilla through the above-quoted phrases.

Another aspect that is expressed and developed at length in the same novel is the view that two characters, Marcos and Andrés, have of women. Marcos, especially, is quite explicit; Andrés acts as a commentator, as a receptor who at times approves, as a balancing factor. According to Marcos,

> Women don't lack the ability to exert themselves, but they tend to apply it to the negative, that is to say that when they don't like something, or everything goes wrong in politics or in the kitchen, then they are capable of such rage, such indignation, such eloquence that you would laugh at Stokely Carmichael. They have their motor accelerated the wrong way, I mean that they are champions when it comes to putting on the brake, I don't know if you follow me. (116)

Another reference that Andrés makes on this subject shows a paternalistic tone, the assuredness of a man who knows women well and can explain their behavior: "I, for instance, don't expect a woman to go crazy over a painting by Max Ernst or over a musical piece by Xenakis; they have their own metabolism, brother, and besides, how are we to tell whether at bottom they are not more enthusiastic than we are, only that you shouldn't confuse exercises with emotion" (115). That is, one shouldn't expect from women certain reactions that belong only to men. The tone of Andrés's words does not go beyond a mere concession: "who knows . . . ," "maybe women . . . ," "perhaps we don't know them as well as . . ."

Lonstein, more removed from women, more impatient than Marcos, confronts Andrés with a precise and centered vision of the problem: "In any case it is fine that you have realized that the mental world of the Argentines is not the whole world, and in the second place that the whole world is not a privilege of the males, anyone can project geometry, you thought that your scheme was acceptable and now you find out that women also have their triangle to say" (344). They have their triangle to say—in some cases. In other cases they exist only as expert translators or in the preparation of sandwiches, a task which they undertake quite often. They also appear as guerrillas, but as such they do not form part of the action of the novel. The "Joda" gives them an opportunity of participating: "In the *Joda* there was no discrimination, why shouldn't the maenads be there preparing sandwiches, even though the bachelors, who were naturally French, expressed their disapproval, which was received with general indifference. Let them come, Roland had finally given in, this will look like a soccer field on a Sunday" (298). It is true: there is no discrimination, especially when it comes to making sandwiches. It's all right; only the French (bachelors, at that) are opposed to women's participation. Finally, even though reluctantly, women are accepted. And thus woman surmounts another obstacle and takes a big step forward in her search, in her struggle to defeat the "old woman," and to make the "new woman" emerge. The sandwiches she makes will help her greatly in her undertaking.

Woman, in her established and accepted role, is more an observer than a participant; she is more passive than adventurous, and much more repressed than man in expressing herself. This last characteristic is developed in the scene where everyone goes to see Lonstein's mushroom:

> They are all the same, the coephori protested, it was worth seeing, it is an extraordinary mushroom, a scientific phenomenon, but none of the women said that it was beautiful, that it grew just like that which they were all thinking about, and naturally Heredia was the one to establish the analogy, it is precisely what happens to me when I see a good miniskirt, the *lapsus* grows at once, great applause from the coephori. You talk to them about pricks and they get all upset, Lonstein said resentfully. (182)

The only one of the women who cannot be accused is Ludmilla, who answers with her phrase "red prick and hairy cunt." On saying that, she gains Heredia's respect and Oscar is stupefied. Heredia respects her for being a woman who dares to pronounce these words; Oscar is stupefied because a woman is not expected to pronounce them. But even this phrase of Ludmilla's, which could rescue her from the verbal inferiority of women, is attacked by Marcos: "You make use of that phrase all the time, but I don't know if you realize that it is quite vulgar / Andrés and Patricio said it was in style / You save it only for big occasions" (284). As soon as a woman surmounts an obstacle, man puts a stop to her, pushes her back again. Marcos observes that, with the exception of the Chilean *pico*, which is a rare example of masculinization, all the Latin American or Argentine terms for the male sexual organ are feminine in grammatical gender. This linguistic peculiarity could partially explain man's aggressive feelings. The fact that the part of him that makes him a *man* should be designated in feminine terms could explain an unexpressed resentment, a grudge that he holds against woman. All women, even a man's mother, are therefore guilty of feminizing his virility.

Women take a step forward and are placed in a more salient position in the two most recent works by Cortázar. In "Homage to a Young Witch" (1972)[3] the writer discovers Rita Renoir through a road that leads him to the world of the comic strips. In that world he discovers Valentina, yes, "pretty Valentina, Valentina all thighs and breasts, of course I'm joking and I'm not placing you on the shelf of Emma Bovary and not even Scarlett O'Hara" (75). Valentina shares a special section along with other heroines such as Barbarella and Phoebe Zeit-Geist, but she is obviously above them, in the same way that Rita Renoir surpasses them all. Cortázar, without having even seen her personally, already admired her "for intellectual reasons," having seen some photographs in a magazine which led him to say to himself "but then this woman, this consumer's object from the Lido and the Crazy Horse" (76). He discovered in the photographs the first open rebellion, a whipping aimed at all the audiences who paid to see her and applauded her while they scorned her. Then he goes on to describe the experience of seeing Rita Renoir on stage, a shuddering experience in front of an uncensored body, while she danced and made love to an invisible devil:

> The witch comes forward on the stage, and her body, which has known the art of showing itself to a point that neither Valentina nor the managers of cabarets will ever transgress, is going to be possessed by the looks of an audience that cannot believe it, that darkly fears that delegation of powers which gives it the supreme right to objectify at its complete will one of the most beautiful women of our times. (78)

As he is witnessing the most daring of stripteases, the writer feels the birth of the new man through this experience: "The man, yes, old emblem of the phoenix rising from the ashes of an error of twenty centuries; yet no longer another phoenix but a different bird, another way of looking at oneself, another road to orgasm and the word, another building of the socialism of the liberated body, without guilt" (79).

Rita Renoir surpasses shy Valentina: "Rita Renoir, sick and tired of the conventional striptease, goes beyond the apparent limits of the erotic toward the obscene, knowing that this road against all convention is equivalent for her and, hopefully, for others, to the abolition of the limits, to the denunciation of its deepest lie" (79). It is a question now of trying to understand what is happening on the stage if something of the old man has been destroyed, of learning to love the body in its entirety, of learning to look at it with the look of the new man. But which body is it we are looking at? *It is the body of the woman*, even though the writer mentions "our body and all bodies." It is the body of the woman on the stage which has motivated the writer to express what he has witnessed, to find the new man this time through an erotic experience. As a conclusion to the text, Cortázar says: "I don't like easy praise, I'm just saying that, since two nights ago, I have a respect for Rita Renoir that I don't always have for many women who are dressed from head to toe" (80). The writer feels the need to communicate his experience to the readers, to the male readers especially. It is not a question of women's being passive females or of their being shocked by the description or of their not understanding it. It is not that. I simply ask: Can a woman feel a rebirth as a "new woman" after such an experience as the one narrated, or is this rebirth reserved only for men?

We also find another woman in Cortázar's recent *Fantomas contra los vampiros multinacionales*.[4] Because of the mysterious disappearance of books and the burning of the libraries all over the world, Fantomas gets in touch with the greatest contemporary writers. The narrator wonders who they are. The answer lies in an order Fantomas gives to his secretary Libra. (Once more, the roles fit in with tradition: the master is a man, the secretary a woman; the master commands, the secretary obeys.) The greatest contemporary writers are Julio Cortázar, Octavio Paz, Alberto Moravia and Susan Sontag. Although listed last of the four, at least a woman is included among the best writers. And when she happens to be the only one who has found out the true conspiracy, the men do not understand what she is talking about. They need to arrive at the discovery of truth through reasoning; Susan has arrived through her own means (intuition?) before anyone else. The men, although they do not understand, accept what she proposes to them. "The matriarchate makes itself felt and I obey," Julio explains to Alberto. Woman does not need to explain her actions, and man does not require her explanations. It is the obedience to a group that every day is asking for more of what rightfully belongs to it; screaming more and more loudly, it makes itself heard, and it is the one entity that can find the truth.

At the end of this narration there is a small blond boy sitting on the curb. Like Manuel, he symbolizes the utopia that can be fulfilled in the future, the newest of new men, with the morning sun shining on his blond hair, a new man in the dawn of the new day. And the woman?

---

[1] *62: Modelo para armar*, Buenos Aires, Sudamericana, 1968, p. 67. Subsequent references are to this edition. The translations are my own.

[2] *Libro de Manuel*, Buenos Aires, Sudamericana, 1973, p. 302. Subsequent references are to this edition. The translations are my own.

[3] In *El Urogallo*, 6, nos. 31–32 (January-April 1975), pp. 72–80. Subsequent references are to this edition. The translations are my own.

[4] Mexico City, Excelsior, 1975.

Ontological Fabulation: Toward Cortázar's Theory of Literature

By SARA CASTRO-KLARÉN

> *Apenas soy aquel que ayer soñaba.*
> A. Machado, *Campos de Castilla*

> *The symbolic function must always be ahead of its object and finds reality only by anticipating it in imagination.*
> Maurice Merleau-Ponty, *Signs*

It is almost a commonplace to say that modern literature is nurtured by the suspicion of language. The word is no longer thought to be an unequivocal "representation" of the object, and thought is not conceivable as independent of the phenomenon of language.[1] Furthermore, language itself has proven to be grounded in an opaque resistance to the tools of analytical reason. The ensuing radical mistrust of reason and of the possibility of knowledge has done away with the visible world of empirical epistemology and realism as its corollary in the arts. With the realization that neither the world of our sensory perception nor our knowledge of it can ever be held to be absolutely independent of the perceiver, the writer is now engaged in the pursuit of an invisible world. The ruses and murky secrets of the word, the sign or form have become the central concern of the artist's craft. If the writer or the speaker is to comprehend language, he must dwell in it and above all he must use it critically.

Julio Cortázar writes within this critical awareness of language and of form in general. His work—short stories, "novels," "essays"—embodies simultaneously the suspicion and the investigation of the mind and therefore of man. He conceives of man as a "monstrous fabulating machine" forever weaving in the loom of form or, if you wish, in his dialectic encounter with the world. Although in *Ultimo round* he openly acknowledges the generating force of all his work to be metaphysical,[2] we must not misunderstand and think that Cortázar is in search of some ideal principle whereby everything, including man, can be explained to the satisfaction of our reason. His search is indeed ontological,[3] but this simply means that what the author of so many "fantastic" and humorous texts is after is a revelation of man and his proclivity for invention, his tendency to establish a dialectic with the Other. Cortázar conceives of the fissures created by and in between the acts of writing and reading as a singularly appropriate standpoint from which to dwell on man's movement toward an ever new image of himself and the world.

My purpose here is to show that Cortázar's keen exercise of the critique of form (novel, essay, poem) and his overt, challenging and even cruel relationship to his reader are exceptionally conscious and successful representations of contemporary epistemology—sometimes broadly labeled as phenomenology. It holds that the matrix of the world's reality or meaning, be it scientific or poetic, rational or magic, rests on man's imagination. Moreover, man, although the source of meaning in his encounter with the world, is himself also invisible; and thus his being is inescapably invention or, as Cortázar would have it, it is "writing, that is to say, a fable."[4] Cortázar expects us to greet this unsettling proposition with great joy and laughter, as his *cronopios*[5] often do, for he believes that if man should become aware of his free and "porous" condition, he might be able to harbor seriously the hope of finding himself. Such a state of awareness would lead to what he calls an "epiphany."

Because Cortázar claims—and I think correctly so—that his writing is a search for being and that being for him and, he hopes, for his reader comes about in the exercise of the critical imagination, I have chosen to call his esthetic praxis and theory "ontological fabulation." It recognizes no *a priori* limits or conditions to man's knowledge or invention of his own being, and it obviously rejects any deterministic postulates such as human destiny or human nature. Because it is basically an ontology of becoming, the symbols Cortázar finds most emblematic of his position and search are the sponge and the chameleon.[6] Ontological fabulation makes no claim about man other than 1) a recognition of the porous (sponge-like) condition of his consciousness and his acts (full of something other than itself = phenomenological intentionality) and 2) a sense of a constant longing to be the Other (chameleon-like) or simply to be ("ausia de ser").

Unlike most other Latin American writers, with the principal exceptions or Jorge Luis Borges and Octavio Paz, Cortázar has frequently made esthetics the topic of his concern. He has explicitly tried to deal with a general poetics in "Para una poética"[7] and with a theory of the short story in *La vuelta al día*. One could say, however, that starting with *Rayuela* most of his work is implicitly or explicitly dedicated to the exploration of esthetic problems and to the elaboration of an esthetic theory for his own oeuvre. *Rayuela*, for instance, is not just the critique of realistic narrative or even of discourse in general, but is also and necessarily "in some way the philosophy of my short stories, an inquiry on the nature of what determined in the course of many years their material or their impuse" (*La vuelta al día*, p. 25). With each subsequent work Cortázar seems to have embarked on a critique of his previous writing. *Rayuela* is an alternate form or a critique of *Los premios*, just as *La vuelta al día* assembles reflections on *Rayuela*, and *Ultimo round*, describing an ever-widening circle, encompasses the critique of *62: Modelo para armar*, itself an experiment on some of Morelli's reflections on the novel. In *La vuelta al día* he says that writing for him is "a kind of constant play, which explains—if not justifies—much of what I have written or lived. People criticize in my novels . . . an *intellectual search* of the novel itself, which would be a kind of continuous commentary on the action and many times the action of a commentary" (p. 21).

Steady and successful in his struggle to erase the Western division between the rational and the irrational, the physical and the metaphysical, the tragic and the comic, Cortázar has imbedded esthetics into the linguistic object. Nevertheless, one can discern two main postulates to his theory of literature. 1) Fundamentally, Cortázar posits a porous, non-substantial, open structure for the self, the world and knowledge. At the root of this vision of porousness is a feeling of incompleteness (*falencia*), of dislocation (*descolocación*; see *La vuelta al día*, pp. 21, 25), of estrangement (*extrañamiento*; see *Ultimo round*, p. 42), which leads the poet to an awareness of existing alongside or parallel to something "other" (*lo otro*). 2) This in turn implies the eternal presence of the Other as the orientation of being. Cortázar maintains that the poet "thirsting for being" (*La vuelta al día*, p. 212) in the act of creation, manages to fuse his anxious being to the ontological qualities of the contemplated object which, thus subjected to the process of creation, relinquishes its entity to the enrichment of the poet's being. The

Other is that which is able to release alien degrees of being to the enrichment of the specific human condition.[8] Thus the poet is in search for the possession of reality at the ontological level of being in order to expand his own sense of being.

For Cortázar, reality, meaning, knowledge, whatever we may choose to call it, is not found there, at the goal line of a chase; rather, "it is always [found] *between*, interstitially . . . [and] the only thing capable of aiding its *progress* (toward it) is the provocation of interstitial eruptions without any pretention of encompassing the entire surface of the phenomenal sponge" (*Ultimo round*, p. 108). "Reality" would seem to be conceived of as a phenomenon in constant dynamic realization, and it should therefore not be conceived of as static in perception. It is, rather, a question of provoking or discovering "las fisuras de lo aparencial" (*La vuelta al día*, p. 24).

In *Ultimo round*, discussing his theory of the short story, Cortázar acknowledges Mallarmé's work on the theory that meaning resides in the articulation of what is between the signs, in the gaps and intervals created by them. Nevertheless he chooses to quote from a Hindu text, perhaps in order to suggest the universality of the theory itself, which states that "reality glitters" when consciousness of the interval has simultaneously eliminated both "things" (*Ultimo round*, pp. 108–109). In the same text Cortázar finds further corroboration for his own orientation toward gaps and the Other in Felisberto Hernandez's dictum on the obligation of the writer to write not only about what he knows but also about *lo otro*. The task of the writer is then "to reach the limit between that which is known and the Other, because there is a beginning of transcendence."[9]

The Other leads a life of silence in the existing intervals among all "things" (perceptions, acts, feelings, thoughts, objects). Thus, according to Felisberto and Cortázar, the artist must seek to articulate the silent meaning of what resides in the interval between objects (= perceptual forms). Speaking of the relation existing between signs, Merleau-Ponty says that "signs taken singly do not signify anything and . . . each of them does not so much express meaning as mark a divergence of meaning between itself and other signs" (*Signs*, p. 39). If we extend this statement to cover larger "things" or forms such as the types that Cortázar experiments with—character/spasmodic character, plot/chance events, Spanish/gliglish; poem/permutating poem—we will find that "meaning" is not contained in either of the two parallel forms[10] or "things," but rather in the gap of consciousness of forms created by their lateral existence.

From the above we can infer that Cortázar supposes a "reality" that is fundamentally discontinuous, porous and dynamic[11] and an epistemology that shares those same characteristics. Jazz, especially in its compositional dynamism, has been one of his favorite analogies for his sense of reality. In the fluid, forever-becoming structure of the improvised jazz melody he finds liberation from "the crab of *the identical* to gain the sponge of porous simultaneity" (*La vuelta al día*, p. 7). The sponge's fundamental characteristic is of course its net- or weblike structure. It is full of gaps, and one cannot say whether it is the links separated by gaps or the gaps separated by links which determine our image of the sponge. Because it is paradoxically made of gaps and because it is therefore open and porous, it is obligated to exist in an osmotic relationship with everything that it is and is not full of at the same time. The sponge exhales and inhales otherness,[12] and in doing so it violates the main Aristotelian principles of being: a fixed and limited unity in space and a complete identicalness in all its aspects. Even if we were to squeeze out the sponge, it would still be full of air and not of "itself"; thus like man it is irrevocably oriented to be sensitive to what it is not.

To say that reality, meaning or being is porous like a sponge amounts to stating that the known formulated meaning exists webbed in together with the unknown and the nonsensical. They cannot be considered self-exclusive or for that matter linearly ordered, for they are paired in a sort of constant flux of mutual need. A porous sense of reality or meaning implies therefore an unstable, changing vision of knowledge which is basically self-generating and self-determining. But we must not assume here that knowledge leads a life different from or independent of man. Knowledge is simply a dimension of man, and whatever we may say about it, we are by implication saying the same of man. If knowledge or signification is self-generating, it is because man is never content to rest with what is constituted. On the contrary, man is forever moving on toward that which he is not (*lo otro*), toward a world which does not as yet exist but which may exist in the intervals, in the gaps of his porous condition.

This notion of self-generating and self-determining knowledge or reality is neither unique nor original to Cortázar. It has been at the root of the epistemology of contemporary science especially since the theory of relativity taught us to think of objects as being essentially in movement and not "naturally" at rest. The Aristotelian conception of substance becomes untenable in view of the fact that exchanges in energy determine modification in matter and modifications in matter condition exchanges in energy. Energy has to be regarded, then, as an integral part of substance, and so we have to conceive of substance as an unstable, porous and dynamic phenomenon given in time. Substance is no longer a discrete, identical, spatially fixed object, but rather something more like form (perception of a set of relations).[13]

The dissolution of substance is also a phenomenon in contemporary chemistry. At the infinitesimal level of chemical substance, at which point being would be expected to be most empirically objective and fixed, it paradoxically appears to be a scientific category in itself. Writing on the false realism of chemistry, Gaston Bachelard says that chemical elements are concretions of circumstances selected in the application of a general law, because a powerful *a priori* force developed within previous knowledge guides the experiment. The objectively real in science becomes, then, nothing but a *realization* or the manifestation of form (in Cortázar's language, it would be called an epiphany), inasmuch as it is a formulation oriented toward the unknown but imbedded in the scientific structure which anticipated it. In organic chemistry, for instance, the DNA chain was known before the nature of the links could be spelled out. The series were known before the substances themselves. Bachelard makes the point that, as a result, the reality of "the substance was dethroned, as it were, by the rigor of the method, for true chemical substances are the products of technique rather than bodies found in reality" (*The Philosophy of No*, pp. 45–50 passim). The real in chemistry is, then, a realization or a formulation and in that sense no different from any plastic or linguistic form.

Thus it seems that, in science, becoming is the undertow of being. What was at one point believed to be the unalterable substance of an object has been demonstrated to be a figment of man's capacity for formulation, that is to say, the product of man's subjective projection of order and of relation. In Cortázar's mind, which, as noted, holds that everything is writing or fable, the scientist's creation of reality is no different from the writer's commitment to explore and expand the notion of reality, for they are both engaged in inventing or fabulating the world and man himself. Invention for Cortázar comes about within the desideratum of the unknown (*lo otro*), which is prompted by the feeling that something is amiss or absent (*falencia*) and yet already present in the gaps or interstices. It is the force of what is known or of the existing form, culled by the unknown which it both contains and is surrounded by, that brings forth what Cortázar calls the birth of a crystal, the "realization" of a phenomenon, an "epiphany." In this regard he says that his writing is guided by a sense of incompleteness or dislocation, "and since I write from an interstice, I am always inviting others to look for theirs and see through them the garden where the trees bear fruits which are, of course, precious stones" (*La vuelta al día*, p. 21). His "incomplete" or "unfinished" novels, essays and poems, then, are a reminder to all men—his readers—of their own need to engage in invention, which is held to be the hallmark of being human.

However, invention or fabulation should not be equated with the unbridled or forgetful babbling of free association. Cortázar is proposing and is relying on a rigorous sense of play and invention which must be "faithful to the theme which it struggles with, transforms and refracts" (*La vuelta al día*, p. 7). Invention therefore is not a simple capricious denial of the known and a displacement toward any new image whatsoever, because as it moves from the form to the "anti-form" or to the unknown, it is critically thoughtful of the form it parallels and transforms. Critical writing or fabulating, for the author of *Rayuela*, is similar to non-Euclidian mathematics,[14] inasmuch as the latter does not abandon Euclidian principles but recognizes them instead as a positive error or point of departure. Cortázar would find that the thrust of Bachelard's "philosophy of no"[15] makes the case for a critical epistemology of science, which supports his own idea that to "fabulate" is to "choose the profile, almost the absence of the theme, evoking it as perhaps matter evokes anti-matter" (*La vuelta al día*, p. 7).

The fiction that Cortázar writes is a challenge and a mockery of the empirical epistemology of nineteenth-century realism and twentieth-century everyday understanding of the world, but it is not born out of a simple egotistical desire to do something "new" or escape the "real" world into "fantasy." Quite to the contrary, Cortázar is trying to write with a living awareness and with a desire to create a world in harmony with the scientific "facts" and theories of his own times. Like Jarry, one of his dearest inspirational *cronopios*, the author of *La vuelta al día en ochenta mundos* seems only too aware of the meaning of contemporary science. Moreover, he believes that "nothing can better cure us of anthropocentrism, author of all our ills, than to take a look at the physics of the infinitely large or small" (*La vuelta al día*, p. 17). The world of ordinary perception—Euclidian localization, fixed identity, time and space—must give way to a living consciousness of the world of becoming and of the invisible, to the world of the macro-objects (black holes) and micro-objects (electrons, radiation), in which our everyday sense of space, time and being breaks down (see *La vuelta al día*, pp.

64 ff.) Inside a black hole, for instance, time and space become interchangeable, so that to remain in one place is as impossible as to stop the "passage" of time. Bodies entering or falling into a black hole would be stretched out like a string (perhaps like the spasmodic characters of *Rayuela* or *62*) and would then disintegrate, but the image of the disappearing body would linger at the fringes of the hole where light does not have enough energy to escape, preserving at its periphery a margin of shadows.

If contemporary science and philosophy (for example Merleau-Ponty's *Phenomenology of Perception*) hold that one can no longer conceive and speak of the world in terms of things but only in terms of arrested phenomena constantly being constituted in time, how could anyone continue to write as if the world of naïve sensory perception were indeed the way the world is perceived? We seem to have here a turning of the tables, and such reversal rests on the proposition "as if." Empiricism and its concomitant descriptive and psychological realism seem now to be based on the implausible "as if" assumptions of our everyday routine, whereas Cortázar's "fabulation" is trying to depict a world more attuned with what we actually "know" about language, thinking, perception and scientific "truths." If, as urged by Bachelard, we leave "sensory perception to its purely affective role, its role as an auxiliary in everyday action, [we] shall thus conclude with a determination of a phenomenon in space which is *thought* and in time which is [also] *thought*" (*Philosophy of No*, p. 94).

Cortázar's sense of writing is to navigate in a world in which neither time nor space is an *a priori* category for "objective" reality or the self, but simply thought. Without the barrier of localization in space, and having done away with the false "before and after" order of causality as an explanation for the way things are or come about (character, plot, story), Cortázar is ready to plunge, in the company of his reader, into "las más vertiginosas aventuras humanas" (*Ultimo round*, p. 70). To make the passage enjoyable as well as to assure a good chance of reaching the interstices (the gaps within the sponges)—the islands of our destination—timid imagination must be prepared to embark in the charting of this invisible world of realization. The journey from the sold and luminous beaches of the known to the uncharted location of the interstices will be full of exhausting intellectual games of exploration and experimentation.

With *Rayuela*, his *roman comique*, he attempts the assault, or rather the persuasion to the idea that "Everything is writing, that is to say, a fable.... Our possible truth must be an *invention*, that is to say, scripture, Nuestra verdad posible tiene que ser invencion, es decir escritura, literatura, pintura, agricultura, pscicultura, in this world" (chapter 73). For him literature is not art, beauty or morals; it is the creation of images or perceptual phenomena which in themselves are the world. The scientist and the writer have an identical task: namely, experimenting, as if there were no referent outside of thought. Man's world—the only one possible—is then invented, and it grows with the pace of imagination.[16] In writing, Cortázar experiments with what he calls "rotting writing" (*Rayuela*, ch. 94)—and I would add rotting categories such as book, sequence, plot, cause and effect, character, motivation—hoping that the process of decomposition will reveal the elements in isolation and also the gaps existing among them. However, as Bachelard has shown to be the case for chemical substances, this process of decomposition by which the elements are shown as such eventually demonstrates that the elements themselves disintegrate into the insubstantiality of thought. So while Cortázar is hoping to get away from the sedimented layers of habit and traditional use of language by letting them decompose to their purest elements, he finds only more thought and more mind. The great gain will, however, be the very recognition of this process, for as the mind encounters itself in unsuspected attitudes and activities, the sense of being vibrates in creative imagination.

If our thought can be referred only to more thought and if our "knowledge" is fabulation or invention in an invisible world, then art cannot be thought ever to be a "reflection" of any "real world." It is an effort destined to show the transparency of the mind or, if you wish, of the object; for one constitutes the other, and the passage of this eternal, reciprocal constitution is the imagination. Unfortunately, we learn to accept only too quickly a dichotomy between the "real" and the "unreal," and so we think of imagination as part of the unimportant and useless unreal, forgetting in some cases and never realizing in others that without the imagination we could not even get through our plans for the routine of the day. Imagination does not differ from reality. It is reality itself (it is the rear of the house we see, even though we do not actually *see* it while standing in front of it; it is the *mancuspias*, the imaginary beings in the short story "Cefalea" whose unseen and intangible torments are only too "real" to the readers and characters of *Bestiario*), and as such it has come to dominate the preoccupations of the artist. Invention and/or imagination have become the very subject of the novel. Novels such as Nabokov's *Transparent Things* or Cortázar's *62* depict a world of detail, to be sure; but the detailed actions, objects and characters do not amount to familiar constructs or designs. The world of known attributes such as fixed location, substance, oneness, quality, relation, function, has given way to a world of sensory invisibility and philosophical insubstantiality, free to be seen—that is, invented —in the act of fabulation. It is this fabulation which the pursuers (Persio and Medrano in *Los premios*, Michel in "*Las babas del diablo*", Oliveira in *Rayuela*, Calac in *62*) are trying to exercise and which the reader is mockingly but seriously challenged to explore in *Rayuela*, *La vuelta al día* and *Ultimo round*. The world neither precedes nor awaits man, but exists in relation to man's ability or will to make it manifest. The same statement in Cortázar's language would assert that "the world is a figure, it has to be read. By read let us understand generated" (*Hopscotch*, ch. 71).

The awareness of the Other, for Cortázar, is concomitant with an irresistible displacement toward its *possession* (*Rayuela*, ch. 78). It moves the poet like a gold-fever rush for ontological enrichment. But if ontological possession (*Ultimo round*, p. 42), the poet's ultimate goal, is born out of the desire for the unknown and yet suspected (*entre-visto*) Other, it will not come about by means of inspiration or naïve intuition: "To be something or . . . to sing the being of something presupposes knowledge" ("Para una poética," pp. 134–35). Before the poet can attempt to possess otherness—the starfish, let us say—he must be steeped in the knowledge of it. However, we must not forget that knowledge is itself grounded in the imagination, so that for ontological knowledge to be possession, as Cortázar would have it, the poet must engage his fundamental tool and resource: the imagination. The starfish will secrete being as the poet in his attempt to possess it invents it. Only when the imagination is at play can the starfish "appear," and only then can the poet adhere his sense of misstatement (*falencia*) and his sense of incompleteness (*ser poroso*) to the starfish's being. It is also at that moment that the poet's mad race to fusion with the "other" rests satiated in temporary completeness and discovery. For Cortázar, then, there is indeed another world, but it is right here, imbedded in the present, in man's inability to coincide with himself. Man must seek to make the "other world" manifest in order to adhere himself to the recognition of the future in the present.

As man fabulates the Other in his longing for it, he is actually fabulating his own being. The imagination necessary for this kind of fabulation carries the fabulator far ahead of conscious contemplation or rigid analytical reflection to reveal the invisible to him in a sort of reverie. Both poetic and scientific imagination are united in this commitment to the invisible and the necessity to invent in order to know. As Bachelard reminds us: "It is in the area of dialectical surrationalism that the scientific mind *dreams*. It is here and nowhere else that analogical dreaming comes into being, dreaming which ventures into thought . . . which seeks illumination of thought by thought, which finds a sudden intuition beyond the veils of informed thought" (*Philosophy of No*, p. 32). But this is not to forget that the fabulating imagination departs from an interstitial vision and that because of its intermediary location (within the gap) it will bring into play both evocating and invocating powers. It is part of the "magical and playful mentality which applies itself to a rupture in the knowledge of all that there is on the other side of the great Habit . . . , because to play poetry is to play fully" (*Ultimo round*, p. 66).

To "play" poetry is to play with the immanence of the imaginary in the "real," it is to engage in reverie, in analogical dreaming. Without speaking of intervals, Bachelard (*L'air et les songes*) believes the real to be a conductor of reality or realization. The imagination erodes and superimposes other images of the real onto ordinary perception. The "real" is then rendered "porous," and it is at that moment that the mind enters the sway of reverie, that solitary meditation "in contact with the world, which is written, and indeed forms itself in the act of writing."[17] Reverie paradoxically unites the joys of evasion and the presence of cogito, for it gathers being around the dreamer. The cogito of reverie is immediately attached to its object and to its image, giving the dreamer the sense of fulfillment of his "porousness" in completion with the "other." Bachelard and Cortázar find in reverie (which is to me another form of ontological fabulation) the reconciliation of subject and world, of present and past, of solitude and communication. Moreover, when reverie finally becomes written expression, the beginning of transcendency appears in the encounter the reader makes with the text, because the poet does not confer the past of his image upon the reader and yet his image immediately takes root in the reader. The communicability of an unusual image is a fact of great ontological significance for Bachelard (*On Poetic Imagination*, p. 71), and the French philosopher further asserts that "I can only know man through reading, which allows me to write man by what he writes" (ibid., p. xvii).

It is the making of reading an inescapable ontological act that Cortázar pursues in all his fiction and poetry. He wants his texts to awaken the need for reverie in the reader. He writes so as to probe into the passivity of the reader's consciousness in order to bring about in him the same sense of sudden strangeness (*extrañamiento*), of incompleteness (*falencia*) that moves him to write, that is, to seek his being in the fabulation of the Other (*Rayuela*, chapter 84). Cortázar would like for all his readers to feel the uneasiness of the poet, to say with him "I live and I write threatened by that very laterality, by that true parallax, because I am always a little too far to the left or deeper than I should be in order for everything to materialize satisfactorily in one more day of life without conflicts" (*La vuelta al día*, p. 22). Writing is the instrument that cuts gaps around and into the reader's consciousness. It produces the necessary ungluing (*desaforamiento*) from ordinary routine in order to push him to the verge of the interval, to the moment when the *entre-visión* or *paravisión* may overtake and displace the "normal" flow of his consciousness.

Yet gathering being for himself alone is not enough for Cortázar. Even before the poet is finished with his encounter with the world, with "things" and with his own self as dimensions of the surrounding "otherness," he has become aware of the otherness of his fellow man, of his reader; and it is this otherness that eventually proves the least subject to possession and therefore the most obsessive. If reading could be turned into a phenomenon of mirrored consciousness, then perhaps a fabulating accomplice would have been found for the poet's sense of incompleteness and his solitary search. If reading is an act of equal ontological significance to writing, then the fabulators (writer and reader) can never be said to be dealing in the creation of a false illusion, for the text is the gap paralleled by the two signifiers who dive into the dark searching for being. The fabulator-reader takes his place as a true *semejante*, (fellow man, mirror, reflection), as a "traveling companion . . . , provided that the reading will abolish reader's time and substitute author's time. Thus the reader would be able to become a coparticipant and cosufferer of the experience through which the novelist is passing, *at the same moment and in the same form*" (*Rayuela*, ch. 79). All this will never be accomplished by offering to the reader a polished and closed "work of art." An impregnable form pretending to be fixed and identical to itself would be an invitation to simple vicarious evasion. It would preclude reverie or the culling of the unknown. The ontological act requires that the reader be faced, as the writer was, with "la materia en gestación" (ibid.). Like Cézanne, Cortázar attempts to present the object as it arises in consciousness. His *roman comique*, *poemas permutantes* and *text-assemblages* evoke in the reader a sense of standing before the "matter in gestation." Cortázar will offer his reader "verses made of commonplaces or clichés, given only partially. The empty space will be filled in by the reader, and it will become a poem only insofar as the reader *completes, transforms or creates it*" (*Ultimo round*, p. 65).

These porous, open texts become passages beyond literature. They are artifacts or emerging objects on their way to "realization" of non-Euclidean and non-Kantian dreams[18] in which the dreamer is not a passive spectator of the dreamed self and events but is instead fabulating them as he lives the moment of encounter with Otherness. Actual reading time is no longer divorced from fictional time. Reading Cortázar demands coincidence with lived time. It entails frequent stops at the library, uncomfortable thinking, getting mad and going back to look for the link we think we have just missed because suddenly things have ceased to flow or make sense or because we are unexpectedly laughing at the "tragic" lives of the characters. It is at this point in discomfort that the novice fabulating reader will begin to *desplazarse*, *desaforarse*, *descentrarse* and *descubrirse* in a manner parallel to the writer's experience before the blank page. What follows, according to Cortázar, is a curious extrapolation, by means of which the characters of the *roman comique* or the speaker of the *poemas permutantes* jumps toward us (readers) and we toward them. The "characters" or "events" are actually arrested moments or pieces of the reader's reverie and as such become the realization of self-attributes. As the reader then "realizes" his own fictive being, he gains in ontological possession—that is to say, he experiences an epiphany. Like one of Nabokov's characters in *Transparent Things*, the reader has been forced to "realize" that the landmarks of his conscious self are all structures of his imagination which can be taken up again and again. The objective of Cortázar's writing—to "see" or live the text as the interval in which meaning becomes manifest—is thus accomplished when his reader, his double, his obsessive Other experiences the mutation, displacement and estrangement from the affective ordinary which had initially urged the writer to embark on his search for being. The circle is thus closed in mutual ontological fabulation. The writer "sees" himself in the invisible "other" reader he anticipated; and the reader, unable to coincide with his previous sense of self, has moved to fabulate a new image of himself in his encounter with the text.

[1] "The relation of meaning to the spoken word can no longer be a point by point correspondence that we always have clearly in mind" (Maurice Merleau-Ponty, *Signs*, Richard C. McCleary, tr., Evanston, Il., Northwestern University Press, 1964, p. 43). Language is not a tool the writer uses to communicate a meaning or a reality existing outside of the context of its own discourse; "it is no longer the servant of signification, but the act of signifying itself" (ibid., p. 232).

[2] "My problem continues to be, as you must have sensed it in reading *Rayuela*, a metaphysical one; it is a continual tearing apart between the monstrous error of being what we are as individuals and as peoples in the twentieth century, and the glimpsing of a future in which human society will finally reach that archetype of which socialism gives us a practical vision and poetry offers us a spiritual one" (*Ultimo round*, p. 213).

[3] "Although incapable of political action, I do not renounce my solitary vocation for culture, my stubborn ontological search, or the games of the imagination played in the most vertiginous planes" (ibid., p. 217).

[4] "Todo es escritura, es decir fábula" (*Rayuela*, Buenos Aires, Sudamericana, 1963, chapter 73). The English is from Gregory Rabassa's translation, New York, Pantheon, 1966, as are all subsequent English quotations from the novel.

[5] *Cronopios*: Persons who are inclined to defy and go beyond the established and "reasonable" notion of the real. Cortázar defines them as "fellows gifted with a constructive notion of the absurd" (*La vuelta al día en ochenta mundos*, Mexico City, Siglo XXI, 1969, p. 18).

[6] In reference to the sponge see in *La vuelta al día*, "Así se empieza," pp. 7–9; regarding the chameleon see "Casilla del camaleón," pp. 209–13.

[7] Julio Cortázar, "Para una poética," *La Torre:* *Revista general de la Universidad de Puerto Rico,* 2 (July-September 1954).

[8] "When the poet sings the rose, in the act of poetic creation, he becomes as one with ontological *qualities* which are not really man's. Man, the discoverer of the marvelous, is anxious to reach and become those qualities. His poem is such a fusion. It amalgamates the poet to the single object, which in turn yields its identity and enriches the poet. Because the Other is what can truly give degrees of alien being to the specific human condition" ("Para una poética," p. 133).

[9] Quoting Vitales-Troxler, he affirms: "There is another world, but it is to be found within this one. So that it may reach perfection we must recognize it distinctly and we must adhere ourselves to it. Man must look for his future in the present, and for heaven within himself and above the earth" (*La vuelta al día*, p. 67).

[10] A good illustration, though on a smaller scale, of the relation between form and "anti-form" is the surrealist analysis of the "crisis of the object." It is produced by projecting onto a "realistic" or everyday perception of an object a different, but equally logical, relation of its parts. The resulting "new" object or set of relations does not invalidate the established form—say, "realistic narrative" in the case of *Rayuela*—but it does bring about the realization that that form was no more than one possible way of structuring our perception of the world.

[11] "Crével is right, reality is flexible and porous and the scholastic separation between physics and metaphysics loses all meaning as soon as we refuse to accept the fixed" (*La vuelta al día*, p. 63).

[12] According to Cortázar, *La vuelta al día* participates "in that respiration of the sponge which the fish of memory, fulminating alliances of time and states and materials which society would consider irreconcilable go in and out" (p. 7).

13 Gaston Bachelard discusses and summarizes the dissolution of the fixed identity of objects by stating that "energy is as real as substance and substance is not more real than energy" (*The Philosophy of No*, G. C. Waterson, tr., New York, Orion, 1968, p. 56).

14 Cortázar dreams of creating events and characters whose "behavior" could be drawn in non-Euclidean spatial and temporal terms. To a certain extent *Rayuela* and *62*, with their emphasis on parallel characters (Maga/Talita, Oliveira/Horacio, Horacio/Traveler, Calac/Juan), parallel settings (Paris/Buenos Aires, club/circus, hospital/madhouse) and coreless events (Rocamadour's death, Morelli's accident, Calac's visit to London), are already attempts at insubstantiality and non-Euclidean impossibility of location.

15 "The philosophy of no will . . . be discovered to be not an attitude of rejection, but an attitude of *conciliation*" (*Philosophy of No*, p. 13; my emphasis). "The philosophy of no will permit to sum up simultaneously all experience and all thought concerning the definition of a substance. We wish to define the philosophy of scientific knowledge as an open philosophy, as the consciousness of a mind which constitutes itself by working upon the unknown, by seeking within reality that which contradicts anterior knowledge" (9).

16 The world is not ultimately referable to Aristotelian "real" substance or to a Platonic form. What Cortázar is trying to do, in the wake of Merleau-Ponty's work, is to attempt here and now a reconciliation of the idealism-materialism split. Man is the world because as he faces it, he must devise ways, forms, attitudes, signs to deal with it; but those very forces become the world for man.

17 Bachelard, *On Poetic Imagination and Reverie*, Colette Gaudin, ed. & tr., New York, 1971, p. 22.

18 "The door is under your eye-lids [soul] . . . But one must be able to see it, and in order to see it I propose to dream, because the dream is a displaced present summoned by an exclusively human operation. It is a saturation of present, a fragment of grey amber floating in the future and at the same time pulling away from it—in as much as the dreamer is in his present—and it is stirring up, outside of any Kantian time or space, the disturbed potencies of his being" (*Ultimo round*, p. 51).

A Quest from "Me" to "Us": Genesis and Definition of the Pursuer Motif in Cortázar

By LIDA ARONNE AMESTOY

> *"What world is this I am bound to bear as a burden? What kind of an evangelist am I?"*
>
> Julio Cortázar, "The Pursuer"

The advocates of free literary interpretation ignored science; those of modern logicism betray it. No method can claim to be scientific unless it meets the real nature of its object. As blind as those scientists who some fifty years ago declared nuclear energy a sheer philosophical category, a number of outdated neo-positivists still persist in viewing live symbols as an archaic human mania—a delusion or, at best, a game or device of imagination aimed at disguising our repressed animal impulses (dream fantasies), at evading our historic aims (religious fantasies), at diverting the mind from logic, its presumably superior function (esthetic fantasies). Thus they fail to see that all literary works intertwine two different sorts of discourse, one temporal and the other affective in quality. That is, they fail to grasp the twofold nature of literary language, which at once involves a logical structure founded on word-as-means and an analogical structure founded on word-as-entity. Yet unless one can distinguish between sign and symbol, and unless one admits the epiphanic character of the latter, one is deaf to poetic speech. Hence neither analytical reason nor analogical intuition can alone furnish a valid method to approach an object which involves both functions at once. In reducing literary language to conscious reasoning or to sheer ecstasy, both logicism and intuitionism destroy the object they try to comprehend. As in the electric bulb, here light depends strictly on the contact of the two opposing poles. Finally, such complementarity points to the tight warp of the objective/subjective levels of the literary work, so hat its presumed autonomy becomes questionable.

Occidental narrative, for instance, results from our specific model of civilization, and it is only in this anthropological frame that its specificity can be realized and even discerned. In his Yoknapatawpha cycle William Faulkner foretells the failure of the typical Western human project. The heir to the old rational existential pattern would be the passive, irrational negro (the idiot); the fall would be brought about by the aggressive irrational white man (Absalom himself), when he murdered his own brother—the "hybrid" or properly American man, the true owner of the land, the only man still capable of love. The Macondo cycle brings this fallen hybrid hero back to life and so supports a new (the only possible) human scheme for the future on our continent. Not only this new man's skin but also his whole cosmovision is marked by hybridization, as shown by the works of García Márquez, Fuentes, Carpentier, Paz, Lezama Lima, Rulfo, Arguedas, Marechal, Cortázar. The symbol that best suggests this mental synthesis is the Cross—not a simple addition but a strenuous, impassioned unity of all the polarities which have so far divorced man and culture. Our writers are thus pioneering a genuine universalism which all our sciences ought to hasten to second, lest our ruin become irreversible. Inasmuch as we adopt for our critical approach the binocular view these authors' works embody, we not only assert practically a true objectivity but endorse as well their integral outlook on reality.

*

A thematic constant runs throughout the whole of Cortázar's narrative production, a constant which is constituted early in his poetic play *Los reyes* (The Kings) in practically all its basic variations. One of these is the split house or split "world"; the other is the itinerary or bridging action, which is embodied by a conscious agent (frequently an intellectual type), the Searcher himself, and by a "magic" agent, mediator or true pontifex. The whole scheme may project allegorically upon the field of poetic creation, suggesting the writer's parallel search as a further variation of the same quest.

The Cortazarian motif thus evolves from the traditional moods of classical drama and Promethean romanticism to the present magic modes of narrative without neglecting the ordinary realistic vein, the grotesque, the absurd, and without missing humor. Yet the dominant note is some peculiar immanent mysticism. The will to exert the poet in order to give birth to the real man reveals not simply an intellectual interest in human destiny (anthropology) but a genuine passion of the soul to fulfill it (mysticism). Like the medieval alchemist, the writer Cortázar wants to experience entelechy, not just define it. He tries to work it through the arduous transmutation of words, through the fusion and re-creation of narrative techniques, through the strict depuration of critical reason. His thirst for the live and life-giving word is stated in all his essays; it underlies his poetry and his narrative; it is echoed by his pursuers' perpetual longing. The most heterogeneous courses and resources serve this one aim: the *antilogos* is sought in esthetic rhythm (jazz/poetry) as well as in worldly cacophony; in blind irrationality as well as in the harshest lucidity; through the intellect and through pure animal impulse; through metaphysical ecstasy and through all-too-human behavior; in sheer hedonistic eroticism as well as in mystic love; in fresh fantasy and in compulsive symbolism; now in the exaltation of the ego, now in its utmost degredation; now in ordinary sentiment, now in its sadistic perversion; by giving in to the certainty of the most hopeful or the most anguishing determinism, as well as by exerting supreme human freedom; by way of yogi-like self-alienation and also by way of integral commitment to life and human brotherhood in the Christian manner.

We must notice, however, that such pluralism does not imply existential confusion, as a partial outlook might lead as to think. The Cortazarian searcher often dives beyond the Euclidean space, yet he never disdains ordinary perception. He evolves his soul's eye without ever belittling those on his face. Hence his goalpost should be conceived as the synthesis of all possible polarities. His choice is never exclusive, as these clue lines of an early poem demonstrate: "I am not farther from the street / because my balcony opens out above." The balcony or extroverted eye of the house/ mind involves the street in the same way as this outer, shared world involves the introverted eye embodied by the balcony. Both the house and the street are aspects of the same reality, and the balcony is precisely the common ground, the point where those opposite orders fuse—the personal and the social, the ordinary and the transcendent. In *Hopscotch*, a climax of the quest, this "cross" is explicitly assumed. Indeed no one among us can at will or by decree thwart his archetypal disposition, ineluctably "modern" and "Western"—that is, "Christian"—except at the price of psychotic or psychopathic disintegration. Thus the Cortazarian searcher can abhor God as Jehovah, "that imperious little bird," but will inevitably uphold the Love principle of the New Testament (both tacitly and expressly). All the versions of the quest reveal him as a man who forges his vertical individuation in a horizontal sympathetic embrace of mankind. He knows well that one cannot restore myth at the expense of reason, assert Love by denying love, conquer human essence by despising human existence or create Man by destroying men. The split macro/microcosmic reality upon which this great theme is founded is not a particular trait of the Cortazarian searcher, as some pretend. What defines the Cortazarian pursuer is not his schizoid disintegration (which actually mirrors the typical personality of our century) but his will to overcome it. In this sense the whole of the author's work is a hopeful metaphor for modern man's present predicament.

When the curtain rises at Knossos, the historical birthplace of Western drama, the world is already split: Athens against the Labyrinth, Theseus against the Minotaur, reason against myth. Between the two poles is Ariadne, the spell of poetry, trying to bridge the gap with her magic string. Yet the kings fight, they do not integrate; and the Minotaur is killed, he lets Theseus kill him. In both this early crime and this surrender we find the root of Western tragedy, as Cortázar re-creates it. The Minotaur embodies the mythical, repressed life powers Western man refuses to acknowledge as his own. "A monster has no brothers," says Minos when Ariadne insists on their bonds. However, it is the unconscious force that will rule as king in the long run: "Dead I shall become myself more steadily. . . . There is only one way to kill monsters: to acknowledge them. . . . I shall plunge to indwell the dreams . . . of the ineluctable time of the race. Thence I shall butt your throne, the uncertain scepter of your kinsmen." His ghostly image will now and then burst through men's routine and thwart their conscious projects. Sometimes it may roam the individual psyche ("Ahí pero donde, cómo"), but it may also affect the couple or the family ("Cartas de mamá") or even threaten human society ("Casa tomada"). "Casa tomada" (House Taken Over) is perhaps the story that best symbolizes the retaliation of the repressed powers' respect of the individual man, of his family and of his social group and cultural environment. As such, it foretells the present crisis of our world. As a result of positivistic existential bias our culture has nourished in its very core a sick anticulture of primitive mystic traits whose (self-)destructive and sinister nihilism now threatens life on the planet. The modern Western confusion of the "person" and the "individual," of "humanism" and "anthropocentrism," has led to the present-day misunderstanding of the social as the "antipersonal" and may eventually do away with all humanitarian tenets. Like the protagonists of that early story, the Christian culture is now in danger of being driven out of its own home by the dark, rebellious ghosts of death.

The scenes that follow *The Kings* in the great Cortazarian drama evolve in Paris—the new Babylon—or in one of its multiple substitutes, mainly in Buenos Aires. The split worlds and the pursuer's efforts to integrate them will remain the central issue throughout. Such polarized worlds may be embodied by two places, two different chronological or psychological moments, two characters or groups of characters, two moods of the same protagonist, place or time. Yet they all refer to a common polarity: "this side" (positive) and "the other side" (magic). In some stories disintegration is evident and strictly individual ("Lejana," "Axolotl"); in others it is less explicit ("Carta a una señorita en París," "No se culpa a nadie"); sometimes it projects straight onto the social ("Omnibus," "Los venenos," "La autopista del sur"). However, the inner split always has an outer correlative and vice versa, as seen in several pieces which are openly bivalent ("Circe," "Los pasos en las huellas"). The split may suggest ordinary neurotic alienation ("Casa tomada," "Verano"), acute neurosis ("La banda," "El otro cielo") or even psychosis ("El ídolo de las Cícladas," "Las armas secretas"), and frequently it embodies the conflict on both the existential and the esthetic levels ("Lejana," "Cefalea," "Final del juego," "Las babas del diablo"). But we should note that the stories do not merely aim at a critical diagnosis: they carry out an actual insight, and they accomplish an esthetic and existential move to overcome the divided state. Such a move may tend to embrace the alienated mythic value by either forcing it or taking it in ("Las puertas del cielo," "La isla a mediodía"), but it may also seek to counteract its dangerous regressive pull simply by balancing its destructiveness ("Circe," "Bestiario").

If we are careful to watch the turn that the various scenes of this narrative drama successively give the pursuer's course, we shall notice a gradual and irreversible evolution from a self-centered subject toward an all-embracing subject, from the plain "I" to the complex "we." Regardless of its peculiar motives and its eventual failure or success, the bridging act always leads to the acknowledgment of one or more aspects of the protagonist's inner and/or outer "otherness," so that every new restatement of the split will entangle a wider and deeper issue. After the cowardly escape of "Casa tomada," for instance, the protagonist's exertion to reconcile his ego and its irrational counterpart (the small rabbits) or his person and the prevailing social values (Andrés's ways) implies the recovery of Ariadne's thread, the start of the self's liberating process. "Carta a una señorita en París" (Letter to a Young Lady in Paris) thus sets the course that will reach a climax in *Libro de Manuel*. Whether the meeting of the polarized worlds is forced by determinism (*62: Modelo para armar*) or is consciously wrought (the other three novels), whether the fusion works out or fails, there is always the tacit or obvious mediation of a link character or link object which we have called the "magic agent" (since its action can be explained by synchronicity rather than by causality). This agent is most evident when it assumes its true archetypal image, when it embodies the Jungian anima or psychopomp, that is, when its function is supported by a more or less round feminine character (La Maga and her forerunners or emulators: Celina, Thérèse, Josiane, Talita). Nevertheless, we are mainly interested here in tracing the evolutions of the searcher himself, that is, what we may call the isotopy of the pursuer.

A clear technical concept to define the pursuer's itinerary is "individuation." Starting from a typical schizoid existential split, the whole Cortazarian adventure seems to cover up the successive stages of a process of integration of the conscious and the unconscious, of intellect and myth. As the pursuer overcomes his adolescent egotism through the expansion of his conscious mind, we watch the birth of the "son of man." Again the implicit reference is "Western" or Christian initiation, since the process of inner growth has no other direction than that imposed by natural human archetypes and acknowledges no other initiator than the personal conscience. The stories in *Bestiario* (Bestiary) embody the initial steps. This is a sort of compulsive stage in which the pursuer simply bears the assault of his alienated irrational entities. At first he does not even dare face them ("Casa tomada"); but soon he will come to love and nourish his inner otherness ("Carta a una señorita en París"), even to acknowledge it as a real personal dimension ("Lejana") and to analyze it "scientifically" ("Cefalea"). "Carta a una señorita en París" and "Omnibus" reveal a rediscovery of the social otherness, whereas the essential instinctive forces are faced in "Circe"—Thanatos in its neurotic expression—and in "Las puertas del cielo" (The Gates of Heaven)—primary eroticism. The closing story, "Bestiario," sanctions this insight with a first responsible act tending to offset the destructive inertia of vice, whether sexual (Nene) or intellectual (Luis). Isabel (natural eros) kills Nene (perverted eros or dissociating force) in order to preserve Rema, who stands for true human eros—"love," the integrating principle for both the individual and society. If Theseus and Minos symbolized Western man deprived of his mythical disposition; if the Minotaur represented the poet, that hybrid but still "inharmonious" being (for he keeps alive both his intellectual and his mythic functions but responds to each in a wanton, neurotic fashion); the pursuer reaches in "Bestiario" such elementary inner coherence as will allow him to restore his basic impulse to sustain life.

The volume *Final del juego* presupposes from the start the overlapping of "parks," of the worlds of daily experience and of art (myth). The "I" of the dull businessman and that of the fictional cuckold in "Continuidad de los parques" (Continuity of Parks) are identical, and hence literature can alter the course of events. Also the "I" of the present moment can simultaneously live in the past ("Torito") or in the future ("Sobremesa"). The woman in "El río" (The River) who refuses to integrate her outer otherness through the erotic embrace at once escapes integration with society and her own self by drowning: the river re-creates the inertness of the lovers' bed, where the isolated ego floats alien to the life around it. The volume asserts the basic oneness of reality. Man should just dare to open the "condemned door" to restore communication between ordinary space/time and the mythic space/time of dream, poetry and madness. There are a number of effective passports: the trance of sensual dancing ("Las puertas del cielo"), of Bacchic excitement ("Las ménades"), of fiction ("Continuidad de los parques"), of enervation through insomnia or sex ("El río"), of sheer nonsense ("La banda"), of anesthesia or intense pain ("La noche boca arriba"), of passion ("Todos los fuegos el fuego"), of "alert silence" or contemplation ("La puerta condenada"), of primitive empathy through a mythical symbol ("El ídolo de las Cícladas"), a natural object ("Axolotl") or an esthetic image ("Las babas del diablo"). The trance can also be afforded by jazz (music, in general), by extreme conscious lucidity or by the simple magic of the ordinary (Traveler's circus). "Final del juego" (End of the Game) sums up the passage formula in Leticia's paralysis: it is the partial or total atrophy of the current disposition (rational empiricism) which gives a person rule in the magic realm "beyond the back door of the house." This cycle asserts the unity not only of the intrapersonal worlds but also of being as such. The man who in conscious space/time lies on a modern French surgical board is also a Toltec chased and sacrificed by the Aztecs during their "flower war" ("La noche boca arriba"). By syntonizing certain deep psychic tunes any man can dream somebody else's dreams, live out somebody else's existence or die somebody else's death ("Una flor amarilla"); for at this level the ants *are* the flowers and even the people ("Los venenos"), the successful businessman *is* the baby moaning at night ("La puerta condenada"), the modern scientist *is* the primitive shaman ("El ídolo de las Cícladas"), man *is* the axolotl ("Axolotl").

As far as the course of the search is concerned, there is visible advance in respect to the *Bestiario* cycle. First, the basic teratologic stage has been overcome; once the pursuer acknowledges his animal impulses (his "monsters"), he can freely face his archetypal (that is, his cultural or properly "human") values. Second, in disclosing the mythic or collective stratum of the unconscious mind, the pursuer's ego transcends itself and wakes up to its universal entity. And third, at this stage the search is not compulsion but vocation, deliberate quest—hence its frequent contemplative trends ("El ídolo de las Cícladas," "Axolotl"). But here the quest has conspicuous ethical implications. Unless introspection is actually a mask for pathological psychic detachment (as in the pseudo-spiritual movements now in fashion), the ego's insight of its individual and traditional essence is never deranging but redounds to a deeper understanding of men and of the ordinary aspects of their living. Hence the reevaluation of everyday language and of realistic devices in this and the subsequent cycles. And though the dialectical conflict still shows in such facts as the implicit rejection of extreme differentiation ("Después del almuerzo") or in its romantic overrating ("Final del juego"), the contrasting poles are obviously conceived as complementary, the two "hands" of an unmistakably individual entity ("No se culpe a nadie"). This is sanctioned by the story after which the anthology is named: when in order to own the magic values of existence man disowns its ordinary, dull, "crippled" counterpart, he brings the game to naught.

A number of stories in this volume, along with those in *Las armas secretas* (Secret Weapons), seem to furnish a synthesis for the two previous cycles: namely, the stage of compulsive acknowledgment and that of elaboration of oddity-in-the-ordinary. Yet here the conflict implicit and even stated philosophically on occasion ("La banda") now hinges on the main human relating forces: sex and love. The real family bond in "Cartas de Mamá" is Nico, the dead protagonist, and his ghostly love is the only genuine sentiment. Similarly, Mme Francinet's "hired" sympathy and tears in "Los buenos servicios" (At your Service) prove to be the only feelings that actually involve M. Bebe in that sordid wake which veils and reveals the jealousy and egotism of homosexual intercourse. The harlot trying to seduce the boy for the "vampire" man in "Las babas del diablo" (Blow-Up) provides another metaphor for pseudo-human, parasitic relations. Once again it is the false camera eye, the one that represents the true human vision and feeling. It is not the axis of Woman (Man)/Boy but the axis Photographer/Objective (or Writer/Literary work) that works out the actual relation of the subject with its otherness. The situation of "Cartas de Mamá" (Letters from Mama) is re-created at a wider social level in "Las armas secretas." The real protagonists of the story are not the central characters but the phantoms of the mad World War II, showing how from the collective background of the mind the blind forces of fright and hatred can rule and determine human relations. A prophetic story, indeed, since it points out the persistence of primitive destructiveness in civilized society, as well as the risks of its present eruption.

The two concluding stories of this third anthology round off the figure of the Cortazarian searcher and complete the definition of his peculiar cosmovision. So far two points have proved outstanding: a) the need to integrate man's mythic entity in his current experience, and b) the deranging effect of restoring myth at the expense of empiric reason. Johnny's pretense of having Lan's red dress (the magic value) without Lan herself (the dull empiric reality) brings the whole search in "El perseguidor" (The Pursuer) to naught and means the end of existence. As soon as Pierre chooses the pataphysical order against that of Roland/Babette in "Las armas secretas," pure synchronicity against causality and determinism against free will, he stops being Pierre (he stops being a man) and becomes a bodiless ghost, the schizo-paranoic ego that can feel real only in hatred and death. A basic knowledge of human psychism, or just a daily objective look at the world news may suffice to prevent literary criticism from defining "Las armas secretas" as a purely exotic, historically uncommitted work (as some have dared to). In the light of a true binocular reading Roland and Babette's closing ride and feelings embody the definite reassertion of the social—the aim of the ride is to "reason away" the ghosts and the subsequent hate and fear that break up the couple—as *the* means to fulfill the individual without destroying the human. How could a world which for centuries has mistaken stupidity for common sense now manage to avoid mistaking madness for lucidity?

Cortázar's protagonists stand at times with myopic empiricists, at others with the clairvoyant apprentices of our modern schizophrenic institution. Yet neither in isolation embodies what we have defined as the isotopy of the pursuer. Since this involves an integrating search, it is therefore simultaneously borne by two polar characters or values. Hence the pursuer may often be at the same time the pursued entity (and hence some critics' misconception of the quest as a vicious circle). This is also the reason why the sought magic object may at once function as the guiding power prompting the search (Oliveira-Maga-Oliveira). Hence, finally, the usual double face of the searcher: Hardoy/Mauro, Somoza/Morand, Johnny/Bruno, Oliveira/Traveler, et cetera.

The explicit definition of the quest as an existential game on two tracks carried out by a double-faced subject is best rounded off in "El perseguidor." Obviously the conformist reader, who has never felt at ease with Cortazarian narrative, will tend to share Bruno's bearing and view Johnny as the typically "insane" Cortazarian character. (And indeed, were he a "man" instead of an esthetic function, he should be considered insane.) On the other hand, all modern nonconformists are ready to call Johnny the "actual" man and to class Bruno with the "happy little hogs . . . redeemed by habit, by mechanical behavior." Whether these readers claim to be materialists or spiritualists, they are all fragmentary men; hence they coincide in rejecting Cortázar's latest work. Some expected the pursuer to become a practical politician fully committed in propagandism. Others expected the pursuer to become a detached, yogi-like mystic. Neither of them can therefore understand *Libro de Manuel*, that masterly *conjunctio oppositorum* where the magic of infancy is forged through the sordid notes from everyday adult life, which are in their turn arranged by the magic of an esthete who is at the same time an active protagonist in history's dull routine.

Unless one dares engage both eyes in reading (the eye of empirical reason and the eye of mythical perception), one will hardly notice the Cortazarian pursuer in Bruno-Johnny (Oliveira-Maga) and in this strict array. Lan's red dress, the essential, ineffable truth, is necessary for man to grow "in his own image, after his likeness." Yet Lan's red dress is magic with vulgar Lan inside, because of Lan—the dull, daily appearance of life. This means the inner, individuating quest has a necessary counterpart in extroverted, integrating action. The Word is to become human flesh and dwell among men. The pursuer's secret is the parallel development of soul vision and facial vision. Unless man learns to use both his myth and his reason, he will never be born anew. He will certainly have jumped from surface realism to phantom idealism, from empirical stupidity to Nietzschean alienation; but he will have missed wisdom.

Pursuers

By SAÚL SOSNOWSKI

They are marked by a kind of need, by signs of searching. They are marked by manias of persecution and the desire to imbricate themselves into an ever more rough and elusive filigree. They are marked by the desire for an encounter or the illusion of an encounter. They are Cortázar's characters, and they keep battering against doors which will not open up to thrusts, pleas or violent ejaculations. Every traveler generates a space that may or may not be spanned. Every narrator has the desire to name what eludes him, what holds him back from his fine ending, another passage undone. There is also a certain kind of reader whose escape is the use of carefully aligned spots. Yet flight could also be an extrapolation, a possible confrontation with a mirror: a clash that may send him from his reading back to that inescapable position of viewer, viewing what others are seeing, what they themselves are viewing.

A certain kind of character, and also a certain kind of reader, accedes to the proposition set forth by the narrator, paving the narrator's way. It is bits and pieces in chapters displaying what they will later conceal; bits and pieces, marking the return trip as well, by way of tables of instructions, numbers at the top and at the bottom of the page; a deceptive ease found in titillation, a titillation that anticipates variations of all sorts, openings to passages unknown: darkness within but the flashlight very firmly in hand. Besides, there is always the certainty that the whole thing may not be so bad after all. If it could be a reading that did more than linger in order to fondle the words, then it could—and why not?—get closer, get *us* closer to exploring other territories outside and within the text. To say that a text "se deja leer" (here we clearly enter into what is proposed by *Rayuela*'s Table of Instructions) is no assurance of the easy surrender by the one who is actually charging us for that very momentary spasm and all the analogous echoes of its false counterresponse. A text which is not read but which rather "submits itself to the reader" is inviting an (apparently) easy seduction, opening itself, as it were, to recommendation by those already initiated by the provocative *sobrador*.

This, then, is a seduction to an order whose members are thus pledged as addicts: "So please do come; this text abandons itself to you. I am different, yes, and my 635 pages, my fluctuations, my queasiness, may well frighten you. But just a moment; keep an eye out. I'm letting you decide: why not come a little closer?" The make-up is on just right, and the one about to be seduced seems on the point of falling into the trap. "And if you like it—well, if you dare, and how can you dare not to, as *macho* as you are!—then we'll go deeper, to the limit, no signs that say stop, no looks that hesitate at further penetrations. The book will let itself be read. You may enter confidently, for this is an expert old tongue, not limited to mere adolescent maneuvers."

This book indicates paths, it frames the way, it shows signs, it makes signs on the cards of him who enters trustingly as he accepts the warmly extended hand. The reader is curious, naïve. He can be seduced by a presentable, exotic façade. That particular mechanism leaves out other elements, but these he does not manage to see. He is

already caught in the "babas del diablo," the devil's spittle, already submitting himself
to be possessed, as a virgin would be, by so much "hangustia hexistencial." Now he
begins, first fondling forms, then learning new ways, repeating those variations; and
yet when he's finished, he still has the voids, the same ones felt before between so many
other sheets. No, this partnership will not do. Having submitted is degrading, it is
belittling, he is just some makeshift kind of seduced male-female. He starts over again.
This time the narrator and the reader are in perfect harmony, their tools warmly joined.
They begin new searchings, they fill up other gaps, gaps requiring other mechanisms,
other games, games signaling other types of frameworks, other dimensions and perhaps other ways out. The crests, the ebbs between desire and encounter, fall in and
out. The encounter, the rejection and seeking, the seeking out and possessing: it is a
dynamics that demands and forces constant movement, even though its price be the
abandonment of partial solutions, of the small joys, of the choices which really are not
choices, of the oscillating between cobblestones and threads, of such pains as the warmth
of a bed or the satisfaction of a "well-written" page that will no longer soothe. No time
here for the pause that refreshes and the resultant satisfied smile coming from the other
side of the sheet. If here you are faced with an onslaught of cobwebs, brush them off
and return to penetrate from other angles, or from the same angle but as if for the very
first time. Evidently it is all a question of going backward, the farther back the better.
That way the romantic little marker will move up another compartment with each
new shove, each time closer to heaven, that heaven that survives in the imagination,
boxed in by desire.

Sax and sex and drugs: none of these is an end; each is a possible means of access
to what cannot be articulated. Each demands the presence of someone who is not a victim of self-abuse, the one with the polka-dotted tie, the one to translate this language—if
that's what it is—into something accessible to others—if it is indeed possible. Any
experiment, hallucination or inner vision is a luminous interstice between the blocks
that guarantee that there is no way out, that any encounter (with what? with whom?)
need take place on this ground-level world of ours, need be reduced to a language
which the Contax 1.1.2 would not transmit beyond the initial dry plate, which the
Lettera 22 would not tap out unless a reasoning hand dictated the mediatization. This
mediatization is the obstacle to and the impossibility of direct access. Once again it is
a demented logic which secures the path, the same path to be left for certain experiments, the same path to which one will eventually return. There you will fall down
once and then again, to see it waiting there: peacefully, smug, knowing the only escape
is to that form of order which I use even now to find the understanding wink of my
paredros. Logic is a mischievous witch that knows about an escape from which one
returns only to slide on his own slippery stick. So? One may not know how to tell
something, but yet one must try. Some sequences will get broken up, some will in-
terpolate spaces that the distant reader must bear for there to be a bridge, for him to
be integrated into "the zone" and be seated confidently on "the island," knowing he
is all right: he hasn't gone too far alone; there's a return ticket still ready for those
waiting.

There is someone waiting while the other goes to recover what he feels to be
lost echoes, but it is he who waits who is actually "the man of the species": the poor

dentist who gambles away all he has left; the one at the port who knows the new-comer will bring multicolored vociferousness and an end to domestic tranquility; the biographer too, ever mediocre, who permits a certain access to the pursuer's workshop. There is no reason to question the writer's sympathy for certain characters' desires to abandon what alienates them from the West, to imbricate them into a world whose components do not demand a constant alienation from what is outside man's world. It is obvious that for the writer the quest must begin with a serious questioning of the tools of his trade. It is understandable, moreover, that such a questioning and desire should be translated into multiple debates between his characters, and that these disquisitions—with or without Morelli, but definitely with Johnny-Bruno, Persio-Medrano, Oliveira and the ones we shall see later on—may be the ones to signal, I believe, a sort of resignation to remain on this side, to specify even more the immediate goals that can be achieved with the limited equipment with which our daily alienation provides us.

Let me specify: if in fact Johnny's quest can really arouse our emotions, can induce us to empathize with him to the point of identifying ourselves with what he does not quite manage to say, it is Bruno who stirs up all these reactions through his narration, through his confession in the eyes of Johnny's challenge. Johnny's biography, as trans-mitted through the omissions he himself and Bruno make, is a mask, a false face for the consumer (literally: he who consumes; and therein lies the director of "Las ménades"), a criticism whose point of departure is deception; for not only are the images desired by the public false, they are subserviently acceded to. In spite of this, Johnny himself accepts it all the while ("Está bien tu libro, Bruno"), perhaps in antici-pation of the final request, the one asking to replace his fidelity to his quest with a mask as well. There is no trace of criticism—which is precisely what is open to criticism—in Bruno. His Johnny is a product tailored to the taste of those who wish their images and illusions reinforced by the (apparent) authority of the printed word. The function of unmasking—if the scheme "life and works" is to be adopted—is replaced with the obliging bestseller recipe and the expected translation, with his wife's satisfaction amid the growing good news. The possibility of acting like a critic capable of confronting what Johnny suggests and joining him in his quest is abandoned for the sake of bourgeois complaisance. Johnny is canned and placed on a shelf with a fancy label; Bruno is wrapped in the satisfaction of having got out a new edition with its very apropos appendix about the subject's death.

This is a version of writing which denounces its very self in the simultaneous opening of two channels of reception, showing by means of Bruno's language his own critical inability and affirming the negation of the biographer, not of the instrument he uses. If Johnny attacks the bourgeois concepts of time and order, he does so through words which register them as being of Bruno's world; there is no denouncement, again, of the tool. This same instrument is the one which condemns its user, thus showing its other critical capacity: that of emerging from itself, from its own condemnation and destruction, to recover its original meaning.

And so it is inevitable that one revert to terms like "capacidad poética" and "lenguaje analógico," already analyzed elsewhere. But it is necessary to persevere with a language used not as a mere object for fondling the objects named, leaving them on the periphery, but rather as an instrument which could leave off with the caressing in order to take a virgin look at each of the elements. The result would be an account that would slowly undress the object and face it with the necessity of being uncovered. It would be conventional language, but it would abhor conventional expressions and use them only to attest to that abhorrence: obsolete expressions, the worn-out thoughts of members of sybilline clubs which serve to accentuate their obsolescence and strive for a more advantageous plane. This would redeem certain primal acts, certain types of contact which do not need so much intermediary verbiage just to come together. It means looking for primary colors before looking for intricate configurations, looking for friendly unions for the sheer, although not simple, desire for love. It means La Maga before so much vain disquisition about the reality that Oliveira let slip through his fingers, Berthe Trépat and the punishment of the prodigal son who for so many decades of hypocritical learning refused pity, and it means sorrow and friendship too when faced with so many threads and water basins. It means, then, a primary language as well, not a return to the innocence of a nonexistent twentieth-century Adam, but rather an opening up to a language of moderation, utilized with no more clownish antics of cuff links and tie. It would certainly mean an honest look at our present moment, at history and at such improvements as are possible for us to realize. No, it is not a question of negating a "literary" or "everyday" language, but rather of the "caricature" by which it is so heavily weighted down; it is not a question of denying the history these very words attest to, but rather of examining their potential in a projection toward the future.

These terms, the ones I have just used, are rigorously examined from a viewpoint that would like to deny the very separation they promulgate. Thus they are replaced with notions of "continuous flux" and "abolition of binary systems," new words as old as the past ones, but words which in their impact suggest possible solutions as yet unelaborated and unaccomplished. These possibilities fork out toward other models which thousands of letters serve to coagulate in the rose of the kaleidoscope; they fork out toward the types of traversings that found cities, which through the sobriety of humor establish zones in which there can also be bridges, in which someone simply named Juan can add himself to a growing chain of pursuers. And these models that seek to be must first lapse into words and worn-out patterns, again to be mistreated by so much abuse. It is left for them to readjust, omit the nexuses, drown out all comfort, arouse once again the storehouse of words belonging to the reader-possessor, the reader who must go back to an adult childhood with its puzzles and erotic dolls, the reader-viewer of explicit situations, ones which underline that eroticism and its translations into physical conduct and are not just a road that leads to being (or to the beginning of being), but a language as well, with its own claim on the city.

What is left is rescue, then, through multiple modes of access, gliglical states of coitus, suggestions from "La Señorita Cora," the echoes of pederasts, lesbian encounters (fern/lakes/hills), exaltations and defenses of onanism, all joining Cortázar's central scheme: how can we talk about a new man (new woman?) while this one keeps hiding behind the proverbial fig leaf, while he still believes in a decency defined in terms of what remains hidden. The nostalgic trip back to Eden acquires a double sonority: a return to the moment of embarking upon what Cortázar considers the wrongly-chosen road; a return as well to the moment just before the first bit of shame was felt about the body. A natal beginning, the joy of discovering a world to be possessed without all the cloaks and conventions. Permission granted—by not having asked for it—to utilize verbs and conjugations in their original meanings, to extend bridges toward others, to be a bridge with others. It is also expected that this eliminates the egocentric viewpoint, that it overcomes the *I* and replaces it with the *we*. There is hope for such a view, not based on negating others, not based on oppressing their being in order to advance to a certain position on a gameboard, a gameboard drawn up according to an alien table of instructions.

Each one of Cortázar's pursuers has to follow a certain plan, not always drawn up by him, in order to get closer to his vision of a possible solution. For some of them failure is the final sign; for others the truncated, inconclusive search. Thus we go back to what "El perseguidor" proposes: so many metaphysical goings-on hovering around Oliveira, so many desires for an encounter that he doesn't quite manage to see his discovery until it is lost. At any rate, love and contact with other people would have seemed too superficial to him. Madness? No. Suicide? No again. Rather the useless lucidity of before; once more to seesaw between Ovejero's "Ahá" and "Death to the dog." It is science, it is deceit, it is "el gran hengaño," the great deception. It is also Persio, who is so much the astral poet that even if he does see what is going on in his world he does not participate. It is Medrano, who does participate and so dies. Personal purification, yes, but what did he contribute to Claudia's time or to the others'? They are already resigned to just one more day, just one more beer, and to forgetting. It is Juan, who seeks access and the opening to Hélène, who repeats, however, certain patterns already drawn by Oliveira. But now a fundamental difference is added: we are no longer facing a Club de la Serpiente which does and undoes itself according to certain internal rules fomented by the mediocrity of some of its participants. Now all the lines are extended toward "the zone," toward a total participation in others, of others, toward a coagulation where beings no longer figure as individual entities, but rather are all projected in a single thrust toward the rest. This human coagulation is translated onto a narrative plane in the first thirty-nine pages of a novel, a narrative coagulation from which we will derive all explicative lines, from which we respond to the oneness of the character's city—a look into the kaleidoscope. If the maximum beauty of these "patterns" is not to be found there, then certainly there is at least the possibility of that one encounter in which it is no longer just one "I" magnified over and beyond the others. Another difference, and certainly not an insignificant one, is a greater, more human responsibility toward the desired woman and a corresponding augmentation of the obstacles which put off the encounter.

I don't want to suggest what is commonly known as "the author's trajectory." I do wish to suggest that a greater opening up to others and a greater corresponding recognition of others' presence are shown. It is a recognition of their participation in oneself and one's own conformation as a result of that participation. That is why in the world of "La Joda" Lonstein's refinements can also have a place. This group—with the reservations already formulated elsewhere—develops the will of every member who will be integrated, *from* his participation in communal interests, *with* the presence of the others. Let us note that Lonstein's solitary pleasure is important because it does not stay shut in, because it obliges the "el que te dije" and those who read about it to participate in his opening up. It is not a matter of convincing; it is a matter of accepting—accepting behavior no less esoteric than that of a luminous mushroom's fortunes or that of a Parisian penguin.

If we continue to classify pursuers, the label obviously corresponds to Andrés. His search would appear to pick up where the others' left off, to depart from an encounter of the *I*, from a partial reconciliation with that *I* toward actions with others. It is no longer a question of passive acceptance, but rather of concrete, physical action, though it may remain on a low level of importance. Here it must be pointed out, however, that Andrés will inherit the function of the "el que te dije." The latter being dead, it is Andrés who must continue with "el libro de Manuel." Once again we have a collage that serves to document the moment it is hoped will one day be prehistoric. I say "once again" because it is the same with *Rayuela*, a collage, in part, of the cliché of all those intellectuals who are so well read but so slow to act. In the cases of both *Rayuela* and *Libro de Manuel* it is not so much the collages of Western ideas, of daily acts of terrorism, which linger after having read them, but the overlapping of these notions into a language which denounces them and which allows, or awaits, their destruction.

Again we have a dual reading of the text: a fact and its inscription into a framework denouncing its presence. This results in a single effect: the impact of the fact already denounced, sending the reader back to his previous passive position. A hope may arise: to accentuate indignation. We already know that such a text will convince neither the incredulous nor those who support or tolerate these acts. It will only accentuate the indignation of one already indignant. In any case, it means a nexus between reader and narrator by means of a text, part of whose extrinsic reality they must both share, the reading of a shared language that unites those who empathize with the proposal, the extension of a bridge where one already exists, hope where perhaps it already awaits. Once again: *challenge* and hope for that *response* which starts up the mechanism, a critical reading which requires a pursuer who would act and which proposes an author who assumes language to be an instrument of denunciation, if no longer one of combat.

But it is not only the searching as action which one gets out of Cortázar. There must also necessarily follow a preoccupation with the function, or multiple functions, which language can and must perform. In *Octaedro* these problems reinstate themselves with a fundamental variation in one special instance. In "Liliana llorando" the sick person writes at first to distract himself, but later notices that he is living the written-imagined parts more than his concrete reality, which is what frees him from his death. "Professional deformation" of reality—is he a writer? a journalist?—allows him these luxuries. The words that fill up the void also establish another reality, the one that forces itself upon his will. Here we could drive home the motif of the power of the word as an instrument of creation, as one unleashing other worlds (e.g., the mention of Nico in "Cartas de mamá"), but I prefer to underline for now the distraction aspect and the replacement of one reality by another (neither of which is desired).

In "Manuscrito hallado en un bolsillo" to write is a way of objectifying, of trying to understand something that is not logical, of pushing it onto the written page. If this writing truly does lay down certain arrangements, certain differentiations that to one's initial apprehension were not necessary (cf. "Las babas del diablo"), then to explain what was done is simpler than living it, even if sometimes there is no way to articulate it. The notebook, just like the Métro map (a variant of the module Persio used, a map of Portuguese trains), imposes an order, invents a time outside of the game to which he is bound and which strange forces prevent him from violating, even at the risk of once again having it said that "no se culpe a nadie."

It is "Los pasos en las huellas" which allows us to elaborate another angle of what was suggested by "El perseguidor" about biography as translation. The title itself underlines the other side of the exercise, as indicated in the initial note: "Crónica algo tediosa, estilo de ejercicio más que ejercicio de estilo de un, digamos, Henry James que hubiera tomado mate en cualquier patio porteño o platense de los años veinte." The narrator develops the new steps that will fill up the tracks by using his text against the grain. This will be the mark of the biographer, registered in the figure of the one he studies. Thus there are new cutouts of the double, through analogy, through entry into a world where one very rationally goes to live, with the minor variations of an avatar, what will be denounced by a book and by a discourse (instead of "una flor amarilla").

New also is the change in the poet=pursuer/critic=follower relationship; the critic redeems the deeper meanings of and the reasons for his subject's poetry from beneath the transitory fame where they are buried. There is a redemption, likewise, from a mediocre academic position by means of a "bestseller"—that institution which transforms everyday lives by sanctioning them for acceptance with the use of rubber stamps and ministerial recognition. From the very beginning, then, we have a re-creation by the critic of the miserable life of his subject. This is a double vengeance, to be achieved when the book forces its way onto the popular market.

The text can then become a mirror, the critical text can become a dissembled autobiography, an exorcism of recognized transgressions in the choice of subject studied. A radical difference is drawn between Bruno, the mere follower of a pursuer, and Fraga, who transforms the study of Romero's life into an examination of his own attitudes in the presence of that greatest of literary frauds. A single approximation turns out in opposite directions. The popular image of Johnny is consumed by the public, thus gratifying his critic. His truth is measured in the number of editions printed, the number of contracts for translations. The recipe has had the desired effect. Bruno and his wife are delighted. They will stay in the game. The possible omens that surface when he is confronted with Johnny dissipate upon leaving the vitiated air of his poorly formulated questions, of his non-methodical questing. In spite of all this, the critic accepts Johnny's superiority, recognizing that his road does not allow for both sanity and coexistence with the parasites of the species. Johnny's remarks when faced with his literary image (image: a glossy surface that hides the true model) alter neither the order nor the reception of Bruno's Johnny. No other exists except the one pressed out between the journalistic sheets, written to assure triumph and international contracts. The choice of subject matter suggests no analogies, no likenesses, no common projects; it responds to the needs of the market, to the necessity of pacifying the reader by assuring him that the artist is what he was expected to be. It is a nice easy chair, with no danger of someone's coming up behind with a dagger or with a version that would change everything around.

There is criticism of what in turn sees itself as a critical text (and there is no text that does not do so); there is layer upon layer of powder over the make-up that is already on. It is a text which refers to the scaffolding behind the critique and its reception—a text like "El perseguidor" transmitting criticism through arousal—an entry, in other words, into the critic's workshop, analogous to its multiple productions with the use of marked cards. Writing here is not the instrument of a search or even the search itself, but a way of enveloping it, of organizing it for worldwide acclaim, for fashion's dictates, to affirm it as one more product to be acquired—Rocamadour boutiques, Macondo restaurants. Everything is obtained, digested and expelled in the direction of yet another consumer.

At some point during this process the collision can occur: the gaze that comes peeking out of the looking-glass, the sign demanding a response, the necessity of opting for the continuation of the hallowed deception, or its rejection and thus its payment, with a return to those uncomfortable positions already overcome once. The dissembled biography has assured what was expected. The *arribismo* of the poet is repeated in the *arribismo* of his critic: the same pattern is drawn, the same hallowing result is obtained. It is simply not convenient to alter proven formulas. Every narrated fact is aimed at those who will devour it, those who will translate it into other equally digestible media. Thus criticism alters its own sign: the research, the files, the wording are all mere steps which reiterate the desired result. There is no critical reading, no critical writing. The critic is the beloved lackey of those who read what they would love to have written, and their applause is of a one-handed variety.

At the moment when success does arrive, however, a sincere questioning may occur: it is a gaze without pretexts upon the mirror, reflecting a falsely revered image; it is the official version, the one that will not allow any idols with clay feet to stand. This is the moment for an obeisant smile, or the smile of him who is preparing to make the leap that will annihilate him along with the philistines. Once again desire for authenticity (Medrano), for faithfulness until death (the first Johnny), of at least not tumbling again into the double infamy of repeating alien deceptions. A double glance, too, toward the *I* and toward those who refuse to tolerate the reduction of something newly enlarged to its vile, rapscallion truth. The new image is the one assimilated, and deception by a truth which has already deceived once will not be tolerated. The acceptance/refusal speech for the prize can only be a product of "indisposition," of a bad moment to be later excused.

The temptation is now mine to go back to theories that might bore some, even though they themselves use them. "Me aburren las hipótesis tempoespaciales, las *n* dimensiones, sin hablar de la jerga ocultista, la vida astral y Gustav Meyrink." It is "contactos tempo-espaciales," "uniones posesivas" and faraway but still visited bestiaries. It is approximations through words that exorcise after having hidden other objects, and beings no longer accepting the forces imposed on them. Of course, it is the farce of the poet himself, that succubus possessor who perhaps also desires to arrive at an ending. There is the possibility of definitively falling from an exalted scenario into bed with Susana/Ofelia, an honest acceptance of limitations, an oh so flogged-about inner peace and a small joy—knowing that even from this side, from the side of true simulation, fidelity was possible—the rejection of decisions, terminating in insane laughter (or hunting the pistol so near at hand in the desk drawer).

To read one's favorite writers and stroll through their new books could be a visit to spots which recognize each other in a friendly way, thanks to other frameworks, a visit to figures who point toward unalterable goals, ones which must be confronted because not to do so would be to remain silent forever. Affirming this is in itself a search for some bridge which extends from opposite points toward the middle. Solitary writing and solitary reading have been (theoretically) progressively abandoned in order to move toward a communal encounter—the trip being nothing more than a stage leading back to the others—a direct appeal to the very one now facing these letters.

It is no longer a question of narrating what can be catalogued by a perpetually self-adhering label (nor is it possible to prevent it from sticking of its own accord at times) in order to entertain, to document certain phenomena attributable to diverse causes within and outside of logical paradigms, to write and to leave what is written to the unwitting disposition of the texts. Conscious of the limits imposed by any narrative framework, one appeals directly to the reader, conscious of the fact that a single graphic plane is not enough to explain—isn't that a main part of what it's all about underneath the multiple ludic drawings?—what has been imposed, along with the very imposition, without the intervention of one's will in these encounters. It is necessary to continue finding and testing approximations that would form a bond between participant and the one who lived it all, on a common analogous plane.

From the very first submission to these means of communication we know there will be insurmountable obstacles unless we denounce those means, unless we resort to their very negation, unless we make explicit their insufficiency before those facts demanding clarification in the face of the "ahí pero dónde, cómo." It is here that silence fits in, or a perpetual quest for a formula, the one closest to a faithful translation of what has been accepted, but without so much mediation. Now, and more so each time in Cortázar's works, one must freely receive those signs, which are each time no longer mere paper words, in order to arrive at an immediate contact with the one who, from his side, draws closer and closer to his own version of the encounter, to the sparrow's pecking. Thus one must seek, it seems, total participation, in which writing and the reading of it are no longer two separate exercises, but rather a simultaneous action of translating and assimilating a desired reality.

fueron a izar a la pared de arpillera que miraba hacia →

embocaron mal el santuario y ~~quitaron ademas de~~ Rivadavia, siendo que

como en las pilas de discos

las cajas de herramientas

las carpetas de papeles

la entrada ~~muuuuuuuuuuuu~~

~~el patio~~

~~el llamado~~

~~el recibo del alquiler~~

estaba del otro lado, del lado de la pirámide

DONDE DESDE LO ALTO VEINTE SIGLOS NO OS CONTEMPLAN

y se abría sobre el próximo y movido horizonte de la calle Hipólito Irigoyen.

- Me han jodido el coliflor - decía Juan a Stella que andaba felicísima.- Es lástima, porque si lo llegás a ver cuando estaba recién comprado, seguro que se te refresca el alma.

- Te podés comprar otro mañana - dijo Stella.

- Claro. Como Cocteau a Orfeo: "Mata a Eurídice. Te sentirás mucho mejor después."

- Bueno - dijo Stella.- Yo, en realidad, lo que quise decir ...

- Sí, naturalmente. Ahora que no siempre pasa uno por el mercado del Plata en el momento preciso en que sale a la venta un coliflor así. Fijáte que hacen falta miles de factores en perfecta coincidencia. Si mi colectivo me deja en esa esquina dos minutos después, me pierdo la compra. Lo sé porque cuando lo alcé en mis brazos

- Manfloro de mierda - dijo claramente una voz educada entre la gente.

arrorró mi coli

arrorró mi flor

sí

realmente lo alcé en mis brazos, y justo entonces una señora se lo que-

A page of the original text of *El Examen*, an unpublished novel (1949–50). Photo: Alfredo J. Zamora.

Léonie que mirándome la mano me repitió casi tus mismas palabras. "Ella sufre en
alguna parte. Siempre ha sufrido. Es muy alegre, adora el amarillo, su pájaro es
el mirlo, su hora la noche, su puente el Pont des Arts". (Una pinaza color
borravino, Maga, y por qué no nos habremos ido en ella cuando todavía era tiempo.)

~~Desde ese día empezamos a no vernos.~~ Apenas nos conocíamos y ya la vida urdía
~~todo~~ lo necesario para desencontrarnos minuciosamente. Como no sabías disimular
~~tus gustos~~ me di cuenta en seguida de que no te gustaban las ~~cosas sencillas~~,
salvo que fueran flores o pájaros o ideas, y que para vivirte como yo quería
era necesario cerrar los ojos y ~~empezar a ver~~. Sí, primero ~~las~~ estrellas amari-
llas (moviéndose en una jalea de terciopelo), luego saltos rojos, ~~movimientos
elementales de la luz, de una riqueza increíble~~ que acababan en la firma Klee,
~~como la firma de una araña~~, en ~~el deslumbrado~~ circo Miró, en ~~el fabuloso~~
Vieira da Silva, en ~~Klee un mundo~~ Picasso con las manos en la cintura y un cigarro de hoja a un lado
de la ~~boca~~. Íbamos a los cine-clubs a ver películas mudas, y no ~~entendías~~ absolu-
tamente nada de esa estridencia amarilla donde corrían los muertos, donde todos
estaban y estábamos muertos (vos lo has dicho mejor, Fernando Pereda, y me acuer-
do), pero de repente ~~pasaba~~ Harold Lloyd y te ~~sacudías el agua del sueño, olvi-
dabas tu tristeza de estar tan lejos del pasado inmediato~~, y al final te con-
vencías de que todo había estado muy bien, y que Pabst y que Fritz Lang. Me
hartabas un poco con tu manía de perfección, con tus zapatos rotos, con tu ne-
gativa a aceptar lo aceptable. Comíamos hamburgers en el Carrefour de l'Odéon,
y nos íbamos en bicicleta a Montparnasse, a cualquier hotel, a cualquier almo-
hada. Pero otras veces seguíamos hasta la Porte d'Orléans, conocíamos cada vez
mejor la zona de terrenos baldíos que hay más allá del Boulevard Jourdan,
donde a medianoche se reunían los del Club de la Serpiente. ~~Dejábamos las bi-
cicletas~~ en la calle y nos internábamos de a poco, parándonos a mirar el cielo
porque ésa es una de las pocas zonas de París donde el cielo ~~puede desplegar su
plumaje manchado de rojo~~. Sentados en un montón de basuras fumábamos un rato, y
la Maga me acariciaba el pelo o canturreaba melodías ni siquiera inventadas,
melopeas absurdas cortadas por suspiros o recuerdos. Yo aprovechaba para pensar

A page of the original text of *Rayuela*. Photo: Alfredo J. Zamora.

Bibliography

Bibliography of Works By and About Julio Cortázar

By MARTHA PALEY FRANCESCATO

To attempt a complete bibliography of a writer like Julio Cortázar is a task bordering on the impossible. The term "complete," then, should be preceded by the word "relatively." Once more, several institutions as well as individuals have made this task possible: the Research Board of the University of Illinois has generously and consistently supported this effort; Rosa Turek and Leticia Díaz have helped with the compilation and typing; and the Center for Latin American and Caribbean Studies helped enormously with travel funds to Paris, where Julio Cortázar kindly allowed me to go through several boxes of material, together with Gladys Yurkievich, who at the time was classifying them, and aided me in the perusal of all the items. To all of them, my deepest thanks.

I. WORKS BY JULIO CORTÁZAR

A. Books

Denís, Julio (pseudonym). *Presencia*. Buenos Aires: El Bibliófilo, 1938. [Poems.]

Cortázar, Julio. *Los reyes*. Buenos Aires: Gulab y Aldabahor, 1949. [Dramatic poem.]

———. *Bestiario*. Buenos Aires: Ed. Sudamericana, 1951. 165 pp. [Short stories.]

———. *Final del juego*. México: Los Presentes, 1956. [9 stories.] 2nd. ed., augmented, Buenos Aires: Ed. Sudamericana, 1964. 196 pp. [18 stories.]

———. *Las armas secretas*. Buenos Aires: Ed. Sudamericana, 1959. 222 pp. [Short stories.]

———. *Los premios*. Buenos Aires: Ed. Sudamericana, 1960. 427 pp. [Novel.]

———. *Historias de cronopios y de famas*. Buenos Aires: Ed. Minotauro, 1962. 155 pp.

———. *Rayuela*. Buenos Aires: Ed. Sudamericana, 1963. 635 pp. [Novel.]

———. *Cuentos*. La Habana: Casa de las Américas, 1964. 323 pp. [Collection of stories from *Bestiario, Final del juego, Las armas secretas* and *Historias de cronopios y de famas*.]

———. *Todos los fuegos el fuego*. Buenos Aires: Ed. Sudamericana, 1966. 197 pp. [Short stories.]

———. *El perseguidor y otros cuentos*. Buenos Aires: Centro Editor para América Latina, 1967. 143 pp. [Collection of stories.]

———. *La vuelta al día en ochenta mundos*. México: Siglo XXI Editores, 1967. 214 pp. [Essays, poetry, stories.]

———. *Buenos Aires, Buenos Aires*. Buenos Aires: Ed. Sudamericana, 1968. 224 pp. [Text accompanies photographs of the city taken by Alicia D'Amico and Sara Facio.]

———. *Ceremonias*. Barcelona: Seix Barral, 1968. 295 pp. [Stories from *Las armas secretas* and *Final del juego*.]

———. *62: Modelo para armar*. Buenos Aires: Ed. Sudamericana, 1968. 269 pp. [Novel.]

———. *Casa tomada*. Buenos Aires: Ed. Minotauro, 1969. Pages not numbered. [An edition of the short story translated to graphic design by Juan Fresán.]

———. *Ultimo round*. México: Siglo XXI Editores, 1969. 220 pp. [Essays, stories, poetry.]

———. *Relatos*. Buenos Aires: Ed. Sudamericana, 1970. 647 pp. [Contains the stories of *Bestiario, Final del juego, Las armas secretas*, and *Todos los fuegos el fuego* arranged under the headings "Rites," "Games," and "Passages."

———. *Viaje alrededor de una mesa*. Buenos Aires: Cuadernos de Rayuela, 1970. 62 pp.

[Cortázar's expression of his political views as given at a round-table discussion in Paris, April 1970 on "The Intellectual and Politics."]

———. *La isla a mediodía y otros relatos*. Barcelona: Salvat Editores, 1971. 196 pp. [Contains 12 of Cortázar's better-known stories.]

———. *Pameos y meopas*. Barcelona: OCNOS. Ed. de Sivera, 1971. 135 pp. [Poems written between 1951 and 1958.]

———. *Prosa del observatorio*. Barcelona: Ed. Lumen, 1972. 79 pp. [Text by Cortázar accompanies photographs of the observatory of Jai Singh in Jaipur, Delhi, 1968.]

———. *La casilla de los Morelli*. Barcelona: Ed. Lumen, 1973. 152 pp. [Essays.]

———. *Libro de Manuel*. Buenos Aires: Ed. Sudamericana, 1973. 386 pp. [Novel.]

———. *Octaedro*. Buenos Aires: Ed. Sudamericana, 1974. 165 pp. [Short stories.]

———. *Fantomas contra los vampiros multinacionales—Una utopía realizable narrada por Julio Cortázar*. México: Excelsior, 1975.

———. *Antología*. Trabajo crítico de N. Bratosevich. Buenos Aires: La Librería, 1975.

———. "Estrictamente no profesional." *Humanario*. Buenos Aires: La Azotea, 1976. [Text accompanying photographs by Sara Facio and Alicia D'Amico.]

———. *Alguien que anda por ahí y otros relatos*. Madrid: Alfaguara, 1977. 231 pp. [Short stories.]

B. Translations of the works of Julio Cortázar

1. CZECH

Cortázar, Julio. *Pronásledovatel*. Trans. Kamil Uhlíř. Praha: Odeon, 1966. 166 pp. [*Bestiario*; *Final del juego*; *Las armas secretas* (selec.).]

2. DUTCH

Cortázar, Julio. *De mierenmoordenaar*. Trans. J. A. van Praag. Amsterdam: Van Ditmar, 1967. 142 pp. [*Historias de cronopios y de famas*.]

———. *Brief aan een meisje in Parijs*. Trans. J. A. van Praag. Amsterdam: Meulenhoff, 1969. 155 pp. [*Bestiario* (selec.); *Final de juego* (selec.).]

———. *Het kwijlen van de duivel*. Trans. J. A. van Praag. Amsterdam: Meulenhoff; Bezige Bij, 1969. 202 pp. [*Las armas secretas*; *Todos los fuegos el fuego* (selec.).]

3. ENGLISH

Cortázar, Julio. *The Winners*. Trans. Elaine Kerrigan. New York: Pantheon, 1965. 374 pp. [*Los premios*.]

———. *Hopscotch*. Trans. Gregory Rabassa. New York: Pantheon, 1966. London: Collins, Harvill Press, 1967. 564 pp. [*Rayuela*.]

———. *End of the Game and Other Stories*. Trans. Paul Blackburn. New York: Pantheon, 1967. 277 pp. [Includes stories from *Bestiario*, *Las armas secretas*, and *Final del juego*.]

———. *Blow-up and Other Stories*. Trans. Paul Blackburn. New York: Collier, 1968. 248 pp.

———. *Cronopios and Famas*. Trans. Paul Blackburn. New York: Pantheon, 1969. 161 pp. [*Historias de cronopios y de famas*.]

———. *62: A Model Kit*. Trans. Gregory Rabassa. New York: Pantheon, 1972. 281 pp. [*62: Modelo para armar*.]

———. *All Fires the Fire*. Trans. Suzanne Jill Levine. New York: Pantheon, 1973. 152 pp. [*Todos los fuegos el fuego*.]

4. FRENCH

Cortázar, Julio. *Les gagnants*. Trans. Laure Guille. Paris: A. Fayard, 1961. 384 pp. [*Los premios*.]

———. *Les armes secrètes*. Trans. Laure Guille. Paris: Gallimard, 1963. 227 pp. [*Las armas secretas*.]

———. *Les Discours du Prince-guele*. J. H. Silva, lithographies. Paris: M. Cassé, 1966. 19 pp.

illus. [Fragment of *Ultimo round*. 100 copies printed. Issued in portfolio. Signed by the author and the artist.]

———. *Marelle*. Trans. Laure Guille et Françoise Roset. Paris: Gallimard, 1966. 597 pp. [*Rayuela*.]

———. *La Bande (sculptée) à Reinhoud, vue par Julio Cortázar*. Paris: Galerie de France, 1968. 25 pp.

———. *Gîtes*. Trans. Laure Guille-Bataillon. Paris: Gallimard, 1968. 249 pp. [*Las armas secretas* (selec.); *Bestiario* (selec.); *Final del juego* (selec.).]

———. *Histoires des Cronopiens et des Fameux*. Trans. Pierre Alechinsky. Paris: La Louvière Daily-Bul, 1968. Pages not numbered. [*Historias de cronopios y de famas*.]

———. *Tous les feux, le feu*. Trans. Laure Guille-Bataillon. Paris: Gallimard, 1970. 205 pp. [*Todos los fuegos el fuego*.]

5. GERMAN

Cortázar, Julio. *Das besetzte Haus*. Trans. Edith Aron. Neuwied; Berlin: Luchterhand, 1963. 250 pp. [*Casa tomada*.]

———. *Geschichten der Cronopien und Famen*. Trans. Wolfgang Promies. Neuwied; Berlin: Luchterhand, 1965. [*Historias de cronopios y de famas*.]

———. *Die Gewinner*. Trans. Christa Wegen. Neuwied; Berlin: Luchterhand, 1966, Sonderausgabe, 1969. 468 pp. [*Los premios*.]

6. ITALIAN

Cortázar, Julio. *Le Armi Segrete*. Trans. Cesco Vian. Milano: Rizzoli, 1963. 244 pp. [*Las armas secretas*.]

———. *Bestiario*. Trans. Flaviarosa Nicoletti Rossini. Torino: Einaudi, 1965. 548 pp. [*Bestiario*; *Las armas secretas*; *Final del juego*.]

———. *Il Gioco del Mondo*. Trans. Flaviarosa Nicoletti Rossini. Torino: Einaudi, 1969. 523 pp. [*Rayuela*.]

———. *I premi*. Milano: Einaudi. [*Los premios*.]

———. *Storie di Cronopios e di Famas*. Trans. Flaviarosa Nicoletti Rossini. Torino: Giulio Einaudi, 1971. 157 pp. [*Historias de cronopios y de famas*.]

———. *Il bestiario di Aloys Zötl*. Trans. Flaviarosa Nicoletti Rossini. Parma: Ricci, 1972.

7. NORWEGIAN

Cortázar, Julio. *Seremonier*. Trans. Kjell Risvik. Oslo: Gyldendal, 1970. 221 pp. [*Bestiario*; *Las armas secretas*; *Todos los fuegos el fuego*.]

8. POLISH

Cortázar, Julio. *Tajemna broń. (Opowiadania)*. Trans. Zofia Chądzyńska. Warszawa: Państw. Instytut Wydawniczy, 1967. 226 pp. [*Las armas secretas*.]

———. *Gra w klasy*. Trans. Zofia Chądzyńska. Warszawa: Czytelnik, 1968. 627 pp. [*Rayuela*.]

———. *Dla wszystkich ten sam ogień*. Trans. Zofia Chądzyńska. Warszawa: Czytelnik, 1969. 223 pp. [*Todos los fuegos el fuego*.]

9. PORTUGUESE

Cortázar, Julio. *Blow-up e Outras Histórias*. Trans. Maria M. Fernandes Ferreira. Lisboa: Europa-América, 1968. 208 pp. [*Las armas secretas*.]

———. *O Jôgo da Amarelinha*. Trans. Fernando de Castro Ferro. Rio de Janeiro: Civilização Brasileira, 1970. 521 pp. [*Rayuela*.]

10. RUMANIAN

Cortázar, Julio. *Sfîrșitul jocului*. Trans. Irina Ionescu și Dumitru Țepeneag. București: Editura pentru literatură universală, 1969. 376 pp. [*Las armas secretas; Historias de cronopios y de famas* (selec.).]

11. SWEDISH

Cortázar, Julio. *Slut på leken. Noveller.* Trans. Jan Sjögren. Stockholm: Bonnier, 1969. 231 pp. [*Bestiario*; *Final del juego*; *Las armas secretas.*]

C. *Reviews, articles, stories, essays, poems by Julio Cortázar*

Denís, Julio (pseudonym). "Rimbaud." *Huella*, 2 (1941).

Cortázar, Julio. "La urna griega en la poesía de John Keats." *Revista de Estudios Clásicos* (Universidad de Cuyo), Año 2, Núms. 49–61 (1946), 45–91.

——. "Enrique Wernicke: *El señor cisne.*" *Los Anales de Buenos Aires*, Núms. 20–22 (oct-dic, 1947), 158. [Reseña.]

——. "Notas sobre la novela contemporánea." *Realidad*, 3, Núm. 8 (mar-apr, 1948), 240–246.

——. "Muerte de Antonin Artaud." *Sur*, Núm. 163 (mayo, 1948), 80–82.

——. "François Porché: *Baudelaire—Historia de un alma.*" *Sur*, Núm. 176 (jun, 1949), 70–74. [Reseña.]

——. "Graham Greene: *The Heart of the Matter.*" *Realidad*, 5 (ene-feb, 1949), 107–112. [Reseña.]

——. "Leopoldo Marechal: *Adán Buenosayres.*" *Realidad*, 5 (mar-abr, 1949), 232–238. [Reseña.]

——. "Un cadáver viviente." *Realidad*, 5 (mayo-jun, 1949), 349–350. [Sobre el surrealismo.]

——. "Irracionalismo y eficacia." *Realidad*, 6 (set-dic, 1949), 250–259. [Reflexiones sobre el capítulo "Existencialismo y nazismo" de *Valoración literaria del existencialismo* por Guillermo de Torre.]

——. "Octavio Paz: *Libertad bajo palabra.*" *Sur*, Núm. 182 (dic, 1949), 93–95. [Reseña.]

——. "Cyril Connolly: *La tumba sin sosiego.*" *Sur*, Núm. 184 (feb, 1950), 61–63. [Reseña.]

——. "Situación de la novela." *Cuadernos Americanos*, 3, Núm. 4 (jul-ag, 1950), 223–243.

——. "Victoria Ocampo: *Soledad sonora.*" *Sur*, Núms. 192–194 (oct-dic, 1950), 284–297. [Reseña.]

——. "Los olvidados." *Sur*, Núms. 209–210 (mar-abr, 1952), 170–172. [Reseña.]

——. "Louis, enormísimo cronopio." *Buenos Aires Literaria*, Año 1, Núm. 6 (mar, 1953), 32–37.

——. "Gardel." *Sur*, Núm. 223 (jul-ag, 1953), 127–129.

——. "Carlos Viola Soto: *Periplo.*" *Buenos Aires Literaria*, Núm. 15 (dic, 1953), 57–63. [Reseña.]

——. "Para una poética." *La Torre*, Núm. 7 (jul-set, 1954), 121–138.

——. "Poemas." *Cuadernos del viento*, Núm. 17 (dic, 1961), 264–267. [13 poems.]

——. "Algunos aspectos del cuento." *Casa de las Américas*, Núms. 15–16 (1962–1963), 3–14. [Reproducido parcialmente en *El Escarabajo de Oro*, Núm. 21 (dic, 1963), 13, 16–19.]

——. "Reunión." *El Escarabajo de Oro*, Año 6, Núms. 26–27 (feb, 1965), 2–3, 6, 14, 16–17.

——. "Carta a J. Carnevale." *Cero*, Núms. 3–4 (mayo, 1965), 37.

——. "Sobre Leopoldo Marechal." *El Escarabajo de Oro*, Núm. 30 (1966), 66–67, 74.

——. *Buenos Aires de la fundación a la angustia.* Buenos Aires: Ediciones de la flor, 1967. [A series of short selections from leading authors, including Cortázar, about Buenos Aires.]

——. "Casilla del camaleón." *Indice*, Año 21, Núms. 221–223 (1967), 10–11.

——. "de Julio Cortázar a Francisco de la Moza." *Revista de la Universidad de México*, 21, Núm. 12 (ag, 1967), 31.

——. " 'La embajada de los cronopios' y 'El avión de los cronopios.' " *Cuadernos de Marcha* (Montevideo), Núm. 3 (1967), 11–13. [Fragmento de *La vuelta al día en ochenta mundos.*]

———. "Julio Cortázar al 'Che.' " *La Estafeta Literaria*, Núm. 383, 18 nov 1967, pp. 9. [Poem.]

———. "Los testigos." *Insula*, Núm. 252 (nov, 1967), 16. [Relato.]

———. "El viaje." *Indice*, Año 21, Núms. 221–223 (1967), 14–16. [Cuento.]

———. "Yo podría bailar ese sillón -dijo Isadora." *El corno emplumado* (México), Núm. 21 (ene, 1967), 8–12.

———. "Carta a Fernández Retamar (I)." *Primera Plana*, Núm. 281, 14 mayo 1968, pp. 72–74.

———. "Carta a Fernández Retamar (II)." *Primera Plana*, Núm 282, 21 mayo 1968, pp. 76–77.

———. "Marcelo del Campo, o más encuentros a deshora." *Eco, Revista de la cultura de occidente* (Bogotá), Tomo 18, 2 (dic, 1968), 117–20.

———. "Mensaje al hermano." *Casa de las Américas*, Núm. 46 (1968), 6.

———. "Noticias del mes de mayo." *La Cultura en México*, Supl. de *Siempre*, Núm. 829, 14 mayo 1969, pp. iv–vii. ["Collage de recuerdos."]

———. "Del cuento breve y sus alrededores." *El Urogallo*, Num. 0 (dic, 1969), 71–77.

Collazos, Oscar, Julio Cortázar y Mario Vargas Llosa. *Literatura en la revolución y revolución en la literatura*. México: Siglo XXI Editores, 1970. 118 pp. [Ensayos de polémica.]

Cortázar, Julio. "Selección de *Bestiario*." *Setenta años de narrativa argentina: 1900–1970*. Madrid: Alianza, 1970, pp. 157–165.

———. "So shine, shine, shoe-shine boy." *Casa de las Américas*, Núm. 63 (1970), 103–105.

———. "720 círculos." *Revista Iberoamericana*, 37, Núm. 74 (ene-mar, 1971), 13–15. [Poema dedicado a Octavio Paz.]

———. "Algunos aspectos del cuento." *Cuadernos Hispanoamericanos*, Núm. 255 (mar, 1971), 403–416.

———. "Policrítica a la hora de los chacales." *Los Libros*, Núm. 20 (jun, 1971), 9–10. [Poema referente al "caso Padilla."]

Benedetti, Mario, Alejo Carpentier, Julio Cortázar, Miguel Barnet, et al. *Literatura y arte nuevo en Cuba*. Barcelona: Ed. Estela, 1971.

Cortázar, Julio, et al. *KO en el séptimo round*. México: Ed. Extemporáneos, 1972. 199 pp. [Anthology of stories about prize fighting.]

Cortázar, Julio. "Respuesta a comentarios de David Viñas, en carta dirigida a Saúl Sosnowski." *Hispamérica*, Núm. 2 (dic, 1972), 55–58.

———. "Alejandra." *Desquicio* (Paris), otoño 1972. [Sin paginación; poema.]

———. "Mi ametralladora es la literatura." *Crisis*, 1, Núm. 2 (jun, 1973), 10–15.

———. Retratos y autorretratos. Buenos Aires: La Azotea, 1973, pp. 45–46. [Texto de Julio Cortázar y fotografías de Alicia D'Amico y Sara Facio.]

———. "An Approach to Lezama Lima." *Review 74*, 12 (1974), 20–25. [Translated from the Spanish by Paula Speck.]

———. "Estamos como queremos o los monstruos están entre nosotros." *Crisis*, 1, Núm. 11 (mar, 1974), 40–44.

———. "Liliana llorando." *Crisis*, 1, Núm. 11 (mar, 1974), 45–58. [Cuento.]

———. "Please, wristwatch, please." *Crisis*, 1, Núm. 11 (mar, 1974), 46–47. [Poema.]

———. "Homenaje a una joven bruja." *El Urogallo*, Año 6, Núms. 31–32 (ene-abr, 1975), 72–80.

———. "Donde dije digo . . ." *Indice*, Núms. 327–328 (abr, 1973), 39.

———. "Carta abierta a Pablo Neruda." *Revista Iberoamericana*, Vol. 39, Núms. 82–83 (ene-jun, 1973), 21–26.

———. "La noche de Mantequilla." *Cambio* (México), Núm. 2 (ene-mar, 1976), 29–35. [Cuento.]

———. "Viaje a las fronteras de la realidad." *Siete Días Ilustrados* (Buenos Aires), Año

9, Núm. 460, 9–15 abr 1976, pp. 54, 58, 60. [Principales pasajes del texto "Estrictamente no profesional," incluido en *Humanario*.]

————. Review of Néstor Sánchez: *Cómico de la lengua*. *Cambio*, No. 2 (ene-mar, 1976), 86–87.

————. "The Present State of Fiction in Latin America." *Books Abroad*, 50, No. 3 (Summer 1976), 522–532. [Article translated from the Spanish by Margery A. Safir.]

————. "Politics and the Intellectual in Latin America." *Books Abroad*, 50, No. 3 (Summer 1976), 533–540. [Article translated from the Spanish by Mary E. Davis.]

————. "Second Time Around." *Books Abroad*, 50, No. 3 (Summer 1976), 517–521. [Story translated from the Spanish by Gregory Rabassa.]

D. Cortázar as Translator

Bremond, Henri. *La poesía pura*. Buenos Aires: Ed. Losada.

Chesterton, G. K. *El hombre que sabía demasiado*. Buenos Aires: Nova.

Defoe, Daniel. *Robinson Crusoe*. Buenos Aires: Vian.

Gide, André. *El inmoralista*. Buenos Aires: Argos.

Giono, Jean. *Nacimiento de la odisea*. Buenos Aires: Argos.

Houghton, Lord. *Vida y cartas de John Keats*. Buenos Aires: Imán, 1955.

Mare, Walter de la. *Memorias de una enana*. Buenos Aires: Argos.

Poe, Edgar Allan. *Obras en prosa*. Traducción, introducción y notas por Julio Cortázar. Ediciones de la Universidad de Puerto Rico. Madrid: Revista de Occidente, 1956. 2 volúmenes.

Poe, Edgar Allan. *Cuentos*. La Habana: Ed. Nacional de Cuba, 1963. 398 pp.

Poe, Edgar Allan. *Aventuras de Arthur Gordon Pym*. La Habana, Cuba: Instituto del Libro, 1968. [*The Narrative of Arthur Gordon Pym of Nantucket*.]

Poe, Edgar Allan. *Eureka*. Madrid: Alianza, 1972.

Stern, Alfred. *Filosofía de la risa y del llanto*. Buenos Aires: Imán, 1950.

Stern, Alfred. *La filosofía existencial de Jean-Sartre*. Buenos Aires: Ed. Imán.

Yourcenar, Marguerite. *Memorias de Adriano*. Buenos Aires: Ed. Sudamericana, 1955.

II. INTERVIEWS WITH JULIO CORTÁZAR

Benasco, Rodolfo. "Explica a Julio Cortázar." *Bibliograma*, Núms. 35–36 (1967).

Bottone, Mireya. "Cortázar en el testimonio." *Boletín de Literaturas Hispánicas*, Núm. 6 (1966), 85–92.

Díaz Martínez, Manuel. "Cuatro preguntas a Julio Cortázar." *La Gaceta de Cuba*, feb 1967, pp. 3.

Flores, Margarita G. "Siete respuestas de Julio Cortázar." *Revista de la Universidad de México*, 21, Núm. 7 (mar, 1967), 10–13.

Guibert, Rita. "Un gran escritor y su soledad." *Life en español*, 7 abr 1969, pp. 43–55. [Respuestas a una serie de preguntas formuladas por escrito por Rita Guibert en nombre de *Life*.]

Guibert, Rita. *Seven Voices*. New York: Alfred A. Knopf, 1973.

Hernández, Ana María. "Conversación con Julio Cortázar." *Nueva Narrativa Hispano-americana*, 3, Núm. 2 (set, 1973), 31–40.

Hildebrandt, Martha. "Entrevista: Julio Cortázar." *Textual* (Lima), Núm. 7 (jun, 1973), 52–54.

Lazar, Josette. "About Julio Cortázar." *New York Times Book Review*, 21 Mar 1965, pp. 5.

Martínez, Tomás Eloy. "La Argentina que despierta lejos." *Primera Plana*, Núm. 103, 27 oct 1964, pp. 36–40.

Schneider, Luis Mario. "Entrevista a Julio Cortázar." *Revista de la Universidad de México*, 17, Núm. 8 (apr, 1963), 24–25.

Schneider, Luis Mario. "Sobre las técnicas, el compromiso y el porvenir de la novela." *El Escarabajo de Oro*, Boletín Núm. 1 (1965), 3.

Urondo, Francisco. "El escritor y sus armas políticas." *Panorama*, 24 nov 1970, pp. 40–50. [Entrevista a Cortázar en Buenos Aires.]

Vargas Llosa, Mario. "Preguntas a Julio Cortázar." *Expreso* (Lima), 7 feb 1965. [Incluida en Simo, Ana María, ed. *Cinco miradas sobre Cortázar*. Buenos Aires: Ed. Tiempo Contemporáneo, 1968.]

Vargas Llosa, Mario. "Entrevista a Julio Cortázar." *Comentarios Bibliográficos Americanos*, 3, Núm. 11 (ene-mar, 1971), 17–19.

III. BIBLIOGRAPHY OF WORKS ABOUT JULIO CORTÁZAR

A. Bibliographies

Bottone, Mireya. "Bibliografía de Cortázar." *Boletín de Literaturas Hispánicas*, Núm. 6 (1966), 93–94.

———. "Bibliografía sobre Cortázar." *Boletín de Literaturas Hispánicas*, Núm. 6 (1966), 95–96.

Paley Francescato, Martha. "Bibliografía de y sobre Julio Cortázar." *Revista Iberoamericana*, 39, Núm. 84–85 (jul-dic, 1973), 697–726.

———. "Selected Bibliography (1938–1976)." *Books Abroad*, 50, No. 3 (Summer 1976), 513–516.

B. Books

1. GENERAL STUDIES OF CORTÁZAR BY ONE AUTHOR

Alsacio Cortázar, Miguel. *Viaje alrededor de una silla*. Buenos Aires: Carpeta Editora, 1971. [Answer to Cortázar's *Viaje alrededor de una mesa*.]

Amícola, José. *Sobre Cortázar*. Buenos Aires: Ed. Escuela, 1969.

Aronne Amestoy, Lida. *Cortázar: la novela mandala*. Buenos Aires: Fernando García Cambeiro, 1972.

Arriguci, Davi Jr. *O Escorpião encalacrado. A poética da destruição em Julio Cortázar*. São Paulo: Editora Perspectiva, 1973.

Curutchet, Juan Carlos. *Julio Cortázar o la crítica de la razón pragmática*. Madrid: Editora Nacional, 1972. [Aparecido por capítulos en *Cuadernos Hispanoamericanos*:
—Núms. 253–254 (ene-feb, 1971), 301–307;
—Núm. 255 (mar, 1971), 561–572;
—Núm. 256 (abr, 1971), 153–164;
—Núm. 259 (ene, 1972), 129–140;
—Núm. 260 (feb, 1972), 330–337;
—Núm. 261 (mar, 1972), 459–479;
—Núms. 263–264 (mayo-jun, 1972), 425–446.]

Escamilla Molina, Roberto. *Julio Cortázar: visión de conjunto*. México: Ed. Novaro, 1970.

Filer, Malva E. *Los mundos de Julio Cortázar*. New York: Las Américas Publishing Co., 1970.

García Canclini, Néstor. *Cortázar. Una antropología poética*. Buenos Aires: Ed. Nova, 1968.

Garfield, Evelyn Picon. *¿Es Julio Cortázar un surrealista?* Madrid: Gredos, 1975.

Garfield, Evelyn Picon. *Julio Cortázar*. New York: Frederick Ungar, 1975.

Genover, Kathleen. *Claves de una novelística existencial (en Rayuela de Cortázar)*. Madrid: Playor, S. A., 1973.

MacAdam, Alfred. *El individuo y el otro. Crítica a los cuentos de Julio Cortázar*. Buenos Aires, New York: La Librería, 1971.

Mastrángelo, Carlos. *Usted, yo, los cuentos de Julio Cortázar y su autor*. Córdoba: Ed. Universidad Nacional de Córdoba, 1971.

Pereira, Teresinka. *El realismo mágico y otras herencias de Julio Cortázar.* Portugal-USA: Nova Era and Backstage Books, 1976.

Rein, Mercedes. *Julio Cortázar: el escritor y sus máscaras.* Montevideo: Ed. Diaco, 1969.

Rein, Mercedes. *Cortázar y Carpentier.* Buenos Aires: Ed. de Crisis, 1974.

Roy, Joaquín. *Julio Cortázar ante su sociedad.* Barcelona: Península, 1974.

Sola, Graciela de. *Julio Cortázar y el hombre nuevo.* Buenos Aires: Ed. Sudamericana, 1968.

Sosnowski, Saúl. *Julio Cortázar: una búsqueda mítica.* Buenos Aires: Ed. Noé, 1973.

Viñas, David. *De Sarmiento a Cortázar.* Buenos Aires: Siglo Veinte, 1970.

2. GENERAL STUDIES OF CORTÁZAR BY SEVERAL CONTRIBUTING AUTHORS

Benedetti, Mario, et al. "Sobre Julio Cortázar." Cuadernos de la revista *Casa de las Américas*, Núm. 3 (nov, 1967), 7–22. Contenido:

> Discusión de la obra de Cortázar por Mario Benedetti;
> "Café conversatorio" celebrado en la Casa de las Américas el 2 de julio de 1965, sobre *Rayuela* de Julio Cortázar. Panel: Ana María Simo, José Lezama Lima, Roberto Fernández Retamar. El "Café conversatorio" fue reproducido en *Cinco miradas sobre Cortázar* bajo el título "Discusión sobre *Rayuela.*"
> "Todos los fuegos el fuego", por Eliseo Diego.

Boletín de Literaturas Hispánicas, Núm. 6 (1966). Contenido:

> Adolfo Prieto, "Julio Cortázar hoy";
> Rosa Boldori, "La irrealidad en la narrativa de Cortázar";
> Gladys Onega, "*Los premios*";
> María Isabel de Gregorio, "*Rayuela*";
> Rosa Boldori, "Sentido y trascendencia de la estructura de *Rayuela*";
> Nelly Donni de Mirande, "Notas sobre la lengua de Cortázar";
> "Cortázar en el testimonio";
> Bibliografía.

Books Abroad, 50, No. 3 (Summer 1976). Contenido:

> Ivar Ivask, "Cortázar's Oklahoma Stomp";
> Evelyn Picon Garfield, "Chronology";
> Martha Paley Francescato, "Selected Bibliography";
> Gregory Rabassa, "Lying to Athena: Cortázar and the Art of Fiction";
> Roberto González Echevarría, "*Los Reyes*: Cortázar's Mythology of Writing";
> Margery A. Safir, "An Erotics of Liberation: Notes on Transgressive Behavior";
> Ana María Hernández, "Vampires and Vampiresses: A Reading of 62";
> Evelyn Picon Garfield, "*Octaedro*: Eight Phases of Despair";
> Martha Paley Francescato, "The New Man (But Not The New Woman)";
> Malva E. Filer, "The Ambivalence of the Hand in Cortázar's Fiction";
> Saúl Sosnowski, "Pursuers."

Giacomán, Helmy F., ed. *Homenaje a Julio Cortázar.* Madrid: Anaya, 1972. Contenido:

> José Lezama Lima, "Cortázar y el comienzo de la otra novela";
> Marcelo Alberto Villanueva, "El salto hacia adelante o la razón de la sinrazón";
> Fernando Alegría, "*Rayuela* o el orden del caos";
> Enrique Giordano, "Algunas aproximaciones a *Rayuela*, de Julio Cortázar, a través de la dinámica del juego";
> John G. Copeland, "Las imágenes de *Rayuela*";
> Angela Dellepiane, "62. *Modelo para armar*: ¿Agresión, regresión o progresión?"
> Ana María Pucciarelli, "Notas sobre la búsqueda en la obra de Cortázar";
> Malva E. Filer, "La búsqueda de la autenticidad";
> Osvaldo López Chuhurra, ". . . Sobre Julio Cortázar";
> Malva E. Filer, "Las transformaciones del yo";
> Antonio Pagés Larraya, "Cotidianeidad y fantasía en una obra de Cortázar";
> Alfred J. MacAdam, "*Los premios*: Una tentativa de clasificación formal";

Richard F. Allen, "Temas y técnicas del taller de Julio Cortázar";

Flora H. Schiminovich, "Cortázar y el cuento en uno de sus cuentos";

Germán D. Carrillo, "Emociones y fragmentaciones: técnicas cuentísticas de Julio Cortázar en 'Todos los fuegos el fuego' ";

Marta Morello-Frosch, "El personaje y su doble en las ficciones de Cortázar";

Joan Hartman, "La búsqueda de las figuras en algunos cuentos de Cortázar";

Wolfgang A. Luchting, "*Todos los fuegos el fuego*";

Martha Paley de Francescato, "Julio Cortázar y un modelo para armas ya armado";

David Lagmanovich, "Julio Cortázar y su pequeño mundo de cronopios y famas";

Roberto Hozven V., "Interpretación de 'El río', cuento de Julio Cortázar";

Saúl Sosnowski, "Conocimiento poético y aprehensión racional de la realidad. Un estudio de 'El perseguidor' de Julio Cortázar";

Luis Bocaz Q., "*Los reyes*, o la irrespetuosidad ante lo real de Cortázar";

Antonio Pagés Larraya, "Perspectivas de 'Axolotl', cuento de Julio Cortázar";

Mary E. Davis, "La estética del éxtasis".

Indice, Año 22, Núms. 221–223 (1967), 9–24. Contenido:

F. Fernández Santos, "Julio Cortázar: cronopio universal";

José Miguel Ullán, "Dos cronopios";

Luis Harss, "Cortázar en su taller";

Félix Grande, "Fragmento para un homenaje a *Rayuela*".

Lagmanovich, David, ed. *Estudios sobre los cuentos de Julio Cortázar*. Barcelona: Hispam, 1975. Contenido:

David Lagmanovich, "Prólogo: Para una caracterización general de los cuentos de Julio Cortázar";

Jaime Alazraki, "Dos soluciones estilísticos al tema del compadre en Borges y Cortázar";

Rodolfo A. Borello, " 'Los buenos servicios' o la ambigüedad de las vidas ajenas";

Alicia Borinsky, "Juegos: una realidad sin centros";

Mireya Camurati, "El absurdo, la risa y la invitación a la aventura: 'Instrucciones para subir una escalera' ";

Juan Carlos Curutchet, "Julio Cortázar, cronista de las eras imaginarias: para una interpretación de 'Todos los fuegos el fuego' ";

Zunilda Gertel, "Funcionalidad del lenguaje en 'La salud de los enfermos' ";

Marta Morello-Frosch, "La relación personaje-espacio en las ficciones de Cortázar";

Martha Paley de Francescato, "El viaje: función, estructura y mito en los cuentos de Julio Cortázar";

Perla Petrich, " 'Instrucciones para John Howell': iniciación al extrañamiento";

Edelweis Serra, "El arte del cuento: 'La noche boca arriba' ";

Saúl Sosnowski, " 'Una flor amarilla', vindicación de vidas fracasadas";

Alfredo Veiravé, "Aproximaciones a 'El perseguidor' ".

Revista Iberoamericana, Núms. 84–85 (jul-dic, 1973). [The complete issue is devoted to Cortázar.] Contenido:

Julio Cortázar, "Un texto inédito de Cortázar. Un capítulo suprimido de *Rayuela*";

Luis Leal, "Situación de Julio Cortázar";

Saúl Yurkievich, "Julio Cortázar: al Unísono y al Dísono";

Fernando Ainsa, "La dos orillas de Julio Cortázar";

Alfred J. MacAdam, "La torre de Dánae";

Joaquín Roy-Cabrerizo, "Claves de Cortázar en un libro olvidado: *Buenos Aires, Buenos Aires*";

Rubén Benítez, "Cortázar: 'que supo abrir la puerta para ir a jugar' ";

Eduardo G. González, "Hacia Cortázar, a partir de Borges";

Alicia Borinsky, "Macedonio y el humor de Julio Cortázar";

Martín C. Taylor, "*Los reyes* de Julio Cortázar: el minotauro redimido";

Silverio Muñoz Martínez, "Otra mirada sobre *Rayuela*";
A. Carlos Isasi Angulo, "Función de las inovaciones estilísticas en *Rayuela*";
Julio Matas, "El contexto moral en algunos cuentos de Julio Cortázar";
Jaime Alazraki, "Homo sapiens vs. Homo ludens en tres cuentos de Cortázar";
Emir Rodríguez-Monegal, "Le Fantôme de Lautréamont";
David Lagmonovich, "Acotación a 'La isla a mediodía' ";
Saúl Sosnowski, "Los ensayos de Julio Cortázar: Pasos hacia su política";
Carlos Martínez, "Ampliando una página de Cortázar";
Ken Holsten, "Notas sobre 'Tablero de dirección' en *Rayuela* de Julio Cortázar";
Martha Paley de Francescato, "El *Libro de Manuel*";
Lucille Kerr, " 'El individuo y el otro.' Crítica a los cuentos de Julio Cortázar";
Martha Paley de Francescato, "Bibliografía de y sobre Julio Cortázar."

Setecientos monos (Rosario), Año 2, Núm. 7 (dic, 1965). Contenido:
Adolfo Prieto, "Julio Cortázar hoy";
Rosa Boldori, "Cortázar: una novelística nueva";
Gladys Onega, "Cortázar: personajes y misterio."

Simo, Ana María, ed. *Cinco miradas sobre Cortázar*. Buenos Aires: Ed. Tiempo Contemporáneo, 1968. Contenido:
Panel: Ana María Simo, José Lezama Lima y Roberto Fernández Retamar, "Discussión sobre *Rayuela*";
Mario Vargas Llosa, "Preguntas a Julio Cortázar";
Julio Cortázar, "Carta de Julio Cortázar a R. Fernández Retamar" [aparecida en el diario *Espreso* (Lima), 7 feb 1965].

Tirri, Sara Vinocur y Néstor Tirri, eds. *La vuelta a Cortázar en nueve ensayos*. Buenos Aires: Carlos Pérez, 1968. Contenido:
Noé Jitrik, "Notas sobre la 'Zona sagrada' y el mundo de los 'otros' en *Bestiario* de Julio Cortázar";
Manuel Durán, "Julio Cortázar y su pequeño mundo de cronopios y famas";
Alain Bosquet, "Las realidades secretas de Julio Cortázar";
Alejandra Pizarnik, "Nota sobre un cuento de Julio Cortázar: 'El otro cielo' ";
Antonio Pagés Larraya, "*Los premios*";
Graciela de Sola, "*Rayuela*: una invitación al viaje";
Guillermo Ara, "Cortázar cronopio" [Notas sobre *La vuelta al día en ochenta mundos*];
Luis Gregorich, "Julio Cortázar y la posibilidad de la literatura";
Néstor Tirri, "El perseguidor perseguido".

C. Doctoral Theses

Arrone de Amestoy, Lida. "*Rayuela*, otra manera del compromiso literario." Mendoza, 1970.

Bates, Merrit W. "Dos autores, cuatro novelas." Universidad Nacional del Litoral, Rosario-Santa Fe-Argentina, 1968.

Bates, Merrit W. "Dos autores, cuatro novelas." Universidad Nacional del Litoral, Rosario-Santa Fe-Argentina, 1968.

Baxt, Linda Cummings. "Game in Cortázar." Yale, 1974.

Beaulien-Camus, Catherine. "Recherches sur Julio Cortázar. Aspects d'une biographie." Faculté de Lettres de Nanterre, 1974.

Brody, Robert. "Julio Cortázar in his *Rayuela*." Harvard, 1971.

Bruchi, Liliane. "Aspetti di *Rayuela* nella narrativa di Julio Cortázar." Università degli Studi di Firenze, 1972–1973.

Chazelle, Marie-Christine. " 'Omnibus,' un cuento de Julio Cortázar. (Edición anotada y estudio crítico)." Toulouse, 1969.

Davis, Mary Eunice. "The Vision of Reality in Selected Novels by Sábato, Cortázar, and García Márquez." Kentucky, 1970.

Dean, Frances Forsythe. "Nonsignificant and Significant Variation in Literary Translation: Comparison and Analysis of Selected English Translations of Julio Cortázar." Texas A and M University, 1972.

Echevarren-Welker, Roberto. "Le monde Romanesque de Julio Cortázar." Université de Paris VIII, 1974.

Galesta, Adele. "Julio Cortázar. L'impegno atraverso il 'fantastico.'" Istituto Universitario di Magisterio, Napoli, 1972–1973.

Garfield, Evelyn Picón. "La influencia del surrealismo francés en la obra de Julio Cortázar." Rutgers, 1972.

Gemis, Francisa. "Le point de vue dans les contes à la première personne de Julio Cortázar." Université de Liège, 1973–1974.

Holsten, Kenneth Alden. "The Metaphysical Search in the Novels of Julio Cortázar." California, San Diego, 1970.

Jarvis, Ana C. "Julio Cortázar: cuentista." California, Riverside, 1973.

Kerr, Lucille. "The Beast and the Double: A Study of the Short Stories of Julio Cortázar." Yale, 1972.

Larisgoitia, Hernani. "Estudio analítico-interpretivo de los cuentos de Julio Cortázar." Wisconsin, 1971.

MacAdam, Alfred John. "The Individual and the Other: A Study of the Prose Works of Julio Cortázar." Princeton, 1969.

MacCoy, Katherine Wallis. "Theory of the Novel in *Rayuela*." Emory, 1970.

Martins, Teresinha Alves Pereira. "Julio Cortázar, Clarice Lispector e la Nova Narrativa Latinoamericana." New Mexico, 1971.

Más, Ramón. "El desarrollo literario de Julio Cortázar." Florida State University, 1975.

Mozejko, Danuta Teresa. "Lectures des contes de Julio Cortázar." Université de la Sorbonne Nouvelle, Paris, 1974.

Muzika, H. M. "*Rayuela*, a Metaphysical Revolution." Liverpool, 1969.

Nelson, Kathleen G. "Julio Cortázar's *Rayuela* as an Existentialist Novel." Catholic University, 1971.

Osta, Winifred. "The Journey Pattern in Four Contemporary American Novels." Arizona, 1970.

Paley Francescato, Martha. "El *Bestiario* de Julio Cortázar: enriquecimiento de un género." Illinois, Urbana-Champaign, 1970.

Petrich, Perla. "Isotopie Initiatique chez Julio Cortázar." Université de Paris VIII, 1976.

Roy-Cabrerizo, Joaquén. "Soledad y amistad, como características argentinas en la obra de Julio Cortázar." Georgetown University, 1973.

Sosnowski, Saúl. "Julio Cortázar, una búsqueda mítica." Virginia, 1970.

Spencer, Sharon D. "The Architectonic Novel: A Study in Structure in Modern Fiction Based Upon Works by Twenty-Three Experimental Novelists From Raymond Roussel to Carlos Fuentes." New York University, 1969.

Toma, Margrit. "Untersuchungen zum Menschenbild in den Werken Julio Cortázars." Universität Rostock, 1973.

Valmaseda Santillana, Tomás. "El lenguaje narrativo de Julio Cortázar." Madrid, 1970.

Villanueva, Alfredo Rafael. "Julio Cortázar's 'Final del juego': A Translation and Critical Study." New York, Birmingham, 1974.

Williams, Lorna Valarie. "La cuentística de Julio Cortázar: teoría y práctica." Indiana University, 1974.

D. Articles and reviews

Acutis, Cesare. "Siamo la somma degli atti degli altri: Cortázar e il suo *Bestiario*." *Quaderni Ibero-Americani*, 42–44 (1973–74), pp. 163–173.

Aid, Frances M. "Case Grammar Applied: Spanish Language and Literature." *Meaning: A Common Ground of Linguistics and Literature*. Proceedings of a University of

Iowa Conference held April 27–28, 1973. Cedar Falls, Iowa. 356 pp. [The article cited contains an example from Julio Cortázar's 'Tema para un tapiz.']

Ainsa, Fernando. "Las dos orillas de Julio Cortázar." *Revista Iberoamericana*, 39, Núms. 84–85 (jul–dic, 1973), 425–456.

Alazraki, Jaime. "Homo sapiens vs. homo ludens en tres cuentos de Cortázar." *Revista Iberoamericana*, 39, Núms. 84–85 (jul–dic, 1973), 611–624.

———. "Cortázar, entre el surrealismo y la literatura fantástica." *El Urogallo*, Año 6, Núms. 35–36 (sept–dic, 1975), 103–107.

———. "Dos soluciones estilísticas al tema del compadre en Borges y Cortázar." *Estudios sobre los cuentos de Julio Cortázar*. Barcelona: Ediciones Hispam, 1975, pp. 23–39. [Reproducido en *Revista Exilio*, 6 (1972), 21–33.]

———. "The Fantastic As Surrealist Metaphors in Cortázar's Short Fiction." *Dada/Surrealism*, No. 5, 1975, pp. 28–33.

Alegría, Fernando. "*Rayuela*, o el orden del caos." *Revista Iberoamericana*, 35, Núm. 69 (sept–dic, 1969), 459–472. [Reproducido en *Homenaje a Julio Cortázar*. Madrid: Anaya, 1972, pp. 81–94.]

Allen, Richard F. "Los temas del tiempo y la muerte en *Todos los fuegos el fuego* de Julio Cortázar." *Duquesne Hispanic Review*, invierno, 1967, 35–50.

———. "Temas y técnicas del taller de Julio Cortázar." *XIII Congreso Internacional de Literatura Iberoamericana*. Caracas: Organización del Bienestar Estudiantil, 1968, pp. 289–296. [Reproducido en *Homenaje a Julio Cortázar*. Madrid: Anaya, 1972, pp. 297–305.]

———. "Julio Cortázar: *Todos los fuegos el fuego*." *Books Abroad*, 42, No. 1 (Winter, 1968), 80–81.

———. "En busca de la novelística de Néstor Sánchez y Julio Cortázar." *Cuadernos Hispanoamericanos*, Núm. 237 (set, 1969), 711–725. [En realidad, es sobre *Nosotros dos* de Sánchez, pero muestra la influencia de Cortázar.]

Alonso, J. M. "Cortázar, Borges and the Loss of Experience." *Review 72* (Winter, 1972), 14–17.

Alves Pereira, Teresinha. "Coincidencia de la técnica narrativa de Julio Cortázar y Clarice Lispector." *Nueva Narrativa Hispanoamericana*, 3, Núm. 1 (ene, 1973), 103–111.

Amorós, Andrés. "Julio Cortázar: *62. Modelo para armar*." *Revista de Occidente*, Núm. 73 (abr, 1969), 123–124. [Reseña]

———. "*Rayuela* (Nueva lectura.)" *Anales de Literatura Hispanoamericana*, Núm. 1 (1972), 281–319.

Anderson Imbert, Enrique. *Historia de la literatura hispanoamericana*, Tomo 2. México: Fondo de Cultura Económica, 1970, pp. 379–383.

———. "Julio Cortázar: *Final del juego*." *Revista Iberoamericana*, 23, Núm. 45 (ene–jul, 1958), 173–175. [Reseña.]

Andreu, Jean L. "*Todos los fuegos el fuego*, les derniers contes de Julio Cortázar." *Cahiers du Monde Hispanique et Luso-Brésilien (Caravelle)*, No. 8 (1967), 153–159. [La traducción de este artículo, "Cortázar cuentista", se publicó en *Mundo Nuevo*, Núm 23 (mayo, 1968), 87–90.]

———. "Pour une lecture de *Casa tomada* de J. Cortázar." *Cahiers du Monde Hispanique et Luso-Brésilien (Caravelle)*, No. 10 (1968), 49–60.

——— et Yves-René Fonquerne. "*Bestiario* de Julio Cortázar: essai d'interprétation systématique." *Cahiers du Monde Hispanique et Luso-Brésilien (Caravelle)*, No. 11 (1968), 112–129.

Anzoategui, Ignacio B. "El anti-Cortázar." *Atlántida*, Núm 1234 (ene, 1970), 58–63. [Respuesta a las declaraciones de Cortázar a *Life*. Es en realidad un violento ataque al escritor, a quien llama "peluquero de señoras," y donde se demuestra un total incomprensión de la obra del escritor y un marcado mal gusto, que le niegan al artículo todo valor crítico.]

Ara, Guillermo. "Cortázar Cronopio. (Notas sobre *La vuelta al día en ochenta mundos*.) *La vuelta a Cortázar en nueve ensayos*. Buenos Aires: Carlos Pérez, 1968, pp. 105–118.

————. *Los argentinos y la literatura nacional*. Buenos Aires: Huemul, 1969, pp. 131–132.

Armani, Horacio. "Algunas vueltas en torno de Cortázar." *La Nación*, Supl. literario, 28 ene 1968, p. 4. [Sobre *La vuelta al día en ochenta mundos*.]

————. "Un viaje imaginario a través de un talento creador." *Clarín*, Supl. literario, 15 feb 1968, p. 5.

Arroyo, Justo. "Julio Cortázar y su *Rayuela*." *Lotería*, Núm 125 (mayo, 1966), 26–30.

Arrufat, Antón. "Julio Cortázar: *Cuentos*." Selección y prólogo por Antón Arrufat. Cuba: Casa de las Américas, 1964, pp. vii–xvi.

————. "*Las armas secretas* de Julio Cortázar." *Casa de las Américas*, Núm. 26 (oct–nov, 1964).

Babín, María Teresa. "La antinovela en Hispanoamérica." *Revista Hispánica Moderna*, Núms. 3–4 (jul–oct, 1968), 523–532. [Study of *Rayuela* as a prime example of the contemporary novel.]

Balla, Andrés. "Clasicismo e innovación en *Cien años de soledad, La casa verde y Rayuela*." *Insula*, Núm. 303 (feb, 1972), 12.

Barberii, Nancy. "*Final del juego* de Julio Cortázar." *Books Abroad*, 39 (Fall, 1965), 440.

Barnatán, Marcos Ricardo. "Julio Cortázar, fantasma y escritor." *Papeles de Son Armadans*, 44, Núm. 132 (mar, 1967), 350–359.

————. "El retorno a Cortázar." *Insula*, Núm. 271 (jun, 1969), 13.

Barrenechea, Ana María. "*Rayuela*, una búsqueda a partir de cero." *Sur*, Núm. 228 (mayo–jun, 1964), 69–73.

————. "La estructura de *Rayuela* de Julio Cortázar." *Litterae Hispanae et Lusitanae*. München: Max Hueber Verlag, 1968, pp. 69–84. [Reproducido en *Nueva Novela Latinoamericana 2*. Buenos Aires: Ed. Paidós, 1972, pp. 222–247.]

Barufaldi, Rogelio. "Soledad y vocación en la última narrativa argentina." *Señales*, Núm. 134 (ene–feb, 1962), 6–9.

Basso, Eleonora. "La música en la obra de Cortázar." *Revista Iberoamericana de Literatura*, 2a. época, Núm. 2 (1970), 51–60.

Bataillon, Laure. "Sur deux tableaux." *La Quinzaine littéraire*, No. 132, 1er. au 15 janvier 1972, pp. 4–5. [About *62. Modelo para armar*.]

Benedetti, Mario. "Julio Cortázar, un narrador para lectores cómplices." *Los Tiempos Modernos*, Núm. 2 (abr, 1965), 16–19. [Reproducido en *Letras del Continente Mestizo*. Montevideo: Arca, 1967, pp. 85–103.]

Benítez, Rubén. "Cortázar: 'que supo abrir la puerta para ir a jugar.'" *Revista Iberoamericana*, 39, Núms. 84–85 (jul–dic, 1973), 483–501.

Bernstein, J. S. "Capítulo 34 de *Rayuela*: Toma de posesión." *Papeles de Son Armadans* (Mallorca), 68, pp. 233–248.

Bernu, Michele. "Essai d'interprétation d'un conte de Julio Cortázar: 'Continuidad de los parques.'" *Cahiers du Monde Hispanique et Luso-Brésilien (Caravelle)*, No. 13 (1969), 23–31.

Bersani, Leo. "*62. A Model Kit*." Trans. Gregory Rabassa. *The New York Times Book Review*, 26 Nov 1972, pp. 7, 43. [Review.]

Bishop, Tom. "Julio Cortázar: *Cronopios y Famas*." Trans. Paul Blackburn. *Saturday Review*, 27 Sept, 969, pp. 26–27. [Review.]

Bjurström, C. G. "Det fantastika i litteraturen; ett samtal med Julio Cortázar." *Bonniers Litterära Magasin*, 38 (maj–juni, 1969), 334–340.

————. "Julio Cortázar. Mon fantastique." *La Quinzaine littéraire*, No. 100, 1er. au 31 août 1970, pp. 16–19.

Blanco, Guillermo. "Todos los fuegos el fuego." *Mapocho* (Santiago de Chile), Núm. 16 (1968), 188–189.

Blanco Amor, José. "Julio Cortázar." *Cuadernos Americanos*, 160, Núm. 5 (set–oct, 1968),

213–237. [Reproducido en *Homenaje a Julio Cortázar*. Madrid: Anaya, 1972, pp. 235–260.]

Block de Behar, Lisa. *Análisis de un lenguaje en crisis*. Montevideo: Ed. Nuestra Tierra, 1969.

Bocaz Q., Luis. "*Los reyes* o la irrespetuosidad ante lo real de Cortázar." *Atenea*, 166, Núm 419 (ene–mar, 1968), 47–55. [Reproducido en *Homenaje a Julio Cortázar*. Madrid: Anaya, 1972, pp. 445–455.]

Boldori, Rosa. "Cortázar = una novelística nueva." *Setecientos monos*, Núm. 7 (dic, 1965).

———. "La irrealidad en la narrativa de Cortázar." *Boletín de Literaturas Hispánicas*, Núm. 6 (1966), 13–27.

———. "Sentido y trascendencia de la estructura de *Rayuela*." *Boletín de Literaturas Hispánicas*, Núm. 6 (1966), 59–69.

Bordelois, Ivonne. "Julio Cortázar: *Los premios*." *Cuadernos del Congreso por la Libertad de la Cultura*, Núm. 55 (1961), 87–88. [Reseña.]

Borello, Rodolfo. "El último combate de Julio Cortázar." *Cuadernos Hispanoamericanos*, Núm. 374 (jul, 1970), 165–173. [Sobre *Ultimo round*.]

———. "Julio Cortázar y lo coloquial en 'Habla coloquial y lengua literaria en las letras argentinas.'" *Anales de Literatura Hispanoamericana*, Núm. 1 (1972), 42–43.

———. "'Los buenos servicios' o la ambigüedad de las vidas ajenas." *Estudios sobre los cuentos de Julio Cortázar*. Barcelona: Ed. Hispam, 1975, pp. 41–57.

Borinsky, Alicia. "Macedonio y el humor de Julio Cortázar." *Revista Iberoamericana*, 39, Núms. 84–85 (jul–dic, 1973), 521–536.

———. "Juegos: una realidad sin centros." *Estudios sobre los cuentos de Julio Cortázar*. Barcelona: Ed. Hispam, 1975, p. 59–72.

Bosquet, Alain. "Les réalités secrètes de Julio Cortázar." *Le Monde* (Courrier Littéraire), 3 ag 1963, p. 7. [Trans. by Sara Vinocur de Tirri and Néstor Tirri, and included in *La vuelta a Cortázar*. Buenos Aires: Carlos Pérez, 1968, pp. 51–54. About *Las armas secretas*.]

———. "La course d'obstacles de Julio Cortázar." *Magazine Littéraire* (Paris), Núm. 94 (nov, 1974), 43.

Botero, Ebel. "El proceso de las identificaciones en tres obras de Julio Cortázar." *Veinte escritores contemporánoes*. Manizales, Colombia: Ebel Botero, 1969, pp. 21–41.

Brody, Robert: "Twos and Threes in Cortázar's *Rayuela*." *The Analysis of Hispanic Texts: Current Trends in Methodology*. New York: York College, CUNY, 1975, pp. 113–129.

Bryan, C. D. B. "Cortázar's Masterpiece." *New Republic*, 154, 23 April 1966, pp. 19–23. [About *Hopscotch*.]

———. "Julio Cortázar: *Cronopios y Famas*." Trans. Paul Blackburn. *The New York Times Book Review*, 15 June 1969, pp. 4. [Review.]

———. "The Deluxe Model." *Review* 72 (Winter, 1972), 32–34. [About *62. A Model Kit*.]

Cammozzi Barrios, Rolando. "Julio Cortázar: *Todos los fuegos el fuego*." *Revista de Occidente*, 2a. época, Núm. 55 (oct, 1967), 115–117. [Reseña.]

Campos, Jorge. "Julio Cortázar: *Rayuela*." *Insula*, Núm. 250 (set, 1967), 11. [Reseña.]

Camurati, Mireya. "El absurdo, la risa y la invitación a la aventura: 'Instrucciones para subir una escalera.'" *Estudios sobre los cuentos de Julio Cortázar*. Barcelona: Ed. Hispam, 1975, pp. 73–81.

Carnevale, Jorge. "Cortázar o el verdadero rostro." *Cero*, Núm. 1 (set, 1964), 29. [Sobre *Final del juego*.]

———. "Cronopiaje." *Cero*, Núms. 3–4 (mayo, 1965), 36.

Carranza, José María. "Julio Cortázar: *62. Modelo para armar*." *Revista Iberoamericana*, 35, Núm. 69 (set–dic, 1969), 557–559. [Reseña.]

Carrillo, Germán D. "Emociones y fragmentaciones: técnicas cuentísticas de Julio Cortázar en 'Todos los fuegos el fuego.'" *Homenaje a Julio Cortázar*. Madrid: Anaya, 1972, pp. 319–328.

Carter, Boyd G. "Palíndromos." *Hispania*, Vol. 52, Núm. 1 (mar, 1969), 137–138.

Castelar, Diana. "*Final del juego*: un libro de cuentos de Julio Cortázar." *Clarín*, Supl. literario, 23 jul 1964, pp. 3.

Castelli, Eugenio. "Cortázar, *Rayuela* y la antinovela." *Moyano. Benedetto. Cortázar*. Rosario, Santa Fe: Ed. Colmegna, 1968, pp. 51–73.

Castillo, Abelardo L. "*Las armas secretas*: cuentos de Julio Cortázar." *El grillo de papel*, Núm. 2 (ene, 1960), 19–20.

Césped, Irma. "El montaje como recurso en *Rayuela*." *Revista Chilena de Literatura*, 5–6 (1972), 111–132.

Cócaro, Nicolás. "De Julio Denís, poeta, a Julio Cortázar." *Las letras y el destino argentino*. Buenos Aires: Ed. Sopena, 1969, pp. 107–110.

———. " 'Casa tomada' por Julio Cortázar." *Cuentos fantásticos argentinos*. Buenos Aires: Emecé Editores, 1969, pp. 155–162.

Coddou P., Marcelo. "Julio Cortázar: *Todos los fuegos el fuego*." *Atenea*, 153, Núm. 413 (jul–set, 1966), 244–248. [Reseña.]

Coleman, Alexander. "Everywhere Déjà Vu." *The New York Times Book Review*, 9 July 1967, pp. 5. [In part, about *End of the Game*.]

Coll, Edna. "Cortázar y su *Rayuela*." *Atenea* (Revista de la Universidad de Puerto Rico en Mayagüez), Nueva Serie, Núm. 2 (jun, 1967), 9–17.

———. "Aspectos cervantinos en Julio Cortázar." *Revista Hispánica Moderna*, Núms. 3–4 (jul–oct, 1968), 596–604.

Concha, Edmundo. "Julio Cortázar: *Todos los fuegos el fuego*." *Anales de la Universidad de Chile*, 124, Núm. 138 (1966), 249–250. [Reseña.]

Concha, Jaime. "Criticando *Rayuela*." *Hispamérica*, Año 4, 1 anejo (1975), 131–151.

———. "Comentario 1." *Hispamérica*, Año 4, 1 anejo (1975), 152. [About his article criticizing *Rayuela*.]

Conte, Rafael. "Doce proposiciones para un festival Cortázar." *Cuadernos Hispanoamericanos*, Núm. 222 (jun, 1968), 590–601. [Sobre *La vuelta al día en ochenta mundos*.]

———. "Julio Cortázar o la esperanza de la destrucción." *Lenguaje y violencia*: *Introducción a la narrativa hispanoamericana*. Madrid: Al-Borak, 1962, pp. 133–156.

Copeland, John G. "Las imágenes de *Rayuela*." *Revista Iberoamericana*, 33, Núm. 63 (ene–jul, 1967), 85–104. [Reproducido en *Homenaje a Julio Cortázar*. Madrid: Anaya, 1972, pp. 131–149.]

Copouya, Emile. "*The Winners* by Julio Cortázar." *Saturday Review*, 27 March 1965.

Cornejo Polar, Antonio. "*Todos los fuegos el fuego*." *Letras*, 80–81 (1968), 71–83.

"Cortázar." *Indice*, Año 21, Núms. 221–223 (1967), 9.

Cortínez, Carlos. "Ampliando una página de Cortazar. (Notas sobre 'Las babas del diablo.')" *Revista Iberoamericana*, 39, Núms. 84–85 (jul–dic, 1973), 667–682.

Courtines, Pierre. "*The Winners* by Julio Cortázar." *America*, 17 April 1965, pp. 581, 583–584.

Csép, Attila. "El papel de lo fantástico en las obras de Cortázar." *Acta Litteraria Scientiarum Hungaricae*, 11 (1969), 281–290.

Cuperman, Pedro. "Relectura de *Rayuela*." *Point of Contact*, I (1975), 84–87.

Curley, Arthur. "Cronopios y Famas." *Library Journal*, 94 (Sept, 1969), 3082.

Curutchet, Juan Carlos. "Apuntes para una lectura de Cortázar." *Cuadernos Hispanoamericanos*, Núm. 223 (jul, 1968), 233–238. [Sobre *Todos los fuegos el fuego*.]

———. "La prehistoria literaria de Julio Cortázar." *Cuadernos Hispanoamericanos*, 253–254 (ene–feb, 1971), 301–307. [Sobre *Los reyes*.]

———. "Cortázar, Años de Aprendizaje." *Cuadernos Hispanoamericanos*, Núm. 255 (mar, 1971), 561–572.

———. "Cortázar: Descubrimiento de una realidad-otra." *Cuadernos Hispanoamericanos*, Núm. 256 (abr, 1971), 153–164.

———. "Cortázar: una mirada al vacío." *Cuadernos Hispanoamericanos*, 259 (ene, 1972),

129–140. [Sobre *Los premios*.]

————. "Cortázar: Metodología de la rebelión." *Cuadernos Hispanoamericanos*, Núm. 260 (feb, 1972), 330–337.

————. "Cortázar: La crítica de la razón utópica." *Cuadernos Hispanoamericanos*, Núm. 261 (mar, 1972), 459–479.

————. "Cortázar: La crítica de la razón pragmática." *Cuadernos Hispanoamericanos*, 263–264 (mayo–jun, 1972), 425–446.

————. "Julio Cortázar, cronista de las *eras imaginarias*: para una interpretación de 'Todos los fuegos el fuego.'" *Estudios sobre los cuentos de Julio Cortázar*. Barcelona: Ed. Hispam, 1975, pp. 83–98.

Charosky, Claudio B. "Cronología de un Derrumbe: Cortázar y Fuentes." *Alacrán Azul*, Núm. 1 (1970), 74–76.

Dalton, Roque. "Historias de cronopios y de famas." *Casa de las Américas*, Núms. 20–21 (dic, 1963), 64–65.

D'Amico, Alicia' y Sara Facio. "Los juegos de Julio Cortázar." *La Nación*, Supl. literario, 4 jun 1967.

Dapaz Strout, Lilia. "Casamiento ritual y el mito del hermafrodita en *Omnibus* de Cortázar." *Anales de Literatura Hispanoamericana*, Núms. 2–3 (1973–1974), 533–553.

Dávalos, Baica. "Buenos Aires el mito." *Revista Nacional de Cultura* (Caracas), 30, Núm. 194 (jul–ag, 1970), 119–120.

Davenport, Guy. " '*End of the Game*' and Other Stories." *National Review*, 19, Núm. 29 (25 July 1967), 811.

Davis, Deborah. " 'All Fires the Fire' by Julio Cortázar." *Review 73*, 9 (Fall, 1973), 69–70.

Davis, Mary E. "Cortázar y Nabokov: la estética del éxtasis." *Homenaje a Julio Cortázar*. Madrid: Anaya, 1972, pp. 481–489.

Delay, Florence. "Julio Cortázar: Enfance du récit." *Critique*, 30 (1974), 1041–1052.

Dellepiane, Angela B. "La novela argentina desde 1950 a 1965." *Revista Iberoamericana*, Vol. 34, Núm. 66 (1968), 237–282.

————. "*62. Modelo para armar*: ¿Agresión, regresión o progresión?" *Nueva Narrativa Hispanoamericana*, 1, Núm. 1 (ene, 1971), 49–72. [Reproducido en *Homenaje a Julio Cortázar*. Madrid: Anaya, 1972, pp. 151–180.]

————. "Otra experiencia para lectores 'salteados': *Libro de Manuel*." *Nueva Narrativa Hispanoamericana*, 5 (ene–set, 1975), 17–34.

Devoto, Daniel. "Julio Cortázar: *Los reyes*." *Realidad*, 6 (set–dic, 1949), 319–321. [Reseña.]

Díaz Plaja, Guillermo. "*Todos los fuegos el fuego* de Julio Cortázar." *La creación literaria en España*. Madrid: Aguilar, 1968, pp. 214–217.

Díaz Ruiz, Ignacio. "Julio Cortázar: La golondrina enfurecida." *Latinoamérica Anuario/Estudios Latinoamericanos*, Núm. 4 (1971), 157–166.

Diego, Eliseo. "Julio Cortázar: *Todos los fuegos el fuego*." *Casa de las Américas*, 7, Núm. 31 (mar–abr, 1967), 122–125. [Reseña.]

Dollen, Charles. "End of the Game." *Best Sellers*, Vol. 27, No. 8 (15 July 1967), 150–151.

Donoso Paraja, Miguel. "Reseña de *Fantomas contra los vampiros multinacionales*." *Cambio*, Núm. 2 (ene–mar, 1976), 88–89.

Durán, Manuel. "Julio Cortázar y su pequeño mundo de cronopios y famas." *Revista Iberoamericana*, 31, Núm. 59 (ene–jun, 1965), 33–46. [Reproducido en *La vuelta a Cortázar en nueve ensayos*. Buenos Aires: Carlos Pérez, 1968, pp. 31–49; y en *Homenaje a Julio Cortázar*. Madrid: Anaya, 1972, pp. 389–403.]

Durand, José. "Julio Cortázar: los cuentos del gigante." *Américas*, 15 abr 1963, pp. 39–43.

Edwards, Jorge. "*Rayuela*." *Anales de la Universidad de Chile*, Núm. 129 (1964), 229–232.

"8 x 8 = Gliglish." *Time*, 29 April 1966, pp. 117–118. [About *Hopscotch*.]

" 'End of the Game' (and other stories)." *Library Journal*, Vol. 92, No. 13 (July, 1967), 2603.

Eyzaguirre, Luis B. "*Rayuela, Sobre héroes y tumbas* y *El astillero*: Búsqueda de la identidad individual en la novela hispanoamericana contemporánea." *Nueva Narrativa Hispano-*

americana, 2, Núm. 2 (set, 1972), 101–118.

Fernández, Henry. "From Cortázar to Antonioni: Study of an Adaption." *Focus on Blow-up.* Roy Huss, ed. New Jersey: Prentice Hall, 1971, pp. 163–167.

Fernández Moreno, César. "La literatura argentina de un galope." *Diálogos*, 40 (jul–ag, 1971), 31.

Fernández Santos, F. "Julio Cortázar, cronopio universal." *Indice*, Núms. 221–223 (1967), 13.

Fèvre, Fermín B. "Julio Cortázar: *Final del juego.*" *Criterio*, Núm. 1462 (oct, 1964), 796. [Reseña.]

———. "*Rayuela.*" *Criterio* (Brasil), Año 37, Núm. 1452 (28 mayo 1964), 397.

———. "Las figuras del zodíaco." *Primera Plana,* Núm. 173 (1966?), 67. [Reproducido en *Atlas* (June, 1966).]

———. "Julio Cortázar: *62. Modelo para armar.*" *Criterio*, Núms. 1565–1566 (feb, 1969), 108–109. [Reseña.]

Figueroa, Esperanza. "Guía para el lector de *Rayuela.*" *Revista Iberoamericana*, 32, Núm. 62 (1966), 261–266.

———. "Dos libros de Cortázar." *Revista Iberoamericana*, 35, Núm 68 (mar–ag, 1969), 377–383. [Sobre *Ceremonias* y *62. Modelo para armar.*]

Filer de Tunkelang, Malva. "Las transformaciones del yo en la obra de Julio Cortázar." *Cuadernos Hispanoamericanos*, Núm. 242 (feb, 1970), 320–334. [Reproducido en *Homenaje a Julio Cortázar.* Madrid: Anaya, 1972, pp. 261–276.]

———. "La búsqueda de autenticidad." *Homenaje a Julio Cortázar.* Madrid: Anaya, 1972, pp. 195–206.

———. "The Ambivalence of the Hand in Cortázar's Fiction." *Books Abroad*, 50, No. 3 (Summer 1976), 595–599.

Flogstad, Kjartan. "Det trivielle som metafysikk: Introduksjon til Julio Cortázar." *Vinduet*, 24 (1970), 188–193.

Flores, Felix Gabriel. "El lirismo metafísico de Julio Cortázar." *Cuadernos Hispano-americanos*, 289–290 (jul–ag, 1974), 7–52.

Fombona, Julieta. "*Rayuela.*" *Revista Nacional de Cultura*, Núm. 180 (abr/mayo, jun, 1967), 79–82.

Ford, Aníbal. "Los últimos cuentos de Cortázar." *Mundo Nuevo*, Núm. 5 (nov, 1966), 81–84. [Sobre *Todos los fuegos el fuego.*]

Foster, David W. "Julio Cortázar: *62. Modelo para armar.*" *Books Abroad*, 43, No. 3 (Summer, 1969), 382. [Reseña.]

Friedmann, Florinda. "*La vuelta a Cortázar en nueve ensayos* y *Cinco miradas sobre Cortázar.*" *Sur*, Núm. 318 (mayo–jun, 1969), 95–97. [Reseña.]

Fuentes, Carlos. "La nueva novela latinoamericana." *La Cultura en México*, Supl. de *Siempre,* Núm. 128, 29 jul 1964, pp. i–vii y xiv–xvii. [Sobre Vargas Llosa, Cortázar y Carpentier. "La caja de Pandora," sobre Cortázar, pp. vii y xiv–xv.]

———. "*Hopscotch* by Julio Cortázar." *Commentary*, Oct 1966, pp. 142–143.

———. "*Rayuela*: la novela como caja de Pandora." *Mundo Nuevo*, Núm. 9 (mar, 1967), 67–69. [Originalmente este artículo fue publicado en *La Quinzaine littéraire.*]

Garavito, Julián. "Julio Cortázar: *Gîtes.*" Trans. Laure Guille-Bataillon. *Europe*, No. 473 (set, 1968), 17–18. [Review.]

García Canclini, Néstor. "La inautenticidad y el absurdo en la narrativa de Cortázar." *Revista de Filosofía,* Núm. 16 (1966), 65–77.

———. "Cortázar: el acceso a la casa del hombre." *La Capital*, 15 nov 1967, pp. 2.

———. "El país de los cronopios." *Primera Plana*, Núm. 262, 2 ene 1968, pp. 49–50. [Sobre *La vuelta al día en ochenta mundos.*]

Garfield, Evelyn Picon. "The Exquisite Cadaver of Surrealism." *Review* 72 (Winter, 1972), 18–21.

Georgescu, Paul Alexandru. "Julio Cortázar, buscador de lo humano." *Studi e Informazione,*

Sezione Letteraria, Serie I, Firenze, 1972, pp. 51–56.

Gertel, Zunilda. " 'La noche boca arriba,' desyunción de la identidad." *Nueva Narrativa Hispanoamericana*, 3, Núm. 2 (set, 1973), 41–71.

———. "Funcionalidad del lenguaje en 'La salud de los enfermos.' " *Estudios sobre los cuentos de Julio Cortázar*. Barcelona: Ed. Hispam, 1975, pp. 99–114.

Ghiano, Juan Carlos. "*Rayuela*, una ambición 'antinovelística.' " *La Nación*, Supl. literario, 20 oct 1963, p. 5.

Gimferrer, Pedro. "Notas sobre Julio Cortázar." *Insula*, Núm. 227 (1965), 7.

Giordano, Enrique. "Algunas aproximaciones a *Rayuela*, de Julio Cortázar, a través de la dinámica del juego." *Homenaje a Julio Cortázar*. Madrid: Anaya, 1972, pp. 95–129.

Goldemberg, Isaac. "Los personajes de Cortázar: ¿Cronopios o famas?" *Razón y fábula*, 14 (1969), 40–46.

Gómez, Carlos Alberto. "Literature y antropología. *62. Modelo para armar* por Julio Cortázar." *La Nación*, Supl. literario, 8 dic 1968, p. 5.

Gómez Paz, Julieta. "Azorín, Cortázar y las nubes." *Insula*, Núm. 331 (jul, 1974), 14.

González, Eduardo G. "Hacia Cortázar, a partir de Borges." *Revista Iberoamericana*, 39, Núms. 84–85 (jul–dic, 1973), 503–520.

———. "Cortázar: Figuras y límites." *Modern Language Notes*, 89 (March, 1974), pp. 232–249.

González, Manuel Pedro. "Reparos a ciertos aspectos de *Rayuela*." *Coloquios sobre la novela hispanoamericana*. México: Tezontle, 1967, pp. 68–81. [Entre otros juicios, González califica a *Rayuela* de "contrahechura," "pastiche," "una invitación al tedio y un eficaz antídoto contra el insomnio," lo cual da una pauta de la calidad del artículo y de la seriedad y objetividad del crítico.]

González Bermejo, Ernesto. "Julio Cortázar. Una apuesta a lo imposible." *Cosas de escritores*. Montevideo: Biblioteca de Marcha, 1971, pp. 91–136.

González Echeverría, Roberto. " 'La autopista del sur' and the Secret Weapons of Julio Cortázar's Short Narrative." *Studies in Short Fiction*, 8, No. 1 (Winter, 1971), 130–140.

———. "*Los Reyes*: Cortázar's Mythology of Writing." *Books Abroad*, 50, No. 3 (Summer 1976), 548–557.

González Lanuza, Eduardo. "Julio Cortázar: *La vuelta al día en ochenta mundos*." *Sur*, Núm. 312 (mayo–jun, 1968), 87–89.

———. "Casualidad y causalidad a propósito de *62. Modelo para armar*, de Julio Cortázar." *Sur*, Núm. 318 (mayo–jun, 1969), 72–75.

Goyen, William. "Destination Unknown. *The Winners* by Julio Cortázar." *The New York Times Book Review*, 21 Mar 1965, pp. 5, 45.

Graciarena, Edmundo. "Primera Plana: La revista y sus armas secretas." *Hoy en la Cultura*, Núm. 17 (nov–dic, 1964), 12.

Grande, Félix. "Fragmento para un homenaje a *Rayuela*." *Indice*, Núms. 221–223 (1967), 22.

———. "Romance del dado y la ratita." *Cuadernos Hispanoamericanos*, 271 (ene, 1973), 105–116.

———. "Nadando en las paredes." *Cuadernos Hispanoamericanos*, 275 (mayo, 1973), 230–236.

Grandi, Carla. "Notas sobre 'El otro cielo' de Julio Cortázar!" *Revista Chilena de Literatura*, 5–6 (1972), pp. 289–299.

Gregorich, Luis. "Julio Cortázar y la posibilidad de la literatura." *Cuadernos de Crítica*, Núm. 3 (ag, 1966), 38–47. [Reproducido en *La vuelta a Cortázar en nueve ensayos*. Buenos Aires: Carlos Pérez, 1968, pp. 119–131.]

Gregorio, María Isabel de. "*Rayuela*." *Boletín de Literaturas Hispánicas*, Núm. 6 (1966), 43–58.

Grossvogel, David I. " 'Blow-up.' The Forms of an Esthetic Itinerary." *Diacritics*, 11, No. 3 (Fall, 1972), 49–54. [Lo mejor que se ha escrito hasta la fecha sobre el cuento de

Cortázar 'Las babas del diablo' y su influencia en la película de Antonioni.]

Guasta, Eugenio. "Los argentinos a través de una novela de Cortázar." *Criterio*, Núms. 1513–1514 (24 dic 1960), 918–921.

———. "Todos los fuegos el fuego." *Criterio*, 39, Núm. 1506 (1966), 636.

Gudiño Kieffer, E. "La novela frente al autor, frente al lector y frente a sí misma." *Explicación de Textos Literarios*, Vol. 2, 2 (1974), 179–182.

Guebenzu, José María. "The reader murder case." *Cuadernos Hispanoamericanos*, Núm. 247 (jul, 1970), 159–164.

Guerrero Mathineitz, Hugo. "La vuelta a Cortázar en 80 preguntas." *Siete días*, Núm. 311 (30 abr–8 mayo, 1973), sin paginación.

Gullón, Germán. "La retórica de Cortázar en *Rayuela*." *Insula*, Núm. 299 (oct, 1971), 13.

Gyurko, Lanin A. "Cyclic Time and Blood Sacrifice in Three Stories by Cortázar." *Revista Hispánica Moderna*, Núm. 4 (oct–dic, 1969), 341–362. [Sobre 'Todos los fuegos el fuego,' 'La noche boca arriba' y 'El ídolo de las Cícladas.']

———. "Fury in Three Stories by Julio Cortázar." *Revista de Letras*, 3 (1971), 511–531.

———. "Authenticity and Pretence in Two Stories by Julio Cortázar." *Bulletin of Hispanic Studies*, 49 (ene, 1972), 51–65.

———. "Hallucination and Nightmare in Two Stories by Cortázar." *Modern Language Review*, 67 (1972), 550–562.

———. "Man as Victim in Two Stories by Cortázar." *Kentucky Romance Quarterly*, 19, No. 3 (1972), 317–335. [Sobre 'Las armas secretas' e 'Instrucciones para John Howell.']

———. "Destructive and Ironically Redemptive Fantasy in Cortázar." *Hispania*, 56 (1973), 988–999.

———. "Truth and Deception in Cortázar's 'Las babas del diablo.'" *Romanic Review*, 64 (1973), 204–217.

———. "Identity and Fate in Cortázar's 62. *Modelo para armar*." *Symposium*, 27 (1974), 214–234.

———. "La fantasía como emancipación y como tiranía en tres cuentos de Cortázar." *Revista Iberoamericana*, 41, Núm. 91 (abr–jun, 1975), 219–236.

———. "Cortázar's Fictional Children: Freedom and Its Constraints." *Neophilologus*, 57 (1973), 24–41.

———. "Guilt and Delusion: Two Stories by Cortázar." *Critique: Studies in Modern Fiction*, 14, No. 3 (1973), 75–90.

———. "Ingeniousness and Deceit in Cortázar's 'Los buenos servicios.'" *Studies in Short Fiction*, 10 (1973), 253–261.

———. "Self-Obsession and Death in Three Stories by Cortázar." *Research Studies* (Washington State U.), 41 (1973), 234–251.

———. "The Bestial and the Demonic in Two Stories by Cortázar." *Revue des Langues Vivants* (Brussels), 39 (1973), 112–130.

———. "Alienation and the Absurd in Two Stories by Cortázar." *Kentucky Romance Quarterly*, 21 (1974), 43–58.

———. "Narcissistic and Ironic Paradise in Three Stories by Cortázar." *Hispanófila*, 50 (ene, 1974), 19–42.

———. "Self-Deception and Self-Confrontation in Cortázar." *Southern Humanities Review*, 8 (1974), 361–373.

Hamilton, Carlos D. "La novela actual de Hispanoamérica." *Cuadernos Americanos*, Núm. 2 (mar–abr, 1973), 223–251. [Sobre Cortázar, pp. 230–233.]

Harris, Yvonne J. "Bestiario." *Books Abroad*, 27 (Spring, 1953), 182.

Harss, Luis and Barbara Dohmann. "Julio Cortázar, or the Slap in the Face." *Into the Mainstream*. New York: Harper and Row, 1966, pp. 206–245.

Harss, Luis. "Cortázar o la cachetada metafísica." *Mundo Nuevo*, No. 7 (ene, 1967), 57–74. [También apareció en *Los nuestros*. Buenos Aires: Ed. Sudamericana, 1967.]

———. "Cortázar en su taller." *Indice*, Núms. 221–223 (1967), 19–24.

Hartmann, Joan. "La búsqueda de las figuras en algunos cuentos de Cortázar." *Revista Iberoamericana*, 35, Núm. 69 (set–dic, 1969), 539–549. [Reproducido en *Homenaje a Julio Cortázar*. Madrid: Anaya, 1972, pp. 339–350.]

———. "El amor y la mujer vistos por Cortázar." *El Urogallo*, Año 3, Núm. 17 (set–oct, 1972), 64–69.

Heker, Liliana. "Concursos ¿o literatura?" *El Escarabajo de Oro*, Año 6, Núms. 26–27 (feb, 1965), 15, 22.

———. "*Rayuela* de Julio Cortázar." *El Heraldo Cultural*, 15, 20 feb 1966, p. 7.

———. "¿Qué opina del *Libro de Manuel* de Julio Cortázar?" *Crisis*, 1, Núm. 1 (mayo, 1973), 17.

Hell, Henri. "Un maître conteur." *L'Express* (Paris), 29 ag. 1963, p. 21. [About *Las armas secretas*.]

Hernández, Ana María. "Cortázar: el libro de Andrés + Lonstein = Manuel." *Nueva Narrativa Hispanoamericana*, 5 (ene–set, 1975), 35–56.

———. "Vampires and Vampiresses: A Reading of 62." *Books Abroad*, 50, No. 3 (Summer 1976), 570–576.

Holsten, Ken. "Notas sobre el 'Tablero de dirección' en *Rayuela* de Julio Cortázar." *Revista Iberoamericana*, 39, Núms. 84–85 (jul–dic, 1973), 683–688.

Huber, Elena. "*Los reyes* de Cortázar y el mito de Teseo." *Clarín* (Cultura y Nación, Buenos Aires), 13 mayo 1976, p. 3.

Hozven V., Roberto. "Interpretación de 'El río,' cuento de Julio Cortázar." *Atenea*, 170 (jul–dic, 1968), 57–77. [Reproducido en *Homenaje a Julio Cortázar*. Madrid: Anaya, 1972, pp. 405–425.]

Incledon, John. "Una clave de Cortázar sobre 62. *Modelo para armar*." *Revista Iberoamericana*, 41, Núm. 91 (apr–jun, 1975), 263–265.

Irby, James E. "Cortázar's *Hopscotch* and Other Games." *Novel: A Forum on Fiction*, 1, No. 1 (Fall, 1967), 64–70.

Isasi Angulo, A. Carlos. "Función de las innovaciones estilísticas en *Rayuela*." *Revista Iberoamericana*, 39, Núms. 84–85 (jul–dic, 1973), 583–592.

Ivask, Ivar. "Cortázar's Oklahoma Stomp." *Books Abroad*, No. 3, (Summer 1976), 503–506.

Izquierdo, Luis. "Leyendo a Cortázar." *Destino*, 28 dic 1968, pp. 62–63.

Jaramillo Levi, Enrique. "Tiempo y espacio a través del tema del doble en 'La isla a mediodía' de Julio Cortázar." *Nueva Narrativa Hispanoamericana*, 4 (1974), 299–306.

Jitrik, Noé. "Notas sobre la 'Zona sagrada' y el mundo de los 'otros' en *Bestiario* de Julio Cortázar." *La vuelta a Cortázar en nueve ensayos*. Buenos Aires: Carlos Pérez, 1968, pp. 13–30.

———. "Crítica satélite y trabajo crítico en 'El perseguidor' de Julio Cortázar." *Nueva Revista de Filología Hispánica*, (México), 22, Núm. 2 (1975), 337–368.

Juin, Hubert. "Les Armes Secrètes." *Les Lettres Françaises* (feb, 1964), 3.

"Julio Cortázar: *Cronopios and Famas*." *Time*, 13 June 1969, p. 105. [Review.]

"Julio Cortázar: *End of the Game and Other Stories*, translated by Paul Blackburn. New York: Pantheon Books, 1967." *Choice*, Vol. 4, No. 4 (1967), 1120.

"Julio Cortázar, *Hopscotch*." *Saturday Review*, 49, 9 April 1966, p. 34.

"Julio Cortázar: *Ultimo round*." *La Nación*, Supl. literario, 11 ene 1970, p. 5. [Reseña.]

Kalda, Alexandre. "Julio Cortázar en Monteforte Toledo." *Arts*, No. 922 (1963), 2.

Kauffmann, Stanley. "Real and Otherwise." *New Republic*, No. 157, 15 July 1967, pp. 22, 36. [About *End of the Game*.]

Kay, Wallace G. " 'As Recollection or the Drug Decide': Images and Imaginings in 'Among School Children' and *Blowup*." *The Southern Quarterly*, 12, No. 3 (April, 1974), 225–232.

Keene, Donald. "Moving Snapshots." *The New York Times Book Review*, 10 April 1966, p. 1. [About *Hopscotch*.]

Kerr, Lucille. "Review of *El individuo y el otro. Crítica a los cuentos de Julio Cortázar* by Alfred MacAdams." *Revista Iberoamericana*, 39, Núms. 84–85 (jul–dic, 1973), 693–695.

———. "Julio Cortázar." *Diacritics*, Vol. 14, No. 4 (Winter 1974), 35–40. [Interview, also participating Roberto González Echevarría and David I. Grossvogel.]

Lafourcade, Enrique. "Julio Cortázar y el neo-culturanismo." *Imagen* No. 83 (oct, 1970), 6–8.

Lagmanovich, David. "*Rayuela*, novela que lo es pero no importa." *La Gaceta*, 29 mar 1964.

———. "Un cuento de Julio Cortázar." *La Gaceta*, 12 dic 1971, 2a sec., p. 1. [Sobre "La isla a mediodía."]

———. "Rasgos distintivos de algunos cuentos de Julio Cortázar." *Hispamérica*, 1, Núm. 1 (jul, 1972), 5–15. [Sobre "Torito," "Bestiario," "Axolotl," "Omnibus," "Después del almuerzo," "La noche boca arriba," "Las puertas del cielo," "Continuidad de los parques."]

———. "Prólogo: Para una caracterización de los cuentos de Julio Cortázar." *Estudios sobre los cuentos de Julio Cortázar*. Barcelona: Ed. Hispam, 1975, pp. 7–21.

———. "Estructura de un cuento de Julio Cortázar: 'Todos los fuegos el fuego.'" *Nueva Narrativa Hispanoamericana*, Núm. 2 (set, 1971), 87–95. [Reproducido en *Homenaje a Julio Cortázar*. Madrid: Anaya, 1972, pp. 375–387.]

———. "La narrativa argentina de 1960 a 1970." *Nueva Narrativa Hispanoamericana*, Vol. 2, Núm. 1 (ene, 1972), 99–117.

———. "Acotación a 'La isla a mediodía.'" *Revista Iberoamericana*, 39, Núms. 84–85 (jul–dic, 1973), 641–655.

Lancelotti, Mario A. "Julio Cortázar: *Final del juego*." *Sur*, Núm. 291 (nov–dic, 1964), 87–89. [Reseña.]

Lask, Thomas. "A Bit of Everything." *New York Times*, 3 May 1966, p. 45. [About *Hopscotch*.]

Lastra, Pedro y Graciela Coulson. "El motivo del horror en 'Octaedro.'" *Nueva Narrativa Hispanoamericana*, 5 (ene–set, 1975), 7–16.

Laut, S. J. "*Hopscotch*." *Best Sellers*, Vol. 26, No. 6 (15 June 1966), 116.

Leal, Luis. "Situación de Julio Cortázar." *Revista Iberoamericana*, 39, Núms. 84–85 (jul–dic, 1973), 399–409.

Lezama Lima, José. "Cortázar y el comienzo de la otra novela." *Casa de las Américas*, Núm. 49 (1968), 51–62. [Reproducido bajo el título "Para llegar a Julio Cortázar" en *México en la Cultura*, Supl. de *Novedades*, Núm. 348 (oct, 1968), ii–vii. También reproducido en *Homenaje a Julio Cortázar*. Madrid: Anaya, 1972, pp. 13–29.]

Liberman, Arnoldo. "*Rayuela*, por Julio Cortázar." *Comentario*, Núm .38 (1964), 95–96.

Lind, Georg R. "Julio Cortázar—um argentino à procura duma nova realidade." *Colóquio* (Rio de Janeiro), No. 6 (mar, 1972), 12–20.

Llopis, Rogelio. "Prologando a Cortázar." *Pueblo y Cultura*, Núm. 30 (dic, 1964), 58–59.

Lockhart, Washington. "El esperanzado desbarajuste de Cortázar." *Marcha*, 15 set 1967, p. 29.

López, Edward. "De Asturias a Cortázar." *O Estado de São Paulo*, Supl. lit., 7 mar 1970, p. 1.

López Chuhurra, Osvaldo. "Sobre Julio Cortázar." *Cuadernos Hispanoamericanos*, Núm. 211 (jul, 1967), 5–30. [Reproducido en *Homenaje a Julio Cortázar*. Madrid: Anaya, 1972, pp. 207–234.]

López-Delpecho, Luis. "C. de Carroll y de Cortázar." *Cuadernos Hispanoamericanos*, Núm. 228 (dic, 1968), 663–674.

López–Morales, Eduardo E. "El libro de los Julios." *Casa de las Américas*, Núm. 30 (1968), 172–178.

Loveluck, Juan. "Aproximación a *Rayuela*." *Revista Iberoamericana*, 34, Núm. 65 (ene–abr, 1968), 83–93.

Luchting, Wolfgang A. "Todos los fuegos el fuego." *Mundo Nuevo*, Núm. 35 (mayo,

1969), 29–35. [Reproducido en *Homenaje a Julio Cortázar*. Madrid: Anaya, 1972, pp. 351–363.]

MacAdam, Alfred. "A Life Without Patterns." *The New Leader*, Vol. 50, Núm. 18 (set, 1967), 19–20. [About *End of the Game and Other Stories*.]

———. "*Los premios*: Una tentativa de clasificación formal." *XIII Congreso Internacional de Literatura Iberoamericana*. Caracas: Organización de Bienestar Estudiantil, 1968, pp. 101–108. [Posteriormente a su comunicación, presentada en la reunión en agosto de 1967, apareció en *Mundo Nuevo*, Núm. 18 (dic, 1967), 38, bajo el título "Cortázar Novelista." Reproducido en *Homenaje a Julio Cortázar*, bajo su título original. Madrid: Anaya, 1972, pp. 289–296.]

———. "El individuo y el otro." *Revista Iberoamericana de Literatura*, 2a. época, Núm. 2 (1970), 3–16. [Sobre los ensayos críticos de Cortázar y especialmente sobre *Los reyes*.]

———. "La simultaneidad en las novelas de Cortázar." *Revista Iberoamericana*, 37, Núms. 76–77 (jul–dic, 1971), 667–676.

———. "Cortázar on Cortázar: A Literary Chronology." *Review* 72 (Winter, 1972), 35–41.

———. "La torre de Dánae." *Revista Iberoamericana*, 39, Núms. 84–85 (jul–dic, 1973), 457–469.

Maddocks, Melvin. "*The Winners*." *Christian Science Monitor*, 6 May 1965, p. 9B.

———. "Hardbound Vaudeville." *The Atlantic*, 223, June 1969, pp. 101–102. [About *Historias de cronopios y de famas*.]

Madrigal, Luis Iñigo. "Julio Cortázar: *Los premios*." *Anales de la Universidad de Chile*, Núm. 123 (3er. trimestre). 212–214. [Review.]

———. "*Rayuela*." *Mapocho* (Santiago de Chile), Núm. 1 (1965), 220–221.

Martin, Horacio? (Félix Grande). "Lisiedros. Espezisología preliminar. 1984 [sic]." *Cuadernos Hispanoamericanos*, 275 (mayo, 1973), 237–242.

Martín, Salustiano. "Re de *Octaedro*." *Reseña*, Núm. 83 (mar, 1975), 7–9.

Martínez, Carlos. "Ampliando una página de Cortázar." *Revista Iberoamericana*, 39, Núms. 84–85 (jul–dic, 1973), 667–682.

Martínez, Tomás Eloy. "Las figuras del zodíaco." *Primera Plana*, Núm. 173, p. 67. [Reproducido en *Atlas*, June, 1966.]

Mastrángelo, Carlos. "'Las babas del diablo,' una nueva era cuentística argentina." *El Contemporáneo*, Núm. 5 (ag, 1969), 9.

———. "Usted, yo, los cuentos de Julio Cortázar y su autor." *Revista de la Universidad Nacional de Córdoba*, Año 10, Núm. 5 (1969), 1085–1137.

Matas, Julio. "El contexto moral en algunos cuentos de Julio Cortázar." *Revista Iberoamericana*, 39, Núms. 84–85 (jul–dic, 1973), 593–609.

Matilla Rivas, Alfredo. "Julio Cortázar: *La vuelta al día en ochenta mundos*." *La Torre*, Núm. 60 (1968), 301–305. [Reseña.]

McMahon, Dorothy. "*Los premios*." *Books Abroad*, 36 (Winter, 1962), 61.

Meinhardt, Warren L. "Descripción de un combate o Julio Cortázar ganador por 'Nocaut' limpio." *Nueva Narrativa Hispanoamericana*, Vol. 1, Núm. 2 (set, 1971), 216–219.

Méras, P. "The Author." *Saturday Review*, 22 July 1967, p. 36.

Micha, René. "Le Je et l'Autre chez Julio Cortázar." *La Nouvelle Revue Française*, No. 140, 1er août 1964, pp. 314–322.

Miguel, André. "Julio Cortázar: *Les Armes Secrètes*." *La Nouvelle Revue Française*, No. 131, 1er novembre 1963, 916–917. [Review.]

Miguel, María Ester de. "Julio Cortázar: *Las armas secretas*." *Señales*, Núm. 114 (oct, 1959), 17–18. [Reseña.]

Millar, Neil. "*Cronopios and Famas*." *Christian Science Monitor*, 3 July 1969, 9.

Miller, Warren. "*Hopscotch*." *Book Week*, 1 May 1966, 12.

Minudri, Regina. "*The Winners*." *Library Journal*, Vo. 90, No. 6 (5 Mar 1965), 1346.

Mirande, Nelly Donni de. "Notas sobre la lengua de Cortázar." *Boletín de Literaturas Hispánicas*, Núm. 6 (1966), 71–83.

Monsiváis, Carlos. "Instructivo para edificar un intersticio que permita encontrarle alguna utilidad a la nota bibliográfica o ¿qué pasaría, Eduviges, si todos los cronopios se llamaran Julio?" *La Cultura en México*, Supl. de *Siempre*, Núm. 306, 27 dic 1967, v. [Sobre *La vuelta al día en ochenta mundos*.]

———. "Bienvenidos al universo Cortázar." *Revista de la Universidad de México*, 22, Núm. 9 (mayo, 1968), 1–10.

Montesinos, Jaime A. "Contra la nada que acecha: Julio Cortázar." *Cuadernos Americanos*, 178 (set–oct, 1971), 237–243.

Morelle, Paul. "*Marelle*, de Julio Cortázar, ou le roman de l'intelligence qui se détruit." *Le Monde* (Paris), 5 April 1967, pp. I, III.

Morello-Frosch, Marta. "El personaje y el doble en las ficciones de Cortázar." *Revista Iberoamericana*, 34, Núm. 66 (jul–dic, 1968), 323–330. [Reproducido en *Homenaje a Julio Cortázar*. Madrid: Anaya, 1972, 329–338.]

———. "Julio Cortázar: From Beasts to Bolts." *Books Abroad*, 44, No. 1 (Winter, 1970), 22–25.

———. "La tiranía del orden en los cuentos de Julio Cortázar." *El cuento hispanoamericano ante la crítica*. Madrid: Ed. Castalia, 1973, 165–178.

———. "La relación personaje-espacio en las ficciones de Cortázar." *Estudios sobre los cuentos de Julio Cortázar*. Barcelona: Ed. Hispam, 1975, 115–124.

Mujica, R. P. Carlos. "¿Qué opina del *Libro de Manuel* de Julio Cortázar?" *Crisis*, 1, Núm. 1 (mayo, 1973), 17.

Mulvey, C. E. "*Hopscotch*." *Commonweal*, 84 (1966), 643–644.

Muñoz Martínez, Silveiro. "Otra mirada sobre *Rayuela*." *Revista Iberoamericana de Literatura*, 2a época, Núm. 2 (1970), 29–49. [Reproducido en *Revista Iberoamericana*, 39, Núms. 84–85 (jul–dic, 1973), 557–581.]

Murena, H. A. "Julio Cortázar: *Rayuela*." *Cuadernos*, Núm. 79 (dic, 1963), 85. [Review.]

Musselwhite, David. " 'El perseguidor,' un modelo para desarmar." *Nuevos Aires*, Núm. 8 (ag/set/oct, 1972), 23–36.

Musto, Jorge. "La zambullida en el embudo." *Temas*, Núm. 13 (jul–set, 1967), 23–30.

Neruda, Pablo. "Con Cortázar y con Arguedas." *El Universal* (Caracas), 17 ag 1969, p. 23.

"Novela espesa con sabias reminiscencias." *Primera Plana*, Núm. 42, 27 ag 1963, p. 34. [Sobre *Rayuela*.]

Novoa, Leopoldo. "Cortázar o cómo venir al Sena permaneciendo en el Plata." *Marcha*, 9 jul 1965, p. 30.

Núñez, Antonio. "Julio Cortázar: *Ceremonias*." *Cuadernos Hispanoamericanos*, Núm. 235 (jul, 1969), 234–236. [Título reúne dos libros de cuentos publicados con anterioridad: *Final del juego* y *Las armas secretas*.]

Nye, Robert. "A Game of Hopscotch." *Manchester Guardian*, Vol. 96, No. 11, 16 Mar. 1967, p. 11.

Ojeda, Jorge Arturo. "Cronopios y Famas." *El Gallo Ilustrado*, Supl. dominical de *El Día*, Núm. 287, 24 dic 1967.

Olaso, Ezequiel de. "El pastor de monstruos." *La Nación*, Supl. literario, 24 mayo 1964, p. 4.

Onega, Gladys S. "Cortázar: personajes y misterio." *Setecientos monos*, Núm. 7 (dic, 1965).

———. "*Los premios*." *Boletín de Literaturas Hispánicas*, Núm. 6 (1966), 29–41.

"On the Hop." *Times Literary Supplement* (London), No. 3393, 9 Mar 1967, p. 181. [About *Hopscotch*.]

Oribe, Basilio. "*Rayuela*." *Criterio*, 37, Núm. 1452 (1964), 397.

Orphée, Elvira. "Julio Cortázar: *Las armas secretas*." *Sur*, Núm. 265 (jul–ag, 1960), 51–54. [Reseña.]

Ortega, José. "End of the Game." *Studies in Short Fiction*, Vol. 6, No. 1 (1968), 109–110.

Ortega, Julio. "Julio Cortázar/*Rayuela*." *La contemplación y la fiesta. Ensayos sobre la novela latinoamericana*. Lima: Ed. Universitaria, 1968, 29–43.

————. "Una novela de Cortázar," *Figuración de la persona*. Barcelona: Edhasa, 1971, 273–277. [On 62. *Modelo para armar*.]

Ortiz, Orlando. "Un atómo de *Rayuela*." *La Cultura en México*, Supl. de *Siempre*, Núm. 825, 16 abr 1969, vi–viii. [Sobre 62. *Modelo para armar*.]

Ostria González, Manuel. "Concepto e imagen del lector en *Rayuela*." *Chasqui*, 2, Núm. 2 (feb, 1973), 22–32.

Oviedo, José Miguel. "Cortázar para recortar y pegar." *La Cultura en México*, Supl. de *Siempre*, Núm. 825, 16 abr 1969, vi–viii. [Sobre 62. *Modelo para armar*.]

Pagés Larray, Antonio. "Julio Cortázar: *Los premios*." *Ficción*, Núms. 33–34 (set–dic, 1961), 165–169. [Reproducido en *La vuelta a Cortázar en nueve ensayos*. Buenos Aires: Carlos Pérez, 1968, 65–73.]

————. "Cotidianidad y fantasía en una obra de Cortázar." *Cuadernos Hispanoamericanos*, Núm. 231 (mar, 1969), 694–703. [Sobre *Historias de cronopios y de famas*. Reproducido en *Homenaje a Julio Cortázar*. Madrid: Anaya, 1972, 277–287.]

————. "Perspectivas de 'Axolotl,' cuento de Julio Cortázar." *Nueva Narrativa Hispanoamericana*, 2, Núm. 2 (set, 1972), 7–24. [Reproducido en *Homenaje a Julio Cortázar*. Madrid: Anaya, 1972, 457–480.]

Palau de Nemes, Graciela. "El espacio como preocupación transcendental y artística en el ensayo de Paz y la narrativa de Cortázar." *El ensayo y la crítica literaria en Iberoamérica*. (Memorias del 14 Congreso Internacional de Literatura Iberoamericana. Kurt L. Levy y Keith Ellis, eds.) Toronto: Universidad de Toronto, 1970, 131–136.

Paley Francescato, Martha. "Julio Cortázar y un modelo para armar ya armado." *Cuadernos Americanos*, Núm. 3 (mayo–jun, 1969), 235–241. [Reproducido en *Homenaje a Julio Cortázar*. Madrid: Anaya, 1972, 365–373.]

————. "Julio Cortázar: *Ultimo round*." *Revista Iberoamericana*, 36, Núm. 72 (jul–set, 1970), 532–534. [Reseña.]

————. "Julio Cortázar: *Casa tomada*." Trans. al diseño gráfico por Juan Fresán. *Revista Iberoamericana*, 36, Núm. 73 (oct–dic, 1970), 670–671. [Reseña.]

————. "*El Libro de Manuel*." *Revista Iberoamericana*. 39, Núms. 84–85 (jul–dic, 1973), 689–691.

————. "El viaje: función, estructura y mito en los cuentos de Julio Cortázar." *Estudios sobre los cuentos de Julio Cortázar*. Ed. Hispam., 1975, 125–137.

————. "Selected Bibliography." *Books Abroad*, 50, No. 3 (Summer 1976), 513–516.

————. "The New Man (But Not the New Woman)." *Books Abroad*, '0:3 (Summer 1976), 589–595.

Paz, Octavio y Julián Ríos. "Modelos para a(r)mar" [sic]. *El Urogallo*, 3, Núm. 15 (mayo–jun, 1972), 33–40.

Peltzer, Federico. "Novela y novedad: dos tentativas argentinas." *La Gaceta* (Tucumán), 1965, s/p. [Sobre *Los burgueses* de Silvina Bullrich y *Rayuela* de Julio Cortázar.]

————. " 'La autopista del sur' de Julio Cortázar." *Lugones* (Córdoba), Año 1, Núm. 1 (1968), 77–88.

"The Perils of Horacio." *Newsweek*, 117, 9 May 1966, pp. 104, 106. [About *Hopscotch*.]

Pereda, Rosa M. "Cortázar: Obra abierta y revolución." *Camp de l'Arpa Revista de Literatura*, 11 (mayo 1974), 8–12.

Petrich, Perla. " 'Instrucciones para John Howell': Iniciación al extrañamiento." *Estudios sobre los cuentos de Julio Cortázar*. Barcelona: Ed. Hispam, 1975, 139–162.

Pezzoni, Enrique. "Transgresión y normalización en la narrativa argentina contemporánea." *Revista de Occidente*, Núm. 100 (jul, 1971), 172–191.

Picon Garfield, Evelyn. "Chronology." *Books Abroad*, 50, No. 3 (Summer 1976), 511–512.

————. "Octaedro: Eight Phases of Despair." *Books Abroad*, 50, No. 3 (Summer 1976), 576–589.

Pinchón Riviere, Marcelo. "Cortázar: De *Rayuela* al *Libro de Manuel*." *Panorama*, Núm. 313 (26 abr–2 mayo, 1973), 60–64.

Pizarnik, Alejandra. "Humor y poesía en un libro de Julio Cortázar." *Revista Nacional de Cultura* (Caracas), Año 25, Núm. 160 (set–oct, 1963), 77–82.

———. "Nota sobre un cuento de Julio Cortázar: 'El otro cielo.'" *La vuelta a Cortázar en nueve ensayos.* Buenos Aires: Carlos Pèrez 1968, 55–62.

Planells, Antonio. "Narración y música en 'Las ménades' de Julio Cortázar." *Explicación de Textos Literarios,* Vol. 2, 2 (1974), 95–99.

Pope, Randolph D. "Dos novelas 'album': *Libro de Manuel* de Cortázar y *Figuraciones en el mes de marzo* de Díaz Valcárcel" *The Bilingual Review/La Revista Bilingüe,* 1, No. 2 (May–Aug, 1974), 170–184.

Prescott, Orville. "*The Winners,* Outward on the Ship of Life." *The New York Times,* 22 Mar 1965, 31.

Prieto, Adolfo. "Julio Cortázar, hoy." *Boletín de Literaturas Hispánicas,* 6 (1966), 5–11.

Pucciarelli, Ana María. "Notas sobre la búsqueda en la obra de Julio Cortázar." *Homenaje a Julio Cortázar.* Madrid: Anaya, 1972, 181–193.

Rabassa, Gregory. "Lying to Athena: Cortázar and the Art of Fiction." *Books Abroad,* 50, No. 3 (Summer 1976), 542–547.

Rama, Angel. "Julio Cortázar: una novela distinta en el Plata." *Marcha,* 17 mar 1961, 22.

Rambures, Jean-Louis de. "Cortázar, le troisième grand de la littérature sud-américaine." *Réalités* (fév, 1968), 88–91.

Reedy, Daniel R. "The Symbolic Reality of Cortázar's 'Las babas del diablo.'" *Revista Hispánica Moderna,* Año 36, Núm. 4 (1970–1971), 224–237.

Rein, Mercedes. "A propósito de 'Las babas del diablo.'" *Revista Iberoamericana de Literatura,* 2a época, Núm. 2 (1970), 17–28.

Revol, E. L. "La vuelta a Cortázar en 80 julios." *Letras del Ecuador,* Núm. 137 (mayo–jun, 1968), 20, 23.

———. "La tradición fantástica en la literatura argentina." *Revista de Estudios Hispánicos,* 2, Núm. 2 (nov, 1968), 205–228. [Habla de Cortázar en extenso.]

———. "Arena en los ojos." *La Nación,* Supl. literario, 6 mayo 1973, p. 6. [Reseña de *Libro de Manuel.*]

Rial, José Antonio. "Reparos a Cortázar." *El Universal* (Caracas), 11 mayo 1969, p. 47.

Ríos, Roberto E. "*Rayuela,* de Julio Cortázar. Argentino. Primera edición, 1963." *La novela y el hombre hispanoamericano.* Buenos Aires: Ed. La Aurora, 1969, pp. 103–116.

Rodríguez Monegal, Emir. "La nueva novela de Latinoamérica. La pluma busca otros horizontes." *Life en español,* 25, Núm. 6, 15 mar 1965, pp. 57, 59.

———. "Erudición cortaziana." *Mundo Nuevo,* Núm. 8 (feb, 1967), 90–91.

———. "Los nuevos novelistas." *XIII Congreso Internacional de Literatura Iberoamericana.* Caracas: Organización de Bienestar Estudiantil, 1968, 33–42.

———. "Le 'Fantôme' de Lautréamont." *Review 72* (Winter, 1972), 26–31. [Reproducido en *Revista Iberoamericana,* 39, Núms. 84–85 (jul–dic, 1973), 625–639.]

Rohon, Guy. "Julio Cortázar: *Marelle.*" *La Nouvelle Revue Française,* No. 173, 1er août 1967, 1113–15. [Review.]

Rojas Guardia, Pablo. "Julio Cortázar: *La vuelta al día en ochenta mundos.*" *Revista Nacional de Cultura,* Núm. 189 (jul–set, 1969), 110–112. [Reseña.]

———. "*La realidad mágica. Ensayos de Aproximación Literaria.*" Caracas: Monte Avila, 1969, 29–33.

Roy-Cabrerizo, Joaquín. "Claves de Cortázar en un Libro Olvidado: *Buenos Aires, Buenos Aires.*" *Revista Iberoamericana,* 39, Núms. 84–85 (jul–dic, 1973), 471–482.

———. "Del doble al amigo en la literatura argentina." *ETC,* Vol. 3, 1 (1974), 3–11.

———. "Fantasía y realidad doble y amigo en tres hitos libros argentinos." *Anales de Literatura Hispanoamericana,* 2 (1974), 191–208.

———. "Julio Cortázar: *Libro de Manuel.*" *Reseña* (Madrid), 72 (feb, 1974), 17–19.

———. "Julio Cortázar en cinco libros de crítica: sobre Lida Aronne Amestoy, Juan Carlos Curutchet, Kathleen Genover, Mercedes Rein, Saúl Sosnowski." *Revista Iberoamericana,*

Núm. 91 (abr–jun, 1975), 338–390.

Ryan, Frank. "*The Winners.*" *Best Sellers*, Vol. 25, No. 1 (1 April 1965), 5–6.

Saez, Jorge Alberto. "Alrededor del hombre en ochenta mundos y tres julios." *Sur*, Núm. 311 (mar–abr, 1968), 87–90.

Safir, Margery A. "An Erotics of Liberation: Notes on Transgressive Behavior." *Books Abroad*, 50, No. 3 (Summer 1976), 558–570.

Salazar Bondy, Sebastián. "Julio Cortázar: *Bestiario.*" *Sur*, Núm. 201 (jul, 1957), 109–110. [Reseña.]

Samuels, Charles Thomas. "Sorting Things Out in 'Blow-up.'" *Review* 72, 7 (Winter, 1972), 22–23.

Sanhueza, Ana María. "Caracterización de los narradores de *Rayuela.*" *Revista Chilena de Literatura*, Núm. 1 (otoño, 1970), 43–57.

Sapota, Marc. "Un fântome d'Edgar Allen Poe revu par Freud." *L'Express*, No. 887, 8–14 juillet 1968, p. 45. [Sobre *Gîtes.*]

Sarduy, Severo. "Del Ying al Yang (Sobre Sade, Bataille, Marmori, Cortázar y Elizondo)." *Mundo Nuevo*, Núm. 13 (jul, 1967), 4–13. [Reproducido en *Escrito sobre un cuerpo. Ensayos de crítica.* Buenos Aires: Ed. Sudamericana, 1969, 9–30.]

———. "Anamorphoses." *La Quinzaine Littéraire*, No. 50, ler au 15 mai 1968, p. 5. [Sobre *Gîtes.*]

Sasturain, Juan. "*Libro de Manuel.*" *La Opinión* (10 mayo 1973), 18. [Reseña.]

Schiavo, Leda y Graciela Reyes. " 'Modelo' y armado en una novela de Cortázar." *Filología*, 15 (1971), 241–250.

Schiminovich, Flora S. "Cortázar y el cuento en uno de sus cuentos." *Nueva Narrativa Hispanoamericana*, 1, Núm. 2 (set, 1971), 97–104. [Reproducido en *Homenaje a Julio Cortázar.* Madrid: Anaya, 1972, 307–317.]

Schmucler, Héctor. "*Rayuela*: juicio a la literatura." *Pasado y Presente*, Núm. 9 (abr–set, 1965), 29–45.

———. "Cortázar, escritor antiliterario." *La Gaceta*, 29 mayo 1966, p. 2.

———. "Notas para una lectura de Cortázar." *Los libros*, Núm. 2 (ag, 1969), 11. [Sobre *62. Modelo para armar.*]

Schneider, Luis Mario. "Julio Cortázar." *Revista de la Universidad de México*, Año 17, Núm. 9 (mayo, 1963), 24–25.

Scholz, Lászlo. "Un octaedro del 'Octaedro' de Julio Cortázar." *Acta Litteraria Academiae Scientiarum Hungaricae*, Tomo 17 (1–2), (1975), 227–238.

Schulman, Ivan A., Manuel Pedro González, Juan Loveluck, Fernando Alegría. *Coloquio sobre la novela hispanoamericana.* México: Fondo de Cultura Económica, 1967.

Schwartz, Kessel. "*Libro de Manuel.*" *Hispania*, Vol. 58, Núm. 1 (mar, 1975), 234–235.

Serra, Edelweis. "Comentario a Julio Cortázar a propósito de *Final del juego.*" *Señales*, Núm. 147 (4o. trimestre 1964), 1–4.

———. "El arte del cuento: 'La noche boca arriba.'" *Estudios sobre los cuentos de Julio Cortázar.* Barcelona: Ed. Hispam, 1975, 163–177.

Servodidio, Mirella d'A. "Facticity and Transcendence in Cortázar's *Rayuela.*" *Journal of Spanish Studies: Twentieth Century*, v. 2, no. 1 (Spring, 1974), 49–57.

Shuttleworth, Martin. "New Novels." *Punch*, 252 (22 mar 1967), 436. [About *Hopscotch.*]

Siles, Jaime. "Cortázar: Análisis de un desmembramiento temporal." *El Urogallo*, 3, Núm. 17 (set–oct, 1972), 70–72.

Siracusa, Isabel. "Informe sobre la literatura argentina en 1969: Panorama de la crítica." *Nueva Crítica*, 1 (ene–abr, 1971), 62–133. [Sobre Cortázar, 78–83.]

Skármeta Vranicic, Antonio. "Trampas al perseguidor." *Mapocho*, Núm. 20 (verano, 1970), 33–44.

"Snapshots of 'Blow-up.'" *Review* 72 (Winter 72), 22–25. [Fragmentos de artículos: 1) Charles Thomas Samuels, "Sorting Things Out in 'Blow-up'"; 2) Stanley Kauffmann,

"The Invisible Immanence of Evil," *Focus on Blow-up*; 3) Rita Guibert, "Cortázar defends Antonioni," *Seven Voices*.]

S[oares], N. J. "Las tribulaciones de Cortázar." *Primera Plana*, Núm. 409, 1 dic 1970, p. 45. [Sobre *Viaje alrededor de una mesa*.]

Sola, Graciela de. "Las galerías secretas de Julio Cortázar." *Señales*, Núm. 154 (3er trimestre 1966), 3–6.

———. "*Rayuela*: una invitación al viaje." *La vuelta a Cortázar en nueve ensayos*. Buenos Aires: Carlos Pérez, 1968, 75–102.

Sommers, Joseph. "Ivan A. Schulman, et al.: *Coloquio sobre la novela hispanoamericana*." *Revista Iberoamericana*, Vol. 34, Núm. 66 (1968), 406–408.

Soriano, Osvaldo. "Reportaje a Julio Cortázar." *La Opinión* (11 mar 1973), 18–20.

Sosnowski, Saúl. "La intuición de la muerte en *Las armas secretas* de Julio Cortázar." *Hispania*, 52 (1969), 846–851.

———. "Conocimiento poético y aprehensión racional de la realidad. Un estudio de 'El perseguidor' de Julio Cortázar." *Nuevos Aires*, 4 (abr, 1971). [Reproducido en *Homenaje a Julio Cortázar*. Madrid: Anaya, 1972, 427–444.]

———. "El compromiso revolucionario de Cortázar: un nuevo 'round.'" *Nueva Narrativa Hispanoamericana*, 2, Núm. 1 (ene, 1972), 211–213. [Sobre *Viaje alrededor de una mesa*.]

———. "Los ensayos de Julio Cortázar: pasos hacia su política." *Revista Iberoamericana*, 39, Núms. 84–85 (jul–dic, 1973), 657–666.

———. "Julio Cortázar: *Libro de Manuel*." *Hispania*, Año 2, 6 (1974), 109–115. [Reseña.]

———. "'Una flor amarilla,' vindicación de vidas fracasadas." *Estudios sobre los cuentos de Julio Cortázar*. Barcelona: Ed. Hispam, 1975, 179–190.

———. "Comentario III." *Hispamérica*, Año 4, 1 (1975), 155–158. [About Jaime Concha, "Criticando *Rayuela*," which appears in the same issue, 131–151.]

———. "Fantomas, Cortázar y los multinacionales." *La opinión cultural* (Buenos Aires), 7 dic 1975, pp. 6–7. [Reprinted in *The American Hispanist*, Vol. 1, No. 4 (Dec, 1975), 12–13.]

———. "Pursuers." *Books Abroad*, 50, No. 3 (Summer 1976), 600–608.

"Southern Crosses." *Times Literary Supplement* (London), No. 3318, 30 Sept 1965, 867–868.

Souza, Raymond D. "Language vs. Structure in the Contemporary Spanish American Novel." *Hispania*, 52 (1969), 833–839. [About Cortázar, 835–836.]

Spector, R. D. "*The Winners*." *Book Week*, 4 April 1965, p. 8.

Speratti Piñero, Emma Susana. "La literatura fantástica en las últimas generaciones argentinas." *La literatura fantástica en Argentina*. México: Imprenta Universitaria, 1957, 73–94. [Libro escrito en colaboración con Ana María Barrenechea.]

Squirru, Rafael. "*Rayuela*." *Américas*, 16, No. 8 (1964), 39.

Stern, Daniel. "*End of the Game and Other Stories*." *Nation*, Vol. 205, No. 8 (18 Sept 1967), 248.

Taglialatela Riccio, Alessandra. "Sopravvivenza e validità del surrealismo (a proposito di *Rayuela* di Julio Cortázar)." *Annali* dell' *Instituto Universitario Orientale, Napoli, Sezione Romanza*, 15, pp 269–278.

"Take it from here." *The Times Literary Supplement* (London), No. 3481, 14 Nov 1968, p. 1286. [About *La vuelta al día en ochenta mundos*.]

Tatum, Charles M. "Sobre Cortázar." *Chasqui*, Vol. 3, Núm. 3 (nov, 1973), 39.

Tavares Rodríguez, Urbano. "Julio Cortázar e a redescoberta do real." *Ensarios de Escrevinar*. Lisbon, 1970, 173–178.

Taylor, Anna Marie. "The 'desdoblamiento' of Oliveira and Traveler in *Rayuela*." *Chasqui*, Núm. 3 (mayo–jun, 1972), 36–40.

———. "Comentario II." *Hispamérica*, Año 4, 1 (1975), 153–154. [About Jaime Concha's article "Criticando *Rayuela*," which appears in the same issue, 131–151.]

Taylor, Martín C. "*Los reyes* de Julio Cortázar: El Minotauro Redimido." *Revista Iberoamericana*, 39, Núms. 84–85 (jul–dic, 1973), 537–556.

Tejera, María Josefina. "Julio Cortázar: *Todos los fuegos el fuego*." *Cultura Universitaria* (Caracas), Núm. 93 (1966), 206–207.

Tirri, Néstor. "El perseguidor perseguido." *La vuelta a Cortázar en nueve ensayos*. Buenos Aires: Carlos Pérez, 1968, 133–161.

Torres-Ríoseco, Arturo. "Notas sobre el desarrollo de la literatura hispanoamericana desde 1916." *Hispania*, Vol. 50, Núm. 4 (1967), 960–961.

Turmen, John H. "*Octaedro*." *Chasqui*, Vol. 4, Núm. 2 (feb, 1975), 63–69.

Turner, Ronald C. "*Hopscotch*." *Library Journal*, Vol. 91, No. 8 (15 April 1966), 2084.

Ullán, José Miguel. "Dos cronopios." *Indice*, Núms. 221–223 (1967), 18.

Urbistondo, Vicente. "Cinematografía y literatura en 'Las babas del diablo' y en 'Blow-up.' " *Los Papeles de Son Armadans*, 71, Núm. 213 (dic, 1973), 229–243.

Uriarte, Fernando. "Julio Cortázar, novelista de Buenos Aires." *Mapocho*, 14, Núms. 2–3 (1966), 57–67.

———. "Aspectos de la novela hispanoamericana actual." *Mapocho* (Santiago de Chile), Núm. 15 (1966), 147–161.

Uribe, Sabilio. "Julio Cortázar: *Rayuela*." *Criterio*, Núm. 1452, 28 mayo 1964, p. 397. [Reseña.]

Valbuena Briones, A. "Una cala en el Realismo Mágico." *Cuadernos Americanos*, Núm. 5 (set–oct, 1969), 233–241. [p. 237 en adelante sobre Cortázar.]

———. "Leyendo las novelas de Cortázar." *Arbor*, Núms. 333–334 (set–oct, 1973), 69–78.

Valdés, Mario J. "Documents and Fiction in Julio Cortázar's *Rayuela*." *Reflexión*, 2–4, 2 (1973), 83–36.

Valentine, Robert. "Borges and Cortázar on Perón's Return to Argentina." *Hispania*, Vol. 56, Núm. 4 (dic, 1973), 1100–1101.

———. "The Artist's Quest for Freedom in *Libro de Manuel*." *Chasqui*, 3, Núm. 2 (feb, 1974), 62–74.

———. "The Creative Personality in Cortázar's 'El perseguidor.' " *Journal of Spanish Studies: Twentieth Century*, v. 2, no. 3 (Winter 1974), 169–191.

Varela, Blanca. "Uno o muchos libros." *Revista Peruana de Cultura*, Núm. 3 (oct, 1964), 130–134.

Vargas Llosa, Mario. "Primitives and Creators." *The Times Literary Supplement* (London), No. 3481, 14 Nov 1968, 1287–1288.

Vásquez Amaral, José. "Julio Cortázar's *Hopscotch* and Argentinian Spiritual Alienation." *The Contemporary Latin American Narrative*. New York: 1970, 157–165.

Vázquez Zamora, Rafael. "Julio Cortázar: *La vuelta al día en ochenta mundos*." *Destino* (Barcelona), 13 mar 1971, 62–64.

Veiravé, Alfredo. "Aproximaciones a 'El perseguidor.' " *Estudios sobre los cuentos de Julio Cortázar*. Barcelona: Ed. Hispam, 1975, 191–218.

"Las verdades de Marechal." *Análisis*, Núm. 393, 25 set 1968, pp. 50–54. [Entrevista; hay algunos juicios sobre Cortázar.]

Villanueva, Marcelo Alberto. "El salto hacia adelante o la razón de la sinrazón." *Homenaje a Julio Cortázar*. Madrid: Anaya, 1972, 31–80.

Viñas, David. "Después de Cortázar: historia y privatización." *Cuadernos Hispanoamericanos*, Núm. 234 (jun, 1969), 734–739. [Incidencia de Cortázar sobre la nueva generación de narradores argentinos: 1) Ricardo Piglia: *Jaulario*—2da ed.: *La invasión*; 2) Aníbal Ford: *Sumbosa*; 3) Germán García: *Nanina*; 4) Néstor Sánchez: *Nosotros dos*; 5) Ricardo Frete: *Dos parientes*; 6) Manuel Puig: *La traición de Rita Hayworth*.]

———. "Cortázar y la fundación mitológica de París" y "Un viaje contradictorio: de *Los premios* a *Rayuela.*" En *De Sarmiento a Cortázar.* Buenos Aires: Ed. Siglo Veinte, 1971, 122–132 y 199–202.

————. "Cortázar y la fundación mitológica de París." *Nuevos Aires,* 1, Núm. 3 (dic–ene–feb, 1971), 27–34.

Vince, Thomas L. "*Hopscotch.*" *America* (jul–dic, 1966), 40.

Vittori, José Luis. "La voluntad de realismo." *Colmegna* (1963), 17–18. [Sobre *Los premios.*]

"*La vuelta al día en ochenta mundos.*" *Siempre* (Supl.), Núm. 757 (dic, 1967), pp. II–IV.

West, Anthony. "*The Winners.*" *New Yorker,* No. 41, 8 May 1965,, 177–178.

West, Paul. "*Cronopios y Famas.*" *Book World,* 17 Aug 1969, pp. 10–11.

"*The Winners* by Julio Cortázar." *Time,* 9 April 1965, p. 112.

Wood, Don E. "Surrealistic Transformation of Reality in Cortázar's *Bestiario.*" *Romance Notes,* 13, No. 2 (Winter, 1971), 239–242.

Yahni, Roberto. "Los conciertos de Cortázar." *Sur,* Núm. 319 (jul–ag, 1969), 56–59.

————. *70 años de narrativa argentina: 1900–1970.* Madrid: Alianza, 1970, 7–16.

Yates, Donald A. "Spun from Fanciful Institutions." *Saturday Review,* 22 July 1967, 36–37. [About "End of the Game."]

Yrache, Luis. "*62. Modelo para armar.*" *Papeles de Son Armadans,* 57, Núm. 170 (mayo, 1970), 205–216.

Yurkievich, Saúl. "Re *Pameos y meopas.*" *Desquicio* (Paris), No. 2 (1972). [No page numbers.]

————. "Julio Cortázar: al Unísono y al Dísono." *Revista Iberoamericana,* 39, Núms. 84–85 (jul–dic, 1973), 411–424.

————. "Los tanteos mánticos de Julio Cortázar." *Revista de Occidente* (Madrid), Núm. 131 (feb, 1974), 154–165.

Zapata, Celia. "Juego de niños: su magia en dos cuentos de Julio Cortázar." *Anales de Literatura Hispanoamericana,* 2, Núms. 2–3 (1976), 667–676.